AA

The Book of LONDON

The Book of
LONDON

Produced by the Publications Division of the Automobile Association
Fanum House Basingstoke Hants RG21 2EA

The Tower

St. Olav

Produced by the Publications Division of the Automobile
Association
Editor Michael Cady
Art Editor Dave Austin
Assistant Editor Jeremy Kirk
Assistant Designer Neil Roebuck MA RCA

Research by the Publications Research Unit of the
Automobile Association
Editorial contributors: Russell P O Beach, Julia Brittain,
Jennifer Chandler, Rebecca King,
and Barbara Littlewood

Original photography by S and O Mathews,
and Martyn Adelman

Picture research by Ikon

All maps by the Cartographic Unit of the Automobile
Association.
Based on the Ordnance Survey Maps, with the permission
of the Controller of HM Stationery Office
Crown Copyright Reserved.

Phototypeset by Vantage Photosetting Co Ltd of
Southampton, England.
Printed and bound in Spain
by Graficromo, S. A. - Córdoba

Contents

Introduction

This book has been designed to enable the reader to travel confidently about London, whether on foot, by public transport above or below ground, or even in the most leisurely way of all – by water. All the different methods of travel in London are explained and there are many full-colour maps, specially drawn by the AA. Equipped with this information, the reader can then use the book to make a choice from London's many entertainments, whether it be strolling round one of the parks, visiting museums or churches, cruising down the Regent's Canal, bargain-hunting in the street markets, or taking a trip to the zoo.

The Book of London is, however, much more than a practical guide – it captures in words and pictures the spirit of London. Here the armchair traveller will find many varied delights, both splendid and quaint, and the tourist can re-live the pleasures of past visits.

A London Compass

A London Compass

London, rich in history, full of pageantry and culture to suit all tastes, with its beautiful shops and parks, characteristic pubs and individual, friendly people, is very much a city for exploring. London welcomes its visitors, and many come to regard it as an old friend, returning time after time to discover new areas, new places to see.

The visitor arriving in London will first need to know how to get about the busy, bustling capital. Fortunately, though Greater London is over 610 square miles in size, twice as large as New York or Paris, it is served by one of the finest transport systems in the world. There are a number of choices. The most scenic way to get about is on top of a double-decker London bus, but the Underground is the quickest. Travel by taxi is the most convenient; by foot or bicycle the most beneficial. The most nerve-racking way to travel is by car, while going by boat is the most relaxing. All these methods of seeing London – even how to take a helicopter tour – are described on the next few pages, including what special offers are available to visitors.

Right: Looking down Regent Street from Piccadilly Circus in the heart of the West End. In the distance, beyond St James's Park, is the Victoria Tower of the Houses of Parliament.

Below: Perhaps the most extensive underground system in the world, the London Underground is a good deal more simple to understand than it looks.

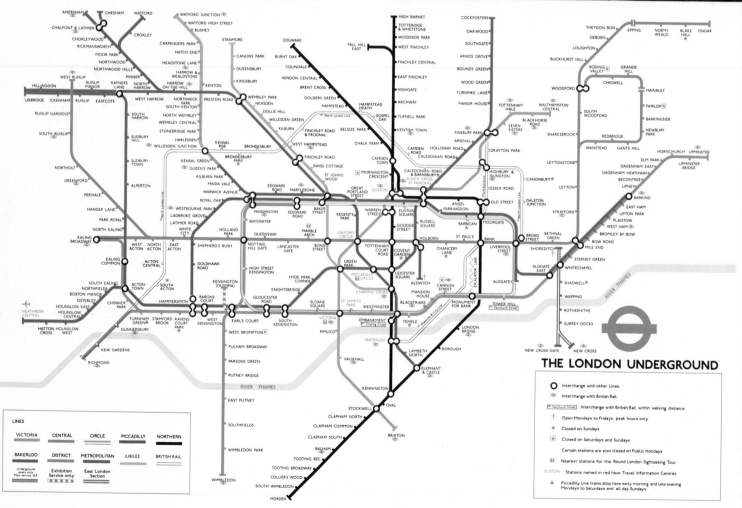

London Transport

London's bus and Underground railway, or 'tube' network, covering an area of some 630 square miles, is controlled by the **London Transport Executive** whose headquarters is at 55 Broadway, Westminster, SW1. This authority maintains travel enquiry offices in central London at the following Underground stations – Charing Cross, Euston, Heathrow Central, King's Cross, Oxford Circus, Piccadilly Circus, St James's Park, Victoria, and at the **British Rail Travel Centre**, Waterloo. These offices are open daily from 08.30–21.30hrs, except Heathrow Central which opens from 05.00–24.00hrs (06.00–24.00hrs Sunday). They can answer queries about travel in London as well as issue tickets and London Transport publications. A 24hr telephone enquiry service (01-222 1234) is maintained at St James's Park, the main enquiry office.

London Transport offers a wide range of concessionary tickets including special tourist 'Go-As-You-Please' and 'Central Tube Rover' tickets in addition to its 'Red Bus Rover' tickets. The 'Go-As-You-Please' tickets give unlimited travel for 4 or 7 days on all red bus routes and the Underground, except for stations beyond Northwood, Harrow & Wealdstone, and Debden. A 'Central Tube Rover' ticket allows unlimited travel for one day between any of the stations on or inside the Circle Line, plus some important ones just outside, such as Earls Court and Waterloo. 'Red Bus Rover' tickets allow unlimited travel for one day on any of London Transport's normal bus services.

What's happened to my...?

If travellers lose anything while travelling on a London Transport bus or train, they should write or apply in person to the **Lost Property Office** at 200 Baker Street, NW1, close to the Baker Street Underground station. This office is open Monday to Friday 10.00–18.00hrs, but is closed on Saturdays and Sundays. The Lost Property Office deals with more than 150,000 items annually and periodically holds an auction to dispose of unclaimed property. A charge is made for reclaimed items to off-set the cost of maintaining the service.

Rush hour

From Monday to Friday the buses and trains of the London Transport Executive carry a daily average of over 6,000,000 passengers. In central London all forms of public transport become extremely crowded between 08.00–09.30hrs and 16.00–18.30hrs when most of London is travelling to and from work. London's rush hour is really most uncomfortable, and if travel can be arranged outside these times, the visit will be considerably more enjoyable. Buses and tubes also get quite busy at lunch-time, but not as bad as during the rush hour.

The Underground

The first 'tube' railway in every sense of the word was opened in 1890 and ran from King William Street to Stockwell employing electricity as its motive power. This had been preceded in 1863 by a sub-surface steam railway and in 1870 by the first 'tube' railway in the world – a subway between Tower Hill and Bermondsey through which ran a cable-operated car. From these small beginnings sprang the network of tube stations used as shelters by many Londoners during both World Wars. At the height of the Blitz during World War II almost 180,000 people were recorded as having taken shelter in the tube on one 1940 September night alone.

The nine lines of the present system now make up one of the largest electric Underground railways in the world. Recent improvements have included the extension of the Piccadilly Line to Heathrow Airport and the opening, in April 1979, of the first stage of the new Jubilee Line.

Getting around on the Tube

As with many capital cities, the quickest and most efficient means of public transport in London is the Underground railway. With more than 275 stations, the Underground covers a wide area reaching out from central London to the suburbs where it rises above ground as an ordinary surface railway. There is almost always an Underground station close at hand throughout London, and trains run frequently between 05.30 and 00.15hrs (until 23.30hrs on Sundays). There are no all-night services, however, and it is important to note that certain stations are closed at weekends. Each station is indicated

Above: At times, particularly during the rush hour, the Underground does seem like an enormous vaccuum-cleaner, sucking people off the street. This rather quaint poster dates from 1927.

Right: A journey on the 'tube' always costs more than the same journey by bus, but it is almost invariably much quicker.

by an illuminated London Transport symbol and every station displays a large-scale version of the Underground map.

Many of the Underground lines are connected with each other by subways at stations where they intersect and also with most main-line railway termini. A list of fares is displayed in every ticket hall but children between 3 and 14 years are charged reduced fares. Tickets are purchased before travel either from the ticket office or from an automatic ticket machine

which takes 5p and 10p coins.

Signs throughout the Underground stations clearly show the way to the line required, but make sure to wait on the correct platform and board the right train by checking the indicator on the platform and on the front of the train. Make sure, also, exactly which train is wanted because from some platforms trains leave for more than one destination. Each car on the train displays a map of the train's route and maps of the network are available from any Travel Enquiry Office.

9

London buses

A regular omnibus service was first seen in London in 1829, following the Parisian precedent. The first omnibuses seated 22 passengers and were horse-drawn. In 1910 a petrol-driven motor bus was introduced and the last horse-drawn bus was withdrawn in 1916. Over the years much development and improvement has gone on. The large tram network of the late 18th and early 19th centuries was succeeded by trolley-buses, and petrol-driven buses gave way to today's fleet of diesel-engined vehicles.

The indomitable London bus is not only one of the most famous in the world, it is also one of the safest. Every bus has to go through this astounding tilt test of 28 degrees to the vertical.

One of the best ways of seeing London is to take a seat on the top deck of one of its famous double-decker buses. The fact that the traffic may be slow on occasions is no great handicap, but offers a wonderful opportunity for leisurely (and inexpensive) sightseeing. Buses operate from about 06.00 to 24.00hrs on most routes, including those connecting the main-line railway stations, and offer a comprehensive service in central London and the suburbs. A number of routes from central London run throughout the night during weekdays, but most do not operate on Saturday nights or Sunday mornings. A main-line station bus, however, connecting Waterloo, Victoria, Paddington, Euston, St Pancras, and King's Cross, runs throughout the year on Sunday nights, and on Friday and Saturday nights between June and September. Detailed bus maps are available at any Travel Enquiry Office or Underground station.

Each bus displays its destination and number on the front. Bus stop signs, which generally give the numbers of buses which stop there, are displayed on a red or white background. A sign with a red background denotes a 'Request Stop' where the intending passenger must stop the bus by raising his hand in good time when the bus approaches. A white background denotes a compulsory stop where all buses stop. At many bus stops there is a panel giving full route details and timetabling information.

The limited-stop 'Red Arrow' service operates on a flat-fare system.

Smoking is not allowed on single-deck buses, and is permitted only on the top deck of double-deckers. Standing is allowed on crew-operated double-deck buses, but is limited to five passengers on the lower deck, or 'inside' as the lower deck is sometimes known, harking back to the days when the top deck had no roof. Standing is not permitted on the top deck, platform or staircase. Passengers may stand on single-deck buses, but the number allowed varies according to the type of service operated.

The red double-decker buses run throughout central London and its suburbs. Single-deck 'Red Arrow' buses provide a fast and frequent limited-stop service on some busy central London routes, connecting the main-line railway termini with the main business areas during the rush hour, and shopping and entertainment centres at other times. Yellow and red 'Shop Linker' buses provide a regular service over a circular route, connecting London's main stores in Kensington, Knightsbridge and the West End. Fares are normally collected by a conductor, but one-man operated buses are in use on some suburban services where passengers enter by the yellow front door and pay the driver. Fares are generally charged according to the distance travelled, but some suburban routes, 'Red Arrow' and 'Shop Linker' buses operate a flat-fare system. Children under 5 travel free and those under 16 years pay a

reduced fare. All tickets should be retained for the duration of the journey because travellers may be requested to produce them at any time by a ticket inspector.

Sightseeing by bus

London Transport operates tours round London in association with National Travel throughout the year. A guided tour of the City, which commences from Victoria Coach Station, takes in St Paul's Cathedral and the Tower of London. The 'Round-London Sightseeing Tour' is an unguided tour of some 20 miles taking in all of London's principal sights. During the summer months open-top buses are used.

London Country and Green Line buses

London Country buses and Green Line coaches have been operating in and around London for many years. Generally the services cover a much wider area than the bus services of London Transport. Green Line coaches run from and across London, linking the capital to various towns and villages in the inner Home Counties. The services, including those running through central London, are frequent, operating from early morning to late at night, but some do not operate on Sunday.

Timetables and maps of Green Line coach routes and boarding points, including those serving Heathrow Airport, are available from the **Green Line Enquiry Office**, Eccleston Bridge, Green Line Coach Station (01–834 6563), or from Travel and Tourist Enquiry Offices. Coaches display their destination and number on the front.

The driver collects the fare and passengers wishing to smoke should sit at the rear of the coach. Children of 5 or under are normally carried free and those from 5 to 13 years are charged half-fare, with certain exceptions determined by the time of travel. To take advantage of some of the special bargain fare offers it is necessary to travel after 09.00hrs on weekdays. 'Golden Rover' tickets allow unlimited travel on any Green Line coach or London Country bus for the whole of the day. 'Outback'

tickets are off-peak cheap day return tickets for those wishing to travel out and back to just one place for a day.

Losses

If you should lose anything while travelling on a Green Line coach or a London Country bus, contact the **London Country Bus Services Ltd**, Bell Street, Reigate, Surrey, *tel* Reigate 42411.

Transport Museum

London Transport maintains a unique collection of vehicles associated with 150 years of public transport in London. The collection includes horse-drawn and motor buses, trams, trolley-buses, rolling stock and a selection of historic posters, signs, tickets and models. The collection has recently been moved to a new site at Covent Garden and is due to re-open in early 1980.

Taxis

The London taxi is one of the friendliest signs a visitor will see. The traditional colour is still black, though in recent years red, blue and yellow vehicles have added a splash of colour to London's fleet. But the distinctive shape remains. Taxis are a salvation for those who get lost; after midnight they are a godsend and the only way to get about. Taxi drivers are also a useful source of information as they know London inside-out – they have to, in order to get their licence.

Nimble in traffic, comfortable to ride in and, it seems, able to turn on a pin-head, London taxis are reasonable in price and can be hailed in the street if the yellow 'For Hire' or 'Taxi' sign above the windscreen is lit up. If (as always seems the case when in a hurry or when it's pouring with rain) there seem to be none about, taxis can be called by telephone. For numbers, see 'Taxi' in the S–Z section of the London Telephone Directory.

It is customary to tip about 10–15% of the fare, or perhaps a little more if the driver has been particularly helpful.

A familiar sight, though not all London taxis are black these days.

British Rail

London's original boundaries were determined by the limited means of transport available. With the development of the railways in the 1800s the population increased and the suburbs spread outwards. By the end of the century the capital was connected to many major cities by a network of different lines, and today's fast and regular rush-hour trains enable workers to commute from places many miles from the capital.

A number of different railway companies competed with each other for business, and each had its terminus on the outskirts of London. Later the railways crept closer and closer towards the city centre, each company trying to get closer than the others. This is why there are so many stations in London today.

After World War II the railway companies were all nationalised to form British Rail, but the flavour of the old rail companies remains in today's different Regions.

Eastern Region

King's Cross Station This is the main London terminal of the Eastern Region for long-distance trains to Scotland and the north, now served by 125-mph high-speed trains. Outer suburban electric services operate as far as Royston. Close to St Pancras station, King's Cross is connected to the Northern, Piccadilly, Circle, Metropolitan, and Victoria lines of the Underground. It was opened by the former Great Northern Railway in 1852, and occupies the site of an old smallpox and fever hospital.

Moorgate Station Inner suburban electric services operate from Moorgate, the main terminus of the Great Northern Electrics line, which utilises a section of the Underground for the initial part of its journey (see map of the Underground, page **8**).

Liverpool Street Station The terminus for East Anglia, it is connected to the Central, Circle, and Metropolitan lines of the Underground. Suburban routes include those to Stratford, Tottenham and Walthamstow.

Fenchurch Street Station The terminus for the Docks and Thames side, it is situated close to the Underground station of Tower Hill. Suburban routes include those to Barking and Woolwich.

London Midland Region

Euston Station Together with St Pancras, Euston is the principal terminus of the London Midland Region and is sometimes referred to as the 'gateway to the North-West'. It is connected to the Northern and Victoria lines of the Underground and suburban routes include those to Hampstead, Queen's Park and Wembley. Rebuilt in the 1960s as part of the region's electrification scheme, the new station was opened by HM Queen Elizabeth in 1968.

St Pancras Station The other principal station of the London Midland Region, it is close to King's Cross station and connected to the Northern, Piccadilly, Circle, Metropolitan, and Victoria lines of the Underground. Designed by Sir George Gilbert Scott for the Midland Railway, it took its name from the boy martyred by Diocletian in AD304. Suburban routes include those to Kentish Town and West Hampstead.

Marylebone Station The station is a terminus for the shorter-distance services to Aylesbury and Leamington. It is on the Bakerloo Underground line and the suburban routes include those to Harrow-on-the-Hill, and the Wembley complex. The last main-line station to be constructed in London, it was built for the Great Central Railway in 1899.

Broad Street Station Adjoining Liverpool Street Station, Broad Street is the main terminus of the London Midland Region's 'North London Line' which runs to Richmond (see map of the Underground, page **8**). The station was originally jointly owned by the London and North Western Railway and the North London Railway and was opened in 1865.

Southern Region

Victoria Station The main Southern Region terminus serving the south coast, it is connected to the Circle, District, and Victoria lines of the Underground. Suburban routes include those to Balham, Battersea, and Streatham. Rebuilt in 1909, the station was altered in the 1920s.

Waterloo Station The main terminus of the Southern Region for the west of England, it is connected to the Bakerloo and Northern Lines of the Underground. It is also the terminus of the Waterloo and City Line (see map of the Underground, page **8**). Suburban routes include those to Feltham and Wimbledon. Waterloo was first opened by the London and South Western Railway Company in 1848.

Two familiar scenes to many City workers. Above right: Rush-hour crowds at Liverpool St Station. Right: The Waterloo and City Line, nicknamed 'the drain'.

Charing Cross Station A terminus of the Southern Region, it is connected to the Bakerloo, Jubilee and Northern lines of the Underground and also with London Bridge Station by way of Waterloo Station. Suburban routes include those to Beckenham and Penge. Built for the South-Eastern Railway Company, it was opened in 1864.

Cannon Street Station The City terminus of the Southern Region, it is connected to the Circle and District lines of the Underground. Closed on Sundays, its suburban routes include those to Deptford and Greenwich. The station was built in 1866 and was partly reconstructed in the 1950s.

London Bridge Station A south bank terminus of Southern Region, it is connected to the Northern line of the Underground. Suburban routes include those to Forest Hill and Sydenham. One of London's first ever railway stations, it was built for the London and Greenwich Railway in 1836 and rebuilt in 1851.

Holborn Viaduct Station A City terminus of the Southern Region near to the Central line Underground station of St Paul's. Closed on Saturday afternoon and Sunday, its suburban routes include those to Elephant & Castle and Herne Hill.

Blackfriars Station This station (closed on Saturdays and Sundays) is on the line from Holborn Viaduct, but also acts as a terminus for some trains. It is connected to the Circle and District lines of the Underground and serves much the same suburban areas as Holborn Viaduct.

Western Region

Paddington The main terminus of the Western Region with 125-mph high-speed trains, the fastest scheduled diesels in the world, serving Bristol and South Wales. The station is connected to the Bakerloo, District, Circle, and Metropolitan lines of the Underground, and its suburban routes include those to Acton and West Drayton. Designed by the famous Victorian engineer Isambard Kingdom Brunel, the station was opened in 1854, replacing an earlier building.

For further train information

The British Rail Travel Centre, 4–12 Regent Street, SW1, is situated in central London near Piccadilly Circus and will assist personal callers with reservations and information about all rail services.

Direct bus services between Heathrow and Victoria Terminal are run by British Airways.

Air transport

London is well served by its airports, to which it is connected by excellent road and rail links. The main London airports, controlled by the British Airports Authority, are Heathrow and Gatwick, supported by auxiliary airports at Stansted, some 30 miles to the north of London, and Luton, 33 miles to the north-west. Both Luton and Stansted airports deal mainly with package-holiday charter flights.

Heathrow Airport

Travellers arriving at Heathrow airport pass through one of the busiest airports in the world. London's main airport, handling millions of passengers a year, it is situated some 15 miles to the west of the centre of London. Heathrow is well connected to London by means of the M4 motorway and is also easily reached by the transport listed below.

Airline bus A regular bus service operated by British Airways runs between the Victoria Terminal in Buckingham Palace Road and Heathrow terminals 1 and 3. Passengers for terminal 2 alight or join the coach at either terminal 1 or terminal 3. Operating from early morning to late evening, the journey takes some 47 minutes.

British Rail A 'Railair' link is operated by British Rail from central London to Heathrow. Passengers departing from Waterloo connect with a Railair link at Feltham which takes them to the airport. Other Railair links to Heathrow are from Euston via Watford Junction, from Paddington via Reading and from Waterloo via Woking.

Green Line Coach Green Line coach services, numbers 701 and 704, operate a regular service from Victoria to the Heathrow Airport Central bus station.

Underground The extension of the Piccadilly Line Underground, opened by HM Queen Elizabeth in 1977, provides a direct link from central London to the airport. Operating from early morning until late at night, but not throughout the night, it provides a service varying in frequency from every 4 minutes at busy times to about every 7½ minutes in the evenings. The London Tourist Board maintains a travel information office with a separate tourist information counter in Heathrow Central Underground station.

Taxi London taxis operate between London and Heathrow airport. The taxi driver is not compelled by law to accept a hiring of more than 20 miles in respect of a journey which begins at Heathrow airport, or a duration of more than one hour.

Gatwick Airport

Gatwick is the second most important airport in the United Kingdom having been greatly expanded and developed in recent years. One of the most convenient ways of travelling to Gatwick is by rail, as the station forms an integral part of the airport terminal building. A frequent train service operates from Victoria, the journey taking some 38 minutes.

Flight-seeing

Once in London an unusual but fascinating way to see the sights is to book a helicopter tour and get a bird's-eye view of the capital. The Bell Jet Ranger of **Helicopter Tours (London) Ltd**, 94 Jermyn Street, SW1, *tel* 01-930 0261, follows the course of the River Thames and gives unrivalled views of central London, especially Big Ben, The Houses of Parliament, St Paul's Cathedral, and the Tower of London. Flights take about 75 minutes.

Driving a car in London

Parking and traffic congestion in central London is a problem and driving can be difficult. Many one-way street systems have been introduced which do create difficulties for the visitor. However, for those unfamiliar with the complexities of London traffic, the two agencies listed below will provide a driver to meet the client at a specific point and drive or guide him in his own car into or across central London or the suburbs. Charges, including expenses, must be paid to the driver at the end of the assignment.

Peaktime Enterprises, 9 Brechin Place, SW7, *tel* 01-373 7306

Chauffeur Services Ltd, 61 Grosvenor Street, W1, *tel* 01-493 0136

For those who still wish to drive themselves and are unfamiliar with conditions in the capital, the best advice is to obtain a copy of the **Highway Code**. When driving in London avoid the rush-hour traffic, which is at its height around 08.00–09.30hrs and 16.00–18.30hrs. Areas to avoid are Buckingham Palace and The Mall between 11.00 and 12.00hrs when the changing of the Guard at the Palace causes traffic delays. Additionally, no cars are allowed to use Oxford Street between 07.00hrs and 19.00hrs from Monday to Saturday.

Car hire

Most of the major car hire firms in London are represented at **Car Hire Centre International**, 23 Swallow Street, W1, *tel* 01-734 7661.

Parking

Street parking in central London is controlled by the Greater London Council's parking policy of meter zones known as the Inner London Parking Area. There are also parking zones in outer London, most of which include meters. The controlled zones are indicated by signs at their boundary points, giving the hours of operation. Special regulations may also apply in areas near to the wholesale markets and where Sunday street markets are held. Street parking other than at officially designated places is prohibited during the specified hours. In many zones, some parking places may be reserved exclusively for residents or other classes of users specified on nearby plates.

Parking meters take 5p or 10p coins but there are differences in charges and variations in the length of time for which parking is allowed. The car must be parked within the limits of the parking bay, indicated by the white lines on the road. It must also face in the same direction as the traffic flow, unless angle parking is indicated by road markings. Payment must be made on arrival, although unexpired meter time paid for by a previous occupant of the space may be used. After the initial payment has been made, additional parking time may not be bought by making any further payments.

Public car parks

There are many public car parks in London including the multi-storey blocks and underground car parks constructed in recent years to ease traffic congestion. Charges vary but information may be obtained from the main operators whose telephone numbers are as follows:

National Car Parks Ltd
01-637 9191
Apcoa Parking Ltd
01-897 6026
Avis Parking Ltd
01-848 8765
Mamos Motor Group Ltd
01-952 7373
ML Car Parks Ltd
01-481 3303

> *When parking a car always remember to secure it against theft and not to leave any valuable property inside.*

London has its fair share of congestion.

London on foot

With its 2,000 years of history, London has much to offer the visitor and probably the best way of getting about and seeing the sights is on foot. Traffic, however, is very heavy in central London and pedestrians must take extra care when crossing the road. Whenever possible use a pedestrian crossing or one of the pedestrian subways which are to be found at many of the busiest crossing points.

An ideal time to explore the capital is in the spring or autumn when most of the crowds have gone. A good idea is to prepare a route in advance and this is quite simple to do. The 'London Walks' section (see pages 37–61) contains a series of 12 easy-to-follow walks, mainly in the central London area and taking in many of the most interesting sights. In addition, several firms organise guided walking tours and this is another way of seeing the sights in and around central London. Details may be obtained from the **London Tourist Board**, 26 Grosvenor Gardens, Victoria, SW1, *tel* 01-730 0791. The London Tourist Board, a regional office of the English Tourist Board, is also able to issue tourist tickets for the bus and Underground and sightseeing tour tickets, in addition to providing general tourist information in several languages. The Board maintains Tourist Information Centres at Heathrow Central Station, the Oxford Street store of Selfridges, and at Harrods in Knightsbridge.

The **British Tourist Authority**, 64 St James's Street, SW1, *tel* 01-499 9325, is the statutory body for promoting tourism in Britain. It maintains a 'Welcome to Britain' Centre for overseas visitors. The Centre has fully-trained staff able to answer all questions about travel in London.

Seeing London by bicycle

A different but not exactly novel way to get about London is to use a bicycle. Traffic, especially in central London, is often congested and the cyclist has a freedom denied the motorist. Additionally, by avoiding the worst of the congestion, the bicycle opens up new areas and creates more time in which to explore them.

There are many firms in London offering a cycle hire service and well able to meet the needs of both the casual and experienced cyclist, whether it be for a three-speed or a ten-speed bike. Most firms can also supply items of cycling equipment, such as lights, tool kits or pumps, and can provide information on sights to see and theatres to visit. Visitors to London may even consider membership of the **Cyclists Touring Club**, 69 Meadrow, Godalming, Surrey, who can supply maps and other useful information. **Rent-a-bike**, Kensington Student Centre, Kensington Church Street, W8, *tel* 01-937 6089, the largest cycle hire company in Britain, are open 7 days a week and offer daily, weekly and monthly or longer periods of rental. The old established firm of **Savile's Cycle Stores Ltd**, 97–99 Battersea Rise, SW11, *tel* 01-228 4279, is open from Monday to Saturday excluding Wednesdays and Bank Holidays. It offers an initial weekly period of rental followed by a daily rate thereafter.

Water transport in London

Much of London's appeal lies in its variety, and the waterways of the capital offer the contrasting energy and bustle of the Thames with the quiet and seclusion of the canals. Both have seen considerable change – passenger liners no longer navigate the Thames beyond Tilbury, and industry has deserted the canals for faster methods of transport.

Silvan peace on the Regent's Canal waterbus.

Canals – the lifeblood of a bygone age

Often hidden in out-of-the-way places, London's canals tend to get overlooked. Where the Thames is wide and sometimes rough, the canals are narrow and peaceful. A product of the Industrial Revolution, they were created in the 18th and 19th centuries to serve commerce and industry. Some were a commercial success, while others, such as the Croydon Canal, were a failure. Opened in 1809 with the intention of linking London Docks to Portsmouth, it got as far as Croydon but now only a short stretch remains. Today the surviving canals in London form a part of either the Grand Union Canal system or the River Lee Navigation.

The Grand Union Canal

The main line of the Grand Junction Canal together with its Slough Arm, the Paddington Canal and the Regent's Canal were amalgamated in 1929 to form the Grand Union Canal. Constructed at the end of the 18th century, the main line of the former Grand Junction Canal starts at Brentford's Thames Lock and links London with the Black Country in the Midlands. Its Slough Arm, one of the last canals to be built in Britain, was opened in 1882. Some 5 miles long, it has three aqueducts but no locks. The Paddington Canal was opened in 1801 to provide a closer link with central London. Leaving the main line at Bulls Bridge, it runs for 13 miles into its terminal at Paddington Basin. Built on one level, the canal has no locks or tunnels.

The Regent's Canal was first suggested in 1802 and finally opened in 1820. Starting from Little Venice, which forms the junction of the Paddington Arm of the Grand Union Canal and the Regent's Canal, it runs into Limehouse Basin, and the stretch between Little Venice and Camden Town is busy with leisure traffic. Passing through Regent's Park, laid out by John Nash for the Prince Regent, the canal runs by the Zoological Gardens with the notable Aviary designed by Lord Snowdon,

opened in 1965. Also running into the Limehouse Basin is the Limehouse Cut, a straight canal built in 1770 to connect the River Lee to the Thames. The Hartford Union, sometimes known as Duckett's Canal, connects the Regent's Canal with the Lee Navigation. The canal was built in 1830, is 1¼ miles long and has three locks.

The Lee Navigation Canal

Starting in north-east London, the Lee Navigation runs from the Thames at Canning Town to Hertford and is some 28 miles long. The river, made famous by the 17th-century writer Izaak Walton in his book *The Compleat Angler*, has been used for navigation since Roman times. Improvements were first made to the navigation in the 15th century as most of London's grain was transported into the capital via the waterway. Until quite recent times London's canals were used commercially, but now only the Lee Navigation is used as such.

As the commercial role of the canals has declined, their recreational value has been realised. Several boats operate regular summer services and many of the canal towpaths have been opened to the public. The boat rides, which began in the early 1950s, operate mainly on the Regent's Canal. Before arranging a canal trip, check first with the operating company to avoid disappointment. The **British Waterways Board** operate a Zoo Waterbus from Little Venice to London Zoo between April and October – for details *tel* 01-286 6101. **Jason's Canal Cruises**, *tel* 01-286 3428, run luncheon and evening trips along the most picturesque part of the Regent's Canal. Using a pair of traditional narrow-boats, they operate from April to October. Regent's Canal cruises may also be taken on the *Jenny Wren*, a traditional narrow-boat, and *Fair Lady*, a cruising restaurant, *tel* 01-485 4433 for details. Another traditional narrow-boat, the *Port A Bella Packet*, operates cruises on the Grand Union and Regent's Canals, *tel* 01-960 5456.

Boat trips on the Thames

Passenger boat services operate a full programme during the summer months and a restricted service in the winter. From Westminster Pier, Charing Cross Pier, and Tower Pier services operate downstream to Greenwich, and from Westminster and Charing Cross Piers downstream to the Tower. Upstream services operate from Westminster Pier to Kew, Richmond and Hampton Court, and from Tower Pier to Westminster. Weekend luncheon cruises are also operated in addition to the normal daily cruises. Full details are available from the London Tourist Board's special **River Boat Information Service**, *tel* 01-730 4812.

Pomp and Circumstance

London's Royal Homes

Quite apart from Buckingham Palace, the most famous royal home in the world, London has several other royal residences. They range from the sumptuous grandeur of Hampton Court Palace to the relative modesty of Clarence House.

Buckingham Palace
The Mall, SW1

Formerly known as Buckingham House, this most famous of royal homes was built in 1703 by the Duke of Buckingham, and subsequently bought by George III in 1762. Nash altered and remodelled it for George IV in 1825, when its name was changed to Buckingham Palace. It was not much used until Queen Victoria came to the throne in 1837, when the court moved here. It has been the London home of the monarch ever since. The east wing, the side the public sees, was added in 1847 and the whole east façade was redesigned in 1913. The west wing remains largely as Nash designed it, but his great gateway, which was to have stood at the end of the Mall, proved too narrow for the State Coach, and the gate was bodily transported to its present site, Marble Arch.

The interior of the palace, with its many splendid rooms, is not open to the public. When in residence, the Royal Family live in the north wing. When the sovereign is in residence, the Royal Standard is flown. Every day in the forecourt at 11.30 am the ceremony of the Changing of the Guard is carried out by the Brigade of Guards.

St James's Palace
St James's Street, SW1

The original palace was started by Henry VII in 1531, and, after the destruction of Whitehall Palace, was the sovereign's official London residence. Foreign ambassadors are still appointed to the Court of St James's. The Gatehouse facing St James's Street is the main remnant of the Tudor building, and has the initials of Henry VIII and Anne Boleyn carved over the doors. The Chapel Royal was originally built by Henry VIII but was much altered in 1837. However, the ceiling by Holbein is original. Several royal marriages have been solemnised here, including those of William III and Mary II, Queen Anne, George IV, Queen Victoria and George V. Every year on 6th January (the Festival of Epiphany) at Holy Communion in this Chapel, an offering of gold, frankincense and myrrh is made on behalf of the Queen by two of Her Majesty's Gentleman Ushers.

In Friary Court the new sovereign is proclaimed from the balcony by the Heralds. Charles II, who was born here, made some additions to the palace, commissioning Wren to add some state apartments facing the park. James II, Mary II, Queen Anne and George IV were all born here. George IV employed Nash to restore and redecorate the palace, but Queen Victoria moved the court to Buckingham Palace when she came to the throne. St James's Palace is now occupied by servants of the Crown, and is not open to the public. However, services may be attended in the Chapel Royal between October and Palm Sunday.

Above: John Nash converted Buckingham House to a palace for George IV in 1825, but the façade dates from 1913. It has been the reigning monarch's London home since Queen Victoria's accession in 1837.

Below: A guard outside Clarence House, the home of Queen Elizabeth the Queen Mother.

Kensington Palace
Kensington Gardens, W8

William III bought what was a town mansion in 1689 and commissioned Wren to alter and improve it. The south wing is the best surviving part of his work. It was enlarged by William Kent for George I, and was the principal private royal residence until George II died here. Queen Victoria was born here and lived in the palace until she became Queen. It is now the residence of Princess Margaret. The State Apartments are open to the public.

Clarence House
Stable Yard, St James's Palace, SW1

Designed by Nash for William IV when he was Duke of Clarence, this house was restored for Princess Elizabeth before her accession in 1952. Princess Anne was born here and it is now the home of Queen Elizabeth, the Queen Mother.

Lancaster House
The Mall, SW1

This massive palace was originally built in the 19th century for the 'grand old' Duke of York, and was acquired by the Duke of Sutherland. Chopin played here before Queen Victoria in 1848. It is now a government hospitality centre and is usually open to the public.

Marlborough House
Pall Mall, SW1

Built by Wren for the Duke of Marlborough, Marlborough House was later occupied by

Above: St James's Palace was the official London residence of the monarch from the 17th to the 19th century.
Left: The astronomical clock at Hampton Court Palace was made for Henry VIII in 1540.

Leopold I of Belgium. In 1850 it became the official residence of the Prince of Wales. George V was born here and after he became King it became the home of Queen Alexandra, Edward VII's widow. The house is now the Commonwealth Centre and is open by appointment.

Queen's House
Romney Road, Greenwich, SE10
The land by the river at Greenwich has belonged to the crown since 1414. Henry VIII was born in the royal palace that was built here, and it was one of his favourite residences. Mary and Elizabeth I were also born here, and during Elizabeth's reign many royal functions were held in the palace.

James I was often here and he gave it to his consort Queen Anne of Denmark, who made a number of extensions. Charles I subsequently gave the palace to his queen, and she employed Inigo Jones to build the Queen's House. By the time Charles II came to the throne, Greenwich Palace was derelict and he pulled it down, at the same time enlarging the Queen's House and the gardens. William and Mary donated all the buildings to the Navy for a hospital, which was built by Christopher Wren. The Queen's House subsequently became the National Maritime Museum (see page 98).

Hampton Court Palace
Hampton Court Road, Kingston
Hampton Court was started by Cardinal Wolsey, Lord Chancellor in the reign of Henry VIII. Intended to be the finest and most extravagant palace in Europe, Wolsey gave it to Henry VIII in a futile attempt to stave off his downfall. Henry was very fond of Hampton Court and he moved in with his

new love, Anne Boleyn, though they were not yet married. He carried out many alterations and improvements to the palace, including a library and the magnificent hammer-beamed Great Hall which still remains.

Hampton Court played an important part in the lives of Henry's wives and his successors. Edward VI's Protectors plotted and quarrelled here, and Mary Tudor spent her unhappy honeymoon within its confines. Elizabeth I's first return to Hampton Court after being imprisoned here by her sister is said to have been for a clandestine meeting with James Hamilton, a potential husband. She added extensively to the gardens with plants brought from the New World by Hawkins, Raleigh and Drake.

When Charles II was restored to the throne he was delighted with Hampton Court and was determined to imitate the grandeur of

Versailles which he had seen during his exile. Both during his reign and that of William and Mary extensive gardens were laid out, in much the same form as they are today. William and Mary also commissioned Wren to convert it into a grand palace on the lines of Versailles, and he built the Fountain Court, the South Front containing the King's State Apartments, the East Front and the Queen's State Apartments. Mary was responsible for the ornamental iron grilles designed by Tijou, and after her death William created the famous Maze.

The last monarch to live in Hampton Court was George II, after which it became a series of 'grace and favour' residences. William IV, and later Queen Victoria, did much restoration work in order to attract paying visitors, and today it can be seen as a grand palace, filled with priceless paintings, tapestries and furniture, set in glorious gardens and resounding with the echoes of great moments of English history.
Also see pages 77 and 144.

Kensington Palace, today the home of Princess Margaret. The State Apartments, which are open to the public, have mementoes of Queen Victoria, who was born and lived here until her accession.

Royal Pageantry

London would be an infinitely poorer place without the splendour and dignity endowed upon it by royal ceremonial. For most people royalty means the Queen, and in the hope of seeing her expectant bystanders are always clustered outside the gates of Buckingham Palace. On these two pages are descriptions of those annual ceremonies which are attended by Her Majesty.

Her Majesty arriving at the State Opening of Parliament in the Irish State Coach.

State Opening of Parliament

late October/early November

In one of London's most colourful pageants, the Queen rides in the Irish State Coach from Buckingham Palace to the Palace of Westminster via the Mall and Whitehall. At Westminster, the Queen and other members of the royal family are greeted by a gun salute fired by the King's Troop of the Royal Horse Artillery. The royal party then enters the Houses of Parliament through the great arch under the Victoria Tower, and the Queen enters the Robing Room. Later Her Majesty emerges wearing the royal robes and the crown, and is conducted, amidst a procession of great officers of state, heralds, and the sound of trumpets, to the House of Lords where she ascends to the throne. The Lords, in their ceremonial robes, are already present and the Speaker and members of the House of Commons are now summoned by the official called Black Rod. After their arrival the Queen makes her speech outlining the government's proposed legislation for the new parliamentary session.

The ceremony has undergone little change since the 16th century and the ritual of the monarch's speech can be traced back to the mid-13th century. A few hours before the Queen arrives, yeomen of the Guard search the vaults of the Houses of Parliament. This exercise has been carried out every year since the unsuccessful Gunpowder Plot of 1605. The actual ceremony of the State Opening of Parliament is not open to the public, but many thousands of people line the processional route to see the Queen arrive and depart in the Irish State Coach.

Her Majesty reading the Queen's Speech in the House of Lords on 15th May 1979.

Trooping of the Colour
second Saturday in June

Held on the Queen's official birthday at Horse Guards Parade, off Whitehall, the Trooping of the Colour is probably the most spectacular military display in the country. This 200-year-old ceremony, with its roots stretching back to medieval times, begins with the Queen riding from Buckingham Palace, wearing the uniform of one of the regiments of which she is Colonel-in-Chief, to Horse Guards Parade, where the Brigade of Guards and the Household Cavalry await her, massed on the parade ground. Her Majesty takes the salute, which is followed by a display of marching and the 'trooping' or carrying of the colours of a selected regiment. Originally the colours were 'trooped' so that the men of the regiment could learn to recognise their own colours. The Queen then leads a contingent of Guards back to Buckingham Palace. The sovereign's official birthday is always held in summer when the chances of good weather are at their best. The custom was begun by Edward VII, whose actual birthday was in November, and has continued ever since. The specially-erected stands around Horse Guards Parade are reserved for ticket holders, but crowds line the Mall in order to see Her Majesty.

Above: The Queen riding side-saddle out of Buckingham Palace.
Below: Horse Guards Parade.

Distribution of the Royal Maundy Money
Maundy Thursday

This ancient ceremony of royal humility, which dates back to the time of Edward III, once included the reigning monarch washing the feet of the poor. The last sovereign to perform this rite was James II. William III delegated the washing to an aide, and the last foot-washing took place in 1754, after which the ceremony consisted of giving specially-minted Maundy pennies first coined in Charles II's reign. Today the Queen distributes two purses, one containing the specially-minted silver Maundy Money, the other containing money which represents the now discontinued gifts of food and clothing, to senior citizens selected from London parishes. The ceremony is held at various alternate locations including Westminster Abbey and Southwark Cathedral.

Remembrance Day Service
on the Sunday nearest to 11th November

A service at the Cenotaph, in Whitehall, to remember the dead of both World Wars, is attended by the Queen, members of the royal family, representatives of the armed services, ex-servicemen's associations and leading politicians. A gun salute is followed by one minute's silence after which wreaths are laid at the Cenotaph.

Daily Ceremonies

Changing the Guard
Buckingham Palace

Perhaps the best known of all London's royal ceremonies, Changing the Guard takes place on the forecourt of Buckingham Palace every day in summer, and alternate days in winter, at 11.30am. Troops from the Brigade of Guards, the Queen's personal bodyguard, take part in the ceremony, which entails the new guard marching from either Chelsea or Wellington Barracks and relieving the old guard from their posts at the Palace.

Mounting the Guard
Horse Guards, Whitehall

This colourful spectacle takes place every morning (11am weekdays, 10am Sundays). A detachment of the Household Cavalry make up the guard, and the new and old guard are drawn up facing Whitehall, changing position at a trumpet call.

The Ceremony of the Keys
Tower of London

At 9.53pm every night the Chief Warder of the Yeoman Warders of the Tower of London lights a candle, collects his escort from the Bloody Tower and locks first the West Gate of the Tower, then the Middle and Byward Tower doors. He returns to the Bloody Tower archway where he is challenged by a sentry. The party then proceeds through the archway and forms up facing the Main Guard of the Tower. At 10pm the Last Post is sounded and the Chief Warder delivers the keys to the Resident Governor and Major in the Queen's House. Applications to attend this ceremony should be made well in advance at the Constable's office in the Tower.

The Ceremony of the Keys is a nightly ritual at the Tower.

Pageantry and Ceremonial

The British need no excuse to hold a ceremony, and their love of pageantry and spectacle is world-famous. London, with its Royal Family, palaces, and City dignitaries, is the scene of a pageant or the enactment of some ancient ceremony virtually daily. Inside the front and back covers of this book is a calendar of major events throughout the year, and described on the following pages is a selection of London's pageantry, ranging from state occasions to smaller, more intimate ceremonies, which all form part of the fabric of London life and tradition.

The band plays and traffic comes to a halt when the Changing of the Guard takes place outside Buckingham Palace.

Annual Ceremonies

Royal Epiphany Gifts Service
6th January

A 700-year-old ceremony in which officers of the royal houshold offer up gifts of gold, frankincense and myrrh in the Chapel Royal, St James's Palace. The gold is subsequently exchanged for currency and distributed to senior citizens.

Old Bailey in Session
early January

The opening session of the Central Criminal Court, Old Bailey, is attended by the lord mayor of London, who leads a procession from the Mansion House to the Old Bailey attended by the sheriffs, the swordbearer, the common crier and the City marshal.

Court of Common Council Service
January

The lord mayor of London and his officers walk in procession from the Guildhall to attend a service at the Church of St Lawrence Jewry, Gresham Street, prior to the first sitting of the newly-elected Court of Common Council which presides over the City of London.

Charles I Commemoration Ceremony
30th January

Each year members of the Society of King Charles the Martyr and the Royal Stuart Society commemorate the execution of Charles I on 30th January 1649. They walk in procession from St Martin-in-the-Fields to the equestrian statue of the King which stands in Trafalgar Square near the entrance to Whitehall.

Blessing of the Throats
3rd February (St Blaise's Day)

Throat sufferers congregate at the Church of St Ethelreda, in Holborn, for a service commemorating St Blaise, Bishop of Dalmatia, who saved the life of a child with a fishbone lodged in its throat while on his way to a martyr's death during the 3rd century.

Scout and Guide Founders' Day Service
on the Saturday nearest to 22nd February

Scouts and guides gather in Westminster Abbey on the shared birthday of Lord Baden-Powell, founder of the Scout and Guide Movement, and his widow. Wreaths are laid on the Baden-Powell memorial.

Cakes and Ale Sermon
Ash Wednesday

Members of the Stationers Company walk in procession from Stationers' Hall to St Paul's Cathedral where their chaplain preaches a sermon in accordance with the wishes of John Norton, a member of the Worshipful Company of Stationers who died during the reign of James I. Cakes and ale are distributed before or after the service.

Oranges and Lemons Children's Service
on or near 28th March

A service to mark the restoration of the bells of St Clement Danes in the Strand, the 'St Clements' of the well-known nursery rhyme 'Oranges and Lemons'. The service is attended by children of the St Clement Danes Primary School and each child receives an orange and a lemon.

Hot-Cross Buns Service
Good Friday

Under the terms of an ancient charity, the morning service at St Bartholomew-the-Great, Smithfield, is concluded by the distribution of money and hot-cross buns to 21 local widows.

Harness Horse Parade
Easter Monday

An extensive display of private and commercial horse-drawn vehicles, featuring all types of horses from shire horses drawing brewers' drays to the pony and trap, which takes place on the Inner Circle, Regent's Park.

London's Pearly Kings and Queens, dressed in their traditional costumes covered in pearl buttons, attend the Costermongers' Harvest Festival at St Martin-in-the-Fields on the first Sunday in October.

On Easter Sunday afternoon in Battersea Park a grand carnival parade takes place, composed of gaily-decorated floats, marching bands and displays of early blooms from the Scilly Islands. The parade has evolved from a custom begun by Queen Victoria when fashionable ladies promenaded through the Park to show off their new spring bonnets.

Spital Sermon Procession
second Wednesday after Easter

The lord mayor of London walks in procession with aldermen and other City dignitaries from the Guildhall to the Church of St Lawrence Jewry where a bishop nominated by the archbishop of Canterbury preaches the Spital Sermon. These sermons have an Easter theme and were preached at St Paul's Cross in the Cathedral churchyard prior to the Great Fire.

John Stow's Quill Pen Ceremony
on or near 5th April

The memorial service for John Stow, who wrote *The Survey of London* in 1598, takes place each year at the Church of St Andrew Undershaft, Leadenhall Street, attended by the lord mayor and other dignitaries. During the service the lord mayor places a fresh quill in the hand of Stow's statue, which depicts him at work on his survey.

Ceremony of the Lilies and Roses
21st May

Representatives of Eton College and King's College, Cambridge, both founded by Henry VI, join in a ceremony at the Wakefield Tower, Tower of London, on the anniversary of the King's murder. Lilies from Eton and roses from King's are placed on the spot where Henry was killed in 1471.

Oak Apple Day
29th May

The Chelsea Pensioners honour Charles II, the founder of the Royal Hospital, on the anniversary of his escape after the Battle of Worcester (1651). His statue is decorated with oak leaves and branches – in memory of the fact that the King hid in an oak tree.

The Knollys Red Rose Rent
24th June

This ceremony commemorates the fining of Sir Robert Knollys in the 14th century for building a footbridge between two of his properties on either side of Seething Lane. In recognition of his recent military service in France the fine imposed was the presentation of a red rose from his garden to the lord mayor every Midsummer Day. Today churchwardens of All Hallows-by-the-Tower carry a red rose to the Mansion House on an altar cushion where it is presented to the lord mayor together with a bouquet of roses for the lady mayoress.

Swan Upping
on or near last Monday in July

The Vintners' and Dyers' Livery Companies have the right, shared with the monarch, of keeping swans on the River Thames between London Bridge and Henley. Swan Upping takes place when the cygnets are about two months old, and entails the Queen's Swan Keeper and the Swan Wardens and Swan Markers of the two companies inspecting all swans and establishing the ownership of the cygnets. These are duly marked by the officials, who wear traditional livery, and operate from skiffs rowed by assistants in striped jerseys and hats.

Swan Upping on the Thames, when swans belonging to the Crown or to the Vintners' and Dyers' companies are marked.

Doggett's Coat and Badge Race

late July/early August

This, the oldest rowing event in the world, was instituted in 1715 by Thomas Doggett, an Irish actor, in honour of the accession to the throne of George I. Today, under the patronage of the Fishmongers' Company, six Thames watermen race against the tide from London Bridge to Chelsea Bridge. The winner of what is sometimes called the 'Watermen's Derby' receives a scarlet livery with silver buttons and a large silver badge on the left arm.

Admission of Sheriffs

28th September

The two sheriffs elected by the livery companies on Midsummer Day, go in full procession together with the lord mayor, senior City officials, and their fellow liverymen, from the Mansion House to the Guildhall. Here the sheriffs are presented with their chains of office.

When a new Lord Mayor of London takes office, he rides in a magnificent coach to the Royal Courts of Justice in the Strand, following a joyous and colourful parade.

Election of the Lord Mayor

29th September

The election of the lord mayor of London has taken place on Michaelmas Day since 1546. After a service in St Lawrence Jewry, the current lord mayor goes in procession to the Guildhall, where he and his aldermen make the final selection from the candidates nominated by the livery companies. After the ceremony the lord mayor and his successor ride in the state coach to the Mansion House to the accompaniment of the City bells.

Quit-Rents Ceremony

late October

This public ceremony, one of the oldest still carried out in London, is held at the Royal Courts of Justice, and involves the City Solicitor making token payment for two properties. The Queen's Remembrancer receives the rents, which take the form of two faggots of wood, a billhook, and a hatchet for land in Shropshire, and six horseshoes and sixty-one nails, for a forge which once stood in the Strand. The ceremony is so old that its origins are obscure.

In thanks for Britain's help to Norway in World War II, the people of Oslo send an enormous tree which is erected in Trafalgar Square every Christmas. Regent Street is also usually illuminated.

Lord Mayor's Show

2nd Saturday in November

This is the day when the new lord mayor publicly takes office. He rides to the Royal Courts of Justice in a ceremonial 18th-century coach, drawn by six horses, attended by a bodyguard of Pikemen and Musketeers, and preceded by a colourful procession of floats depicting some theme related to London's history. This ceremony is at least 600 years old and is the City's most spectacular showpiece. On the following Monday the lord mayor gives a lavish banquet at the Guildhall, attended by the prime minister and the archbishop of Canterbury.

THE LORD MAYOR'S PROCESSION - ROUTE OF

Trafalgar Service and Parade
21st October
A naval parade in memory of the Battle of Trafalgar, 1805, including a march from the Mall to Trafalgar Square followed by a service and the laying of wreaths at the foot of Nelson's column.

RAC Veteran Car Run
first Sunday in November
Cars built between 1895 and 1904 take part in this run which starts from Hyde Park Corner and finishes at Madeira Drive, Brighton. The event dates originally from 1896 when the law compelling motorists to have a man with a red flag walking in front of them was abolished and jubilant drivers destroyed their flags and roared off to Brighton. The first organised Run was held in 1933.

Installation of the Lord Mayor
8th November
The current lord mayor and the lord mayor-elect attend a luncheon at the Mansion House together with liverymen of each of their companies. They then go in procession to the Guildhall where they officially change places and transfer the insignia of office. The two lord mayors then return to the Mansion House to the accompaniment of peals of bells from the City churches.

Festival of St Cecilia
on or near 22nd November
A service is held at St Sepulchre's, Holborn, in honour of St Cecilia, the patron saint of music. Well-known organists and choirs from Westminster Abbey, St Paul's and Canterbury Cathedral combine to provide a feast of church music in a 16th-century ceremony which was revived in 1946 after having died out in the 19th century.

Every three years the choirboys of St Peter ad Vincula whack the boundary stones of their parish with willow canes in the ceremony of 'beating the bounds'.

Christmas and New Year celebrations
Every year a giant Christmas tree is donated to London by the people of Oslo, Norway. It is set up in Trafalgar Square and becomes the focal point for evening carol services from around 16th December onwards. On New Year's Eve the square is the scene of tumultuous celebrations as hundreds see the new year in, many of them demonstrating their joy by dousing each other in the fountains.

The King's Troop, Royal Horse Artillery fires a royal salute in Hyde Park. Salutes are fired in honour of a number of royal occasions, either here or by the Honourable Artillery Company at the Tower.

Occasional Ceremonies

Nosegays for Judges
Whenever a High Court judge hears cases at the Central Criminal Court (The Old Bailey) between May and September, nosegays are presented to all presiding judges. This ceremony dates from the days when evil smells from Newgate Jail pervaded the court during the summer months and judges were given bunches of strong smelling herbs to protect their sensitive noses.

Beating the Bounds
Once every three years (the next in 1981) a service is held on Ascension Day (May) at the Tower of London in the Chapel Royal of St Peter ad Vincula attended by all the dignitaries of the Tower. After the service the Chaplain leads a procession to each boundary stone where he shouts 'Cursed is he who moveth his neighbour's landmark' and the Chief Warder orders the choirboys to beat the stone with their willow wands.

This curious custom dates from the Middle Ages and similar ceremonies are still held in a number of parishes throughout the country. Its purpose (it is thought) was to teach young boys their local parish boundaries.

Gun Salutes
These Royal Salutes take place on various occasions throughout the year such as the Queen's official birthday (June), her actual birthday (21st April), the anniversary of her accession to the throne (6th February), and on other commemorative dates. The guns are fired by the Honourable Artillery Company at the Tower of London, and the King's Troop, Royal Horse Artillery, in Hyde Park.

The Tower of London

Originally built by William the Conqueror to impress and dominate the population of London, the Tower soon became the symbol of ultimate power, the place where even the highest and mightiest in the land could be cast down. Nine centuries later it stands strong, perhaps the most famous castle in the world. Yet for all its stories of imprisonment, torture and execution, its role was for the most part more mundane, being, at various times, the nation's storehouse for weapons, public records, the Crown Jewels, and, of all things, the Royal Menagerie.

Every schoolboy knows that in 1066 William the Conqueror defeated King Harold in the Battle of Hastings – but in that battle William had by no means conquered England. The Norman King knew that the key to the country was the control of London. Fortunately for him he did not have to fight for it. The city dignitaries rode out to meet him and in return for guaranteeing London all its accustomed rights and privileges they offered William the crown, and his Coronation was held on Christmas Day in Westminster Abbey.

William, however, was still wary of London's 'vast and fierce population' and he knew that a show of strength was needed to keep them in check, so he decided to build a great fortress-palace of stone which would dominate the city and forever remind Londoners of the power of the king.

A Royal Fortress

According to popular tradition 1078 marks the start of the building of the original tower (now known as the White Tower). Built of a mixture of Kentish ragstone and expensive Caen stone imported from France, it was, with its sister-fortress at Colchester, the largest building in the country and took about 20 years to build. 900 years later the White Tower remains one of the most outstanding examples of Norman military architecture in Europe. The most notable differences from the original building are Wren's enlarged windows and the extra floor which was added to the interior about 1600.

At the end of the 11th century a simple defensive wall was built round the Tower, and in the reigns of Richard I and John this was extended. All that remains from this period is the Bell Tower, one of the earliest English examples of a polygonal wall-tower. Attempts to create a moat were not very successful as the water went out at low tide. John's successor, Henry III (1216–1272) increased the surrounding walls and fortifications even further, and the Wakefield and Lanthorn Towers date from this time. Henry had the original Tower whitewashed inside and out, from which time it has been called the White Tower. He also started the Royal Menagerie and built the royal residences to the south of the Tower. Henry's son, Edward I (1272–1307), embarked on a

The White Tower, the keep of the Tower of London, stands as an outstanding example of Norman military architecture. It was begun in 1078, and built partly of Caen stone specially imported from France. Sir Christopher Wren remodelled the exterior early in the 18th century.

massive building programme which included a new outer wall, giving the Tower a complex concentric defence system. A Flemish engineer experienced in building dykes was brought in to build sluice-gates to keep the moat filled with water, and an elaborate series of towers with causeways, drawbridges and portcullises defended the landward entrance. Of these, the Lion Gate and Lion Tower have disappeared, but the Middle and Byward Towers still remain. A new entrance from the river, St Thomas's Tower, was later to be known as Traitor's Gate. A new tower to house the inner gate, later called the Bloody Tower, was also built.

Never again was building here undertaken on such a scale, though maintenance and restoration have been carried on ever since, and reflects the changing role of the Tower. By the 16th century it was no longer used as a royal residence and the palace buildings fell into disrepair – more and more it was

becoming infamous as a state prison and place of execution. It was also the traditional place for royal pageants. In addition it housed the Crown Jewels and Royal Menagerie.

Prison of State

It is as the State Prison, mainly reserved for the high and mighty who incurred the displeasure of king or government, that the Tower is best remembered. It had not long been built when, in 1100, Henry I had William II's chief minister Flambard imprisoned within its walls as a punishment for his corrupt practices while in power. The Tower's first prisoner soon escaped, however, using a rope smuggled inside in a jar of wine.

One of the most poignant tales is that of Richard II. Coming to the throne as a boy of eleven in 1377, his first trial came in 1381 when he was besieged in the Tower during the Peasants' Revolt led by Wat Tyler. They wanted the heads of the young King's ministers and while Richard was at Mile End parleying with them, some of them got into the Tower and dragged their oppressors out to their deaths on Tower Hill. Richard managed to persuade the rabble to disperse after Wat Tyler had been killed. In 1387 Richard was once again under siege in the Tower, this time by followers of the nobles who were angered by the power of his favourites. Richard had to agree to the arrest of his friends. Ten years later he turned on the nobles who had brought them down, only to lose support when his cousin Henry Bolingbroke (Henry IV) returned from exile. Eventually Richard was himself imprisoned in the Tower and later sent to Pontefract Castle where he died.

During the 15th century, in the Wars of the Roses, the Tower played a central role. The crown was disputed between the Lancastrian King Henry VI and Yorkist Edward IV, Edward eventually securing it by having Henry murdered in the Wakefield Tower. A tablet on the floor marks the spot where Henry is said to have died while saying prayers, and every year on the anniversary of his death members of King's College, Cambridge, and Eton College, both of which Henry founded, lay lilies and roses there.

Edward IV died in 1483 and the 13-year-old Edward V became king. He and his younger brother were under the protection of the Duke of Gloucester who decided to take the crown himself, becoming Richard III. Later that year the two Princes disappeared, and it was widely rumoured, though still unproven, that the usurper Richard had had them murdered in the Bloody Tower. Nearly two centuries later their bones were found there during demolition work and at Charles II's command were reburied in Westminster Abbey.

The Yeoman Warders, or 'Beefeaters' (French *boufitiers*, guardians of the king's buffet), were formed in 1485 by Henry VII

The Shadow of the Axe

By far the most well-known of monarchs connected with the Tower was, of course, Henry VIII. He had so many people imprisoned there that the French ambassador was moved to say 'when a man is prisoner in the Tower none dare meddle with his affairs, unless to speak ill of him, for fear of being suspected of the same crime'. Some were pardoned, some escaped and some got off with a large fine. For others, though, the only way out was the block. So it was for Henry's second wife, Anne Boleyn, who arrived at the Tower in great ceremony for her coronation in 1533, and again in great tragedy three years later for her trial and execution on Tower Green. His fifth wife, Catherine Howard, suffered the same fate six years later. Sir Thomas More and John Fisher were both imprisoned and executed for refusing to swear the Oath of Supremacy which acknowledged Henry as Head of the Church. Cromwell, Henry's one-time chief minister, went the same way, after he had arranged the marriage with Anne of Cleves, whom Henry detested. Imprisonments and executions did not end with Henry VIII. In Mary I's reign the Tower held for two months one of its most famous prisoners, the Princess Elizabeth, determinedly and characteristically protesting her innocence and loyalty all the while. It was also the time of the saddest of all the Tower executions, that of Lady Jane Grey, the 'Nine Days Queen', who was just a victim of her uncle's power struggle.

Towards the end of Elizabeth I's reign Sir Walter Raleigh, once the Queen's favourite, was imprisoned here for having, without royal approval, married Elizabeth Throckmorton. Later he was set free, but early in the reign of James I, Raleigh became entangled in a plot against the King and back to the Tower he went. There he was to stay for 12 years, where, in the Bloody Tower, he

lived in some comfort writing his *History of the World*, being visited by his friends and family, and being a great public attraction as he walked along the ramparts. He was still under death sentence when James released him in 1616 to find gold in Guiana, but he returned empty-handed and to execution.

The Great Public Attraction

Under the later Stuarts and during the Commonwealth, the Tower was still used as a prison, although less frequently (the last execution, in 1747, was that of the Jacobite rebel Lord Lovat), and from the reign of Charles II its main use was as an arsenal and the headquarters of the Mint (until 1812), the Record Office and the Ordnance Office. By the time of George II the Tower had also become the first national museum, with displays of royal history, weaponry and war trophies open to the general public; the first guidebook was already in existence by about 1750. During the 19th century the popularity of the Tower as a tourist attraction increased with the growth of cheap public transport, although its military function was still important. During both world wars the Tower reverted to its role of state prison for the incarceration of German spies. It is, however, as a repository of nearly 1,000 years of history that the Tower impresses itself on the minds of the thousands of visitors who pass through its gateway every year.

Four of the eight crowns that belong to the Crown Jewels. The jewels are kept in vaults under the Waterloo Barracks at the Tower. The crowns shown in the picture are, from left to right: Queen Elizabeth's, made in 1911; Queen Victoria's, made in 1870; George V's; and Queen Mary's. Both of the latter were made in the early 20th century.

A Tour of the Tower

The shadow of death

In 1465, during the reign of Edward IV, the first permanent scaffold was set up on Tower Hill. It was situated in what is now Trinity Square and its site is marked by a rectangle of bricked paving. This spot, with its blood-drenched memories, now makes a fitting point from which to view the exterior bulk of the Tower. During the last execution here, that of Lord Lovat in 1747, the stand holding the spectators collapsed, killing 12 of them.

Entering the Tower

As the entrance to the Tower is approached from Trinity Square, Tower Moat, which was drained in 1843 and is now partly used as a recreation ground, is seen on the left. The modern entrance to the Tower passes over the stone causeway which was the only entrance by land in the Middle Ages. Part of the outline of the Lion Tower is marked on the roadway between the entrance and the

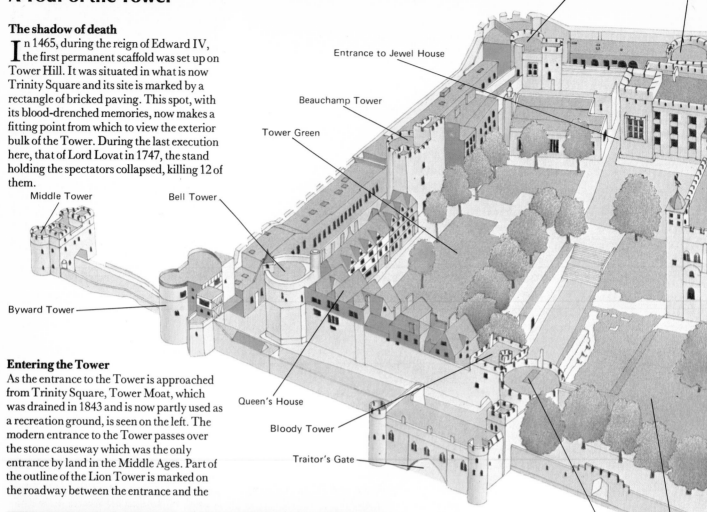

Devereux Tower

Flint Towe

Entrance to Jewel House

Beauchamp Tower

Tower Green

Middle Tower

Bell Tower

Byward Tower

Queen's House

Bloody Tower

Traitor's Gate

Wakefield Tower

Site of Great Ha

The Norman chapel of St John, redecorated by Henry III, but stripped during the Reformation.

Traitor's Gate was the main entrance to the Tower when the Thames was London's principal thoroughfare.

On display in the Tower's Armouries, this suit of armour was made at Greenwich about 1535 for Henry VIII.

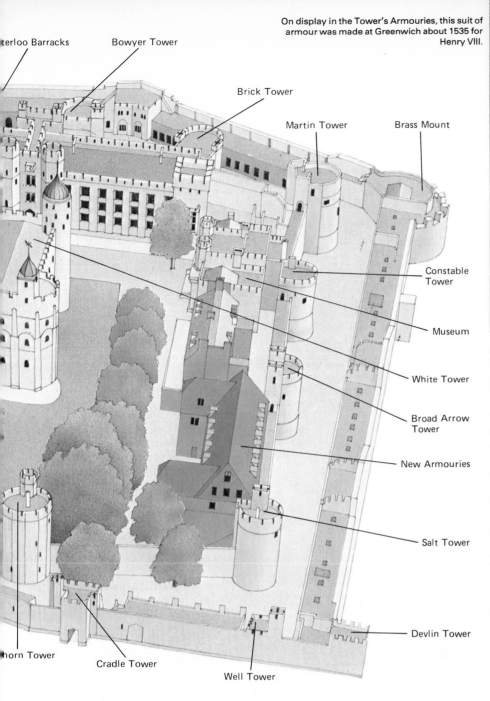

Labels on the illustration:
terloo Barracks
Bowyer Tower
Brick Tower
Martin Tower
Brass Mount
Constable Tower
Museum
White Tower
Broad Arrow Tower
New Armouries
Salt Tower
Devlin Tower
horn Tower
Cradle Tower
Well Tower

Middle Tower. Until 1834 it housed the Royal Menagerie, which included elephants, bears, and as many as 12 lions. Beyond the Middle Tower a causeway crosses the moat to the Byward Tower.

Inside the walls
Dating from the end of the 13th century, the Byward Tower was altered during the reign of Richard II. The timber superstructure on the inside was rebuilt in the early 16th century. Forming part of the Tower's inner defences is the Bell Tower, in which many famous prisoners were detained. Among them were Thomas More, Princess Elizabeth, and the Duke of Monmouth. The curtain wall east of this tower is pierced by the windows of the Lieutenant's Lodgings, now called the Queen's House, and one of these windows lights the Council Chamber, where Guy Fawkes and his fellow conspirators were examined by the Council in 1605 before their public execution at Westminster.

Approaching the block
In the days when the Thames was one of London's principal highways, prisoners were brought by boat from Westminster to the Tower, for execution or imprisonment. They arrived at Traitors' Gate and were escorted up echoing passageways, perhaps to be held in the Bloody Tower. Originally called the Garden Tower, the Bloody Tower was known by its present ominous name as early as 1597 as it was believed to have been the site of the murder of Edward IV and his brother, the Duke of York. Its most famous prisoner was probably Sir Walter Raleigh, who spent 12 years here.

Adjoining the Bloody Tower is the Wakefield Tower, in which the Crown Jewels were kept until 1967, when they were transferred to vaults under the Waterloo Barracks. Most of the Jewels were melted down during the Commonwealth and were subsequently remade for the coronation of Charles II.

The gateway under the Bloody Tower opens out on to Tower Green, where prisoners were executed in surroundings less public than those afforded by the scaffold on Tower Hill. Flanking the Green is the half-timbered Queen's House. In 1941 Rudolf Hess, the deputy leader of the Nazi Party and Hitler's private secretary, parachuted into Britain in an abortive attempt to make what he called an 'honourable' peace. He was detained in the Queen's House while the authorities decided what to do with him.

The White Tower
The nucleus of the Tower of London complex is the White Tower, or keep. It has been a symbol of unassailable power and dominance ever since William the Conqueror built it. It is one of the earliest and largest buildings of its kind in Western Europe, being 90 feet high from ground level to battlements and having walls 15 feet thick. The original Norman windows were enlarged by Sir Christopher Wren, who also added the rather whimsical turrets to the corner towers. Norman architecture at its simplest and most beautiful is displayed in the Chapel of St John, which is situated in the south-eastern corner of the Tower. A magnificent collection of armour is housed in the White Tower, and there are other collections of militaria in the Waterloo Barracks and the Museum.

The City

During the week, the City teems with businessmen, office workers, and a constant surge of traffic. At the weekends it becomes a silent, almost uncanny place, populated only by pigeons and the occasional sightseer. It is a place of sharp contrasts, where venerable old buildings rub shoulders with soaring office blocks of concrete and glass, and where ancient ceremonies are treated just as seriously as business deals involving millions of pounds.

The Origins of the Livery Companies

In 1215 King John signed a charter which gave the citizens of the City of London (that is the area encompassed by the old Roman walls) the right to elect their own mayor annually, rather than accept the choice of the reigning monarch. It was at about this time that the livery companies, who over the centuries have played such a prominent part in the administration of the City, first came into existence. These companies, or guilds, evolved as friendly societies for members of a particular trade or craft, combining this function with the furtherance of their guild's business. As more guilds were founded and those already established became more influential, their leading members took to wearing distinctive costumes or liveries, many of which are still worn during special ceremonies.

The oldest guild is believed to be the Weavers, established in 1184, but most of those still in existence date from the 14th century, by which time they were held in such high esteem that Edward III bestowed royal patronage on them by joining the Linen Armourers (now Merchant Taylors). The original 12 Great Companies – Mercers, Grocers, Clothworkers, Fishmongers, Goldsmiths, Skinners, Merchant Taylors, Haberdashers, Salters, Ironmongers, Vintners, and Drapers – have now been increased to 92.

During World War II only two of the guild halls – the Apothecaries' and the Vintners' – escaped bomb damage, and a number were totally destroyed. Several of the halls which exist today, most of which have been restored or rebuilt, contain historical items including ancient plate, works of art, and fine interior decorations. They are not generally open to the public, but special visits can often be arranged by the City Information Centre in St Paul's Church Yard. Some of the most recent additions to the list of companies are the Builders Merchants (established 1978), and the Actuaries and Insurers (both established in 1979).

Apart from their administrative responsibilities (see below), the livery companies have considerable influence over their trades, being concerned with the binding of apprentices, and trade standards (the Goldsmiths' hallmark still identifies genuine gold and silver articles).

Their benevolent foundations in the sphere of education are marked by the survival of such schools as the Merchant Taylors and the Skinners.

The 15th-century Guildhall is the City's oldest lay building.

The Corporation of London

The City of London is administered by the Corporation acting through the Court of Common Council, which is presided over by the lord mayor. In order to elect this body the City is broken down into 25 wards. Members of the livery companies from each ward elect one alderman and several councilmen to the Court of Common Council. A total of 153 councilmen make up the court together with 25 aldermen. The elected aldermen also form the Court of Aldermen which administers justice within the City.

Each year the liverymen elect two sheriffs for the City, and it is only aldermen who have served as sheriff who are eligible as candidates for the office of lord mayor. On Michaelmas Day the liverymen nominate two such aldermen who are then interviewed by the Court of Aldermen so that one may be selected to stand as lord mayor. This election is followed by the ancient ceremonies of the Installation of the Lord Mayor and the Lord Mayor's Show (see Pageants and Ceremonies on page 22).

The Guildhall

The Court of Common Council meets, by tradition, in the Guildhall. The building dates from 1411, when the livery companies raised money for its construction, but a good deal of restoration was carried out by Wren after the Great Fire, and a new façade was added by George Dance the Younger in 1788. The Great Hall, which was given a new roof in 1953, is now used for the Lord Mayor's Banquet and other civic functions. It has retained its original walls, and is decorated with the colourful shields of the livery companies, the banners of the 12 Great Companies, and several monuments to outstanding figures in the nation's history. At the west end of the Hall stand huge wooden figures of Gog and Magog, legendary British giants who are said to have fought against Trojan invaders around 1000BC. The statues stand over nine feet tall and replace an 18th-century pair which were destroyed during an air-raid in 1940.

Beneath the Hall is a magnificent 15th-century crypt, which has recently been restored and is the largest of its kind in London. The Guildhall also contains a clock museum (see page 98), the administrative buildings where Corporation business is carried out, and the Guildhall Library, founded in 1425, which contains thousands of books, manuscripts, and prints relating to the historical development of London.

The Mansion House

In 1739 the Corporation decreed that the lord mayor should no longer be obliged to provide his own dwelling house, and the architect George Dance the Elder was commissioned to design an official residence. The imposing Palladian-style mansion that he built stands on the corner of Queen Victoria Street. Its principal rooms are the Egyptian Hall, or dining room, and the Salon, which contains 19th-century tapestries and an enormous Waterford glass chandelier. The Corporation plate and insignia are kept in the building and include the 15th-century mayoral chain of office, the 17th-century Sword of State, and the 18th-century Great Mace, which is over five feet long. The Mansion House also contains the Lord Mayor's Court of Justice, which is the only court in the country to be held in a private residence and has its own underground cells. Visits can be arranged by prior application.

Commerce and Financial Institutions

The City has been the hub of London's financial and commercial activities since Roman times. Military campaigns have relied on it for finance: it provided Edward III with money for foreign wars, and Henry V's French campaigns were also funded by City tradesmen.

The Bank of England was founded in 1694 when City merchants decided that an independent national bank would be advantageous to all concerned. It operated from the Grocers' Hall until 1734 when the new building was opened in Threadneedle Street. The building was greatly expanded by Sir John Soane at the turn of the 18th century, and was extensively modernised between 1925 and 1939. The Bank was nationalised in 1946 and has special responsibilities for printing and issuing notes, administering the National Debt, and exchange control.

The vaults traditionally house the nation's gold reserves, and the internal security system is therefore of the highest order. After the Bank was attacked by looters during the Gordon Riots of 1780 the Bank Piquet was instituted, whereby a detachment of Guards marched to the building each afternoon and remained on watch throughout the night. This ceremony continued until 1973 when an electronic security system was installed.

Right: The Lutine Bell at Lloyd's, the world-famous insurance institution which began life in a 17th-century coffee-house. The bell is rung once whenever a ship insured with Lloyd's is sunk or lost at sea.

Below: To those unfamiliar with its ways, the Stock Exchange is a strange and mysterious world, with brokers standing round apparently doing little and messengers scurrying about with slips of paper. From behind a glass panel in the viewing gallery, visitors may watch the scene and come away none the wiser.

The Royal Exchange was opened in 1568 as a meeting place for City merchants. Queen Victoria opened the present building in 1844. No business has been transacted here for over 40 years, but important announcements such as the proclamation of new sovereigns and declarations of war are traditionally made from the broad flight of steps at its entrance.

The Stock Exchange is the modern venue for financial wheelings and dealings. Founded in 1773, it is now housed in a modern building on the corner of Old Broad Street and Throgmorton Street. Its proceedings may be observed by the public from the Visitors' Gallery.

A financier called Edward Lloyd started a shipping underwriting business in a coffee house in Lombard Street in 1691. What began as a small gathering of businessmen grew to become **Lloyd's of London**, which occupies an extensive site in Lime Street. The building's Underwriting Room contains the famous Lutine Bell, salvaged from a frigate which sank in 1799 with a cargo of gold valued at £1,400,000 and insured at Lloyd's. The bell is traditionally rung once for the loss of an overdue vessel and twice for its safe arrival.

The Old Bailey (Central Criminal Court)
The notorious Newgate Prison, which stood on this site, was the scene of public executions between 1783 and 1868 (sentence was subsequently carried out in private until 1901). It was demolished in 1902 and replaced by the Central Criminal Court, which takes its popular name from the street in which it stands. Most of the major trials of this century have been heard here, including those of Crippen, Christie, Haig, and the Kray brothers. The public may view the proceedings in No 1 Court by queueing for a seat in the Visitors' Gallery (entrance in Newgate Street).

The Barbican
This impressive new development, built around the remaining portion of the old Roman wall, is an ambitious scheme to promote the City as a residential area rather than a place to be visited only for the purpose of daily work. It contains high-rise blocks of flats, shops, offices, pubs, the new City of London School for Girls, and the 16th-century church of St Giles Cripplegate. Other features include an ornamental lake, an arts centre, and the new Guildhall School of Music and Drama. The Museum of London (see page 92) lies on the south western extremity of the development.

Information on the City can be obtained from the City of London Information Centre, St Paul's Church Yard, EC4. It is situated opposite St Paul's Cathedral.

St Paul's Cathedral

This magnificent building, created by Sir Christopher Wren after the Great Fire of London in 1666, retains its dignity and grandeur even though it is now overshadowed by enormous tower blocks.

It is a huge structure, 515 ft long and 242 ft across at its widest point, and is elaborately decorated with columns, porticos, and balustrades. The west end of the cathedral is approached by two wide flights of steps and is surmounted by twin towers. The whole building is crowned by a beautiful central dome which rises to 365 ft above ground level and is 112 ft in diameter.

Before the Fire

When clearing the site for the new foundations, Wren found evidence that convinced him that there had been a Romano-British Christian church on the site, although written records go back only as far as AD604.

The cathedral which the Normans began on the site in the 11th century to replace a wooden church was much larger than the present structure and was not finally completed until the 13th century. It became the focal point of religious life in London, but its importance was later to fade as the building was neglected and fell into disrepair. It eventually became a market place for traders and a thoroughfare for pedestrians. By the early part of the 17th

At its completion, Wren's Cathedral dominated the City and its surroundings.

century the cathedral was in a deplorable state, and the great architect Inigo Jones was commissioned to restore it. The Civil War brought the work to a halt, however, and nothing further was done until after the Restoration, when Charles II asked Sir Christopher Wren to draw up plans for a complete restoration of the cathedral. Before any work could be done the Great Fire raged through the City and gutted the building.

Wren immediately drew up plans for a new cathedral, and these were eventually accepted after having first been rejected on the grounds that the designs were newfangled and outlandish. The final stone of the new cathedral was laid by Sir Christopher's son in 1710, only 35 years after the work had begun – a considerable achievement for such a vast undertaking at a time when every stone was cut and put into position by hand. Wren was buried in the crypt of his masterwork in 1723.

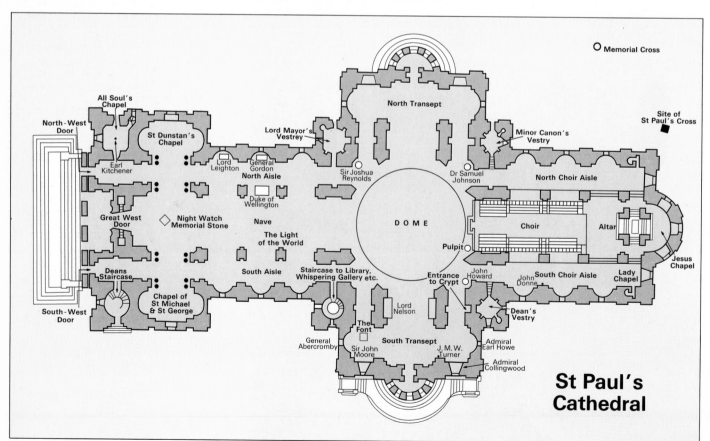

St Paul's Cathedral

Left: The great dome, which contains the Whispering Gallery and frescoes by Sir James Thornhill, is a supreme example of Wren's genius.

Below: Above the choir.

Inside the Cathedral

From the end of the nave there is a superb view along the whole length of the cathedral through the Choir to the High Altar and its ornate canopy. Recorded commentaries describing the cathedral can be obtained from headphones at the west end of the nave. The great dome rises above the centre of the nave. Around its interior is the famous Whispering Gallery, where a message whispered into the wall on one side can be clearly heard 112 ft away on the other side. The Gallery is reached through a doorway in the western corner of the South Transept that leads to the stairs which also give access to the library and the two external galleries of the dome with their panoramic views across London.

In the Choir are the stalls of the St Paul's Cathedral Choir. They are the work of the great 17th-century woodcarver Grinling Gibbons. Beyond the Choir is the focal point of the whole cathedral – the High Altar. It is a modern replacement of the altar which was damaged during World War II, and is an exact copy of Wren's original design.

The cathedral contains numerous chapels, many of which contain exquisite furniture and decorations. Holy Communion is celebrated on most days in the Chapel of St Dunstan, at the western end of the cathedral.

Wren's cathedral originally contained no monuments, but towards the end of the 18th century these began to appear, and now there are several hundred in the building. The oldest is that of the metaphysical poet John Donne (1573–1631), who was Dean of St Paul's from 1621 until his death. It is the only monument to have survived from the old cathedral and is situated in the South Choir Aisle. Almost filling the North Aisle is the huge monument to the Duke of Wellington. He is actually buried in the Crypt, beneath an imposing sarcophagus. The ornate funeral car in which his body was brought to the cathedral stands nearby.

Also in the Crypt is the tomb of Lord Nelson. His coffin lies beneath a black marble sarcophagus that had originally been intended for Cardinal Wolsey, and was also considered for Henry VIII. Standing among the graves of several well-known artists is Wren's own tomb. Above it, his tombstone carries the famous epitaph, 'Lector, si monumentum requiris, circumspice' ('Reader, if you seek his monument, look about you'). Many other tombs and memorials are contained in the Crypt, and also here is the Chapel of the Order of the British Empire, which was dedicated in 1960.

31

Officially, the City of Westminster covers almost all the area known as London's 'West End'. The name Westminster, however, more usually refers to the area immediately around the Houses of Parliament and Westminster Abbey. The site, once known as Thorney Island, is very ancient – a building is known to have stood here in Roman times – and it is said that Mellitus, the first Bishop of London, consecrated a church here in AD616. Later, in about 730, Benedictine monks founded an abbey dedicated to St Peter. This was called West Minster, or 'monastery to the west of London', the name which has been used ever since. Though Westminster today is part of central London, until a few hundred years ago the City of London was confined within the ancient Roman walls and Westminster was an outlying suburb.

The Palace of Westminster

The Houses of Parliament are often called the Palace of Westminster because from the time of Edward the Confessor to Henry VIII the site was the main London residence of the monarch. The Saxon palace in which Edward the Confessor lived was not to the liking of William the Conqueror and he completely rebuilt it. His son, William Rufus, added the 240-ft-long Westminster Hall, probably the largest Norman hall ever built in Europe. It was almost certainly aisled, with timber piers to support the roof.

At the end of the 14th century Richard II remodelled the hall, retaining the lower portions of the Norman walls but adding massive buttresses to support the 600 tons of roof. An outstanding engineering feat in its day, it meant that supporting piers were no longer needed and it is the earliest surviving example of a hammer-beam roof. The hall has miraculously survived almost intact.

Westminster Hall was, of course, part of the royal palace – Old Palace Yard, next to it, was an inner court of the palace – but it was not the original Parliament house. The House of Commons met in the Chapter House of Westminster Abbey until Henry VIII moved to Whitehall Palace in 1529, after which Westminster Palace, including the hall, was turned over to state institutions. Even then the Commons met in the palace's St Stephen's Chapel for some years, while the House of Lords met until 1800 in a chamber at the south end of Old Palace Yard. By the time of Charles I however, the Commons sat in Westminster Hall, and it was here that Charles I was tried in 1649.

The New Palace

Almost all the old palace was burned down in a disastrous fire on 16th October, 1834. All that survived of the medieval buildings were

Westminster

There are more famous London landmarks in Westminster than any other part of the capital. They include Westminster Abbey, the Houses of Parliament, Whitehall, and Downing Street. It has been a sacred site from time immemorial, and the centre of English government for over 900 years. Behind the forbidding façades of the government offices which line Whitehall decisions are made which affect the lives of everyone in Britain.

The architectural detailing of the Houses of Parliament is superb.

Big Ben's 13½-ton bell.

Westminster Hall, the cloister and undercroft of St Stephen's Chapel, and the Jewel Tower. A competition was held at once for the design of a new Parliament building. One of the conditions was that it had to be in either the Gothic or the Elizabethan style. In all, 97 designs were submitted (only six of them Elizabethan) and the winning entry was by Charles Barry; although much of the detailed creative work was done by August Pugin.

The existing Houses of Parliament are basically a series of chambers, lobbies, and offices running parallel to the Thames. The building is 940 ft long, covers eight acres and includes 1100 apartments and over two miles of passages. To the south is the lofty Victoria Tower, 336 ft high. At the north end is the slightly smaller (316 ft), but much more famous Clock Tower known to all as Big Ben. The name actually refers to the mighty 13½-ton bell which strikes the hours. The minute hands on the clock's four 23-ft wide dials are each as tall as a double-decker bus, and it is still wound by hand. It is well known for keeping perfect time – tiny adjustments are made by adding or removing old pennies to or from the mechanism. While Parliament is in session the Union Jack flies from the Victoria Tower by day and by night a light shines from the Clock Tower.

The House of Lords sits in a hall to the south of the central lobby, and at one end, under an elaborate canopy, is the sovereign's throne, used at State Openings. In front of the throne is the Woolsack, a cushion filled with wool, on which the Lord Chancellor sits. The Woolsack is thought to have originated in the reign of Edward III as a symbol of the importance of the wool trade to England.

During World War II Barry's original House of Commons, Commons Lobby and Division Lobbies were destroyed by bombs and have been rebuilt in Gothic style. There are not enough seats in the House of Commons for all the 635 Members entitled to attend, but it was decided to keep the arrangement of the old House because its intimacy is more suited to the British style of politics. The Speaker, who acts as chairman and is elected from the House, sits at one end and presides over debates. The Government and Opposition sit on benches facing each other across the House, the front benches being reserved for Ministers. When a vote is taken, Members file into lobbies on either side of the House, 'Ayes' to the right and 'Noes' to the left.

Parliament

A Parliament of sorts has been in existence since the late 13th century when the reigning monarch presided over a superior court, composed of officials from his own household, plus ecclesiastical and lay magnates, which dealt with national administration. The Commons, which was the brainchild of Simon de Montfort, began to evolve during the reign of Edward III, and by his death in 1377 were firmly established with their own elected Speaker. Officers of State were selected by the monarch until 1696 when William III agreed that the party holding a majority of seats in the House of Commons should form a governing Ministry – the forerunner of the present Cabinet. The Office of Prime Minister was established in the reign of George I, the first incumbent being Robert Walpole.

Parliament was dominated by two political parties – Whigs and Tories (both of which had their origins in the 17th century) – until the late 19th century. In 1828 the Whigs adopted the name Liberals and the Tories that of Conservatives a few years later. Labour candidates first appeared at the general election of 1892. They banded together to form the Labour Representative Committee in 1900, and have been known as the Labour Party since 1906.

Today the Commons has almost full authority for governing the country, though all Bills have to go from there to the House of Lords, where some are amended and passed back to the Commons. Very few are ever rejected. Financial Bills can be delayed for a limited period by the Lords but cannot be thrown out entirely. In recent years no new hereditary peerages have been created, but both men and women can be made Life Peers. Also sitting in the House of Lords are all the archbishops, 24 bishops, and current and retired Lords of Appeal.

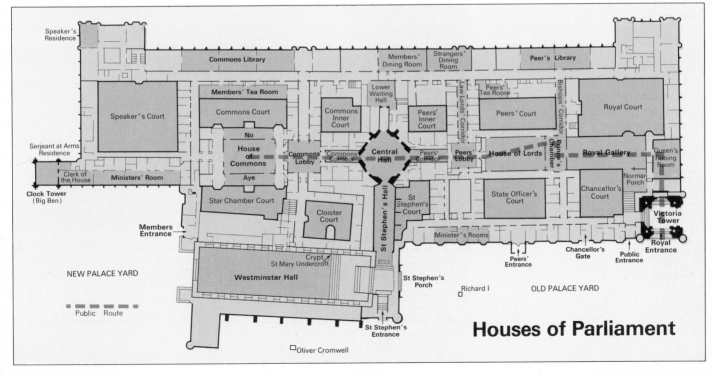

Houses of Parliament

Whitehall

Though the name 'Whitehall' today has come to mean 'Government' to most people, the road called Whitehall which runs from Parliament Square to Trafalgar Square only became the location for the majority of government offices during the early 18th century. No 10 Downing Street became the official residence of the first Prime Minister, Robert Walpole, in 1735, and has been the official home of the Prime Minister ever since. The street also contains the residence of the Chancellor of the Exchequer at No 11, the Government Whips' Office at No 12 (Whips are responsible for the attendance of party members in Parliament), and the offices of the Judicial Committee of the Privy Council – the Court of Appeal for Commonwealth countries which do not have their own.

There are still a number of government buildings in Whitehall itself. At the south end, on the corner of King Charles Street, are the old Foreign and Commonwealth Offices. Farther up, on the same side, is Horse Guards, flanked on either side by the Treasury and the Admiralty. Behind Horse Guards is Horse Guards Parade, where Trooping the Colour takes place.

On the opposite side of Whitehall, at the north end, is Great Scotland Yard, until 1891 the famous Metropolitan Police headquarters. Farther down is the Ministry of Defence, part of which stands behind the Banqueting House. This is the site of the old Whitehall Palace which belonged to Cardinal Wolsey and was seized by Henry VIII in 1529. James I had great plans for rebuilding Whitehall Palace, but owing to lack of funds, the only part which was completed was the Banqueting House, designed in a fine Palladian style by Inigo Jones and erected in 1625. Charles I was executed outside the Banqueting House in 1649. In 1698 the rest of Whitehall Palace was destroyed by fire and was never rebuilt, and William and Mary subsequently took up up residence in St James's Palace.

In the middle of Whitehall stands the Cenotaph, commemorating the dead of the two world wars. Members of the Royal Family and leading politicians lay wreaths at its foot on Remembrance Sunday. Over the years government departments have changed and expanded and a number of offices have moved from Whitehall. The Home Office now has its headquarters in Queen Anne's Gate, and other ministries, such as the Department of Trade and Industry, the Department of Energy and the Department of Transport, are all to be found in neighbouring areas of the City of Westminster.

Westminster Abbey

Edward the Confessor was determined to have the abbey at Westminster enlarged and made the crowning-place of English kings. He lived to see it built but he died the day before his Norman church was consecrated to St Peter on 28th December, 1065, and he was buried behind the high altar. His successor, Harold, was crowned here the following week, and every English sovereign has been crowned here since then. The only exceptions are Edward V and Edward VIII, who were never crowned.

All that remains of Edward the Confessor's building are the Chamber of the Pyx (at one time used as the Royal Treasury) and the Norman Undercroft (which now houses a museum). Henry III added a Lady Chapel to the east end in 1220, but in 1245 decided to rebuild the whole abbey in honour of Edward, by then canonised as St Edward the Confessor. Finished in 1269, the design of the great church was modelled on that of French cathedrals such as Reims and Amiens in much the form it is today. From then until the reign of George III it was the burial-place of all English kings and queens.

Rebuilding work on the nave started at the end of the 14th century and carried on throughout the 15th, though the style and design of Henry III was strictly adhered to. The Lady Chapel was pulled down and replaced between 1503 and 1519 by the splendid Henry VII Chapel at the eastern end. The 225-ft-high towers were added in the mid-18th century by Nicholas Hawksmoor. Much 19th-century renovation has marred the external detail, but the abbey's proportions still give a sense of continuity and permanence. The graceful flying buttresses and the delicately shaped walls of the Henry VII Chapel make it one of the most impressive sights in the capital, particularly when viewed from Parliament Square or Dean's Yard to the south.

Many consider the Chapel of Henry VII in Westminster Abbey to be the supreme example of Perpendicular architecture.

Inside the Abbey

The interior of the abbey is one of the finest achievements of English architecture, though the visitor is hampered in seeing this by the clutter of innumerable monuments and memorials within. Built of Reigate stone with piers of green, grey and purple Purbeck marble, it has the tallest Gothic nave in the country (York Minster's, at 100 ft, is two feet shorter). Although it has been rebuilt, added to, and altered over the years, it is architecturally uniform, with the exception of the Henry VII Chapel which, built of Huddleston stone, is intricately and exquisitely decorated, the highlight being the lace patterns of the fan-vaulting in the roof.

The 1,000 or so monuments have always been a source of controversy. Some say their number ruins the aesthetic appeal of the abbey, while others maintain that without them it would become stark and lose its character. Certainly the memorials provide a history of English monumental sculpture from the 13th to the 19th centuries, and nowhere else are so many great names from Britain's past commemorated under one roof.

The tombs of the monarchs are, as is to be expected, large and elaborate. When Henry III had the abbey rebuilt he provided a magnificent tomb for the remains of Edward the Confessor, and it became a place of pilgrimage. Henry VII's tomb in his chapel was made by the artist Torrigiano – who is

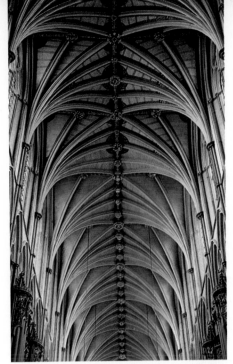

Unlike the majority of English cathedrals, Westminster Abbey displays a marked French influence in the exaggerated height of the nave.

also famous for having given Michelangelo a bloody nose when they were both pupils. In the same chapel Mary Tudor and Elizabeth I are buried together, though the tomb bears the effigy of Elizabeth only. Nearby are monuments to the two little daughters of James I. Sophia, who lived only three days, is commemorated by a little cradle made of alabaster. Sometimes known as Innocents' Corner, here also is the urn holding the remains of the murdered 'Princes in the

Unlike the majority of English cathedrals, Westminster Abbey displays a marked French influence in the exaggerated height of the nave.

Tower', Edward V and his brother Richard.

Since a monument to Chaucer was erected here in 1556 it has been the final accolade for a poet to be commemorated in what is now known as Poet's Corner. Few of them are actually buried within the precincts of the abbey. Among those remembered are Ben Jonson, Shakespeare, Milton, Wordsworth, Keats, and Shelley. There are also memorials to people known in artistic fields other than poetry – such as Sir Walter Scott, Dr Johnson, and G F Handel.

Elsewhere are memorials to the nation's great statesmen, politicians, servicemen, scientists and others. They include statues and commemorations of such eminent people as Pitt, Disraeli and Gladstone, Lord Baden-Powell, General Wolfe and General Gordon of Khartoum. More recent memorials tend to be simple floor-slabs, and these include those honouring Clement Attlee, Ramsay MacDonald, Ernest Bevin and, of course, Winston Churchill.

Westminster Abbey presents a stunning array of historical and commemorative monuments in a setting of outstanding architectural beauty – but it must be remembered that it is still a Christian church with regular services. The abbey is open daily, but when services are being held certain parts are closed to tourists.

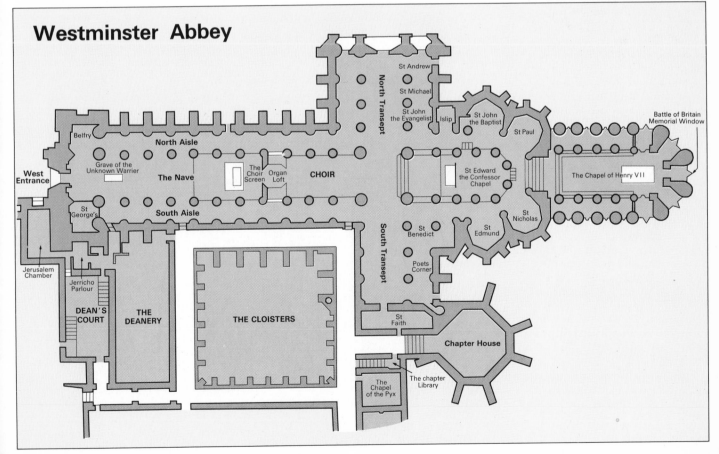

Westminster Abbey

Twelve London Walks

The unassuming doorway of No 10 Downing Street, the London home of the Prime Minister. Next door, at No 11, lives the Chancellor of the Exchequer.

Places in **bold italic** in the route directions are described elsewhere in this book. Of particular relevance to this walk is the section of the book called Westminster (pages 32–35). Names shown in black on the map are described in the text.

Leave Westminster Underground Station and turn right into Bridge Street. Cross Cannon Row, turn right into Parliament Street, and walk up it on the right-hand side.

The Cenotaph

In the centre of Parliament Street is the Cenotaph, a simple yet moving pillar of Portland stone, that was designed by Sir Edwin Lutyens and unveiled in 1920 on the anniversary of Armistice Day. It was originally built to the memory of the men who lost their lives in World War I. Now memorial services for the dead of both world wars are held here every year on the second Sunday in November.

Beyond the Cenotaph Parliament Street becomes Whitehall. Cross the road to reach Downing Street.

Downing Street

This world-famous street was built by Sir George Downing, a secretary to the Treasury, in about 1680. At first it was an unimportant residential street with a pub – the Cat and Bagpipes – on the corner. In 1732 George II offered No 10 to Sir Robert Walpole as a town house and since then it has been the official residence of the British Prime Minister. No 11 is the official residence of the Chancellor of the Exchequer. The buildings themselves have unpretentious Georgian façades, but have been extensively modified inside.

Walk back down Parliament Street to the government offices on the corner of King Charles Street.

Walk 1

Westminster and Millbank

This walk begins in the shadow of the Houses of Parliament, the heart and symbol of Britain's democracy. It then leads to the sequestered peace of Dean's Yard and the elegant charm of the streets round Smith Square. From the Tate Gallery it returns, alongside the Thames, to Parliament Square.

Government Offices

Sir George Gilbert Scott, the distinguished Victorian architect, designed this imposing building. His first designs were in the Gothic style and Lord Palmerston rejected them all. He insisted on something Italian, so Scott bought some books on Italian architecture and 'set vigorously to work to rub up on it', with the results that can be seen today.

At the end of Parliament Street turn right into Great George Street, then left to cross into Parliament Square at the traffic lights.

Parliament Square

In and around Parliament Square there are many statues of British politicians. Foreign statesmen are also represented, and include Field-Marshal Smuts by Jacob Epstein, and (outside the old Middlesex Guildhall) a rumpled figure of Abraham Lincoln. The latter is a copy of the statue by Augustus Saint-Gaudens in Chicago.

Cross Parliament Square.

Middlesex Guildhall

This Renaissance-style building was opened in 1913, and stands on the site of an earlier guildhall. It once functioned as the administrative centre for the old county of Middlesex. The friezes on the façade depict Magna Carta, Henry II granting a charter to Westminster, and Lady Jane Grey accepting the crown from the Duke of Northumberland.

*Leaving the square, cross Broad Sanctuary opposite the entrance to **Westminster Abbey**, and turn right along Broad Sanctuary.*

Methodist Central Hall

Built in 1849-51, the Methodist Central Hall stands across the road in Storey's Gate. It was once a meeting place for the infant United Nations Organization.

Pass to the left of the Westminster Schoolboys' Memorial and bear left through an arched gateway into Dean's Yard. Turn left along the north side of the yard, then right at the entrance to the Abbey Cloisters. Pass the Chapter Office and a gateway on the left leading to Little Dean's Yard and the precincts of Westminster School.

Little Dean's Yard and Westminster School

Westminster Abbey probably had its own school before 1200. When the abbey became a cathedral in 1540, the school became the King's Grammar School, with 40 scholars. It was re-founded by Queen Elizabeth I in 1560. The custom known as the Pancake Greeze is observed here every Shrove Tuesday. The cook, dressed in cap and apron, comes in with a frying-pan and has to toss a pancake over the 16-ft-high iron bar which separates the old Upper and Lower Schools. As it falls, representatives from each form scramble for it, and the boy who gets the biggest piece also gets a guinea from the Dean. On the north side of Little Dean's Yard is Ashburnham House, built shortly after 1662, and

'Peace on thy house, O passer-by' is the motto over the doorway of No 2 Barton Street.

the best example in London of a stately mid-17th-century house.

Leave Dean's yard by the iron gateway in the left-hand corner and turn left into Great College Street. Cross over and turn right into Barton Street.

Barton Street

Barton Street contains some exceptionally well-preserved Georgian houses. Nos 1–14 (except for Nos 2 and 8) are original and carry a tablet dating them to 1722. T E Lawrence ('Lawrence of Arabia') lived at No 14. An inscription on the wall of No 2 reads: 'Peace on Thy House O Passer-by'.

Bear left into Cowley Street, then bear right and walk on, crossing Great Peter Street into Lord North Street, which has attractive 18th-century houses. Turn right into Smith Square.

Looking down over Westminster.

Second-hand bookshops and bookstalls abound all over London, often in the most unexpected places.

Museum of Garden History in memory of John Tradescant, Charles I's gardener. Captain William Bligh, of the *Bounty*, is buried here.

Re-cross Lambeth Bridge, keeping to the right. Turn right into Millbank, then right into Victoria Tower Gardens.

Victoria Tower Gardens

In the thin triangle of Victoria Tower Gardens are the Buxton Drinking Fountain, commemorating the emancipation of slaves in the British Empire in 1834; a statue of the suffragette Mrs Emmeline Pankhurst (1858–1928); and a copy of the famous statue by Auguste Rodin (1840–1917) called 'The Burghers of Calais'.

Emerge from the gardens into Abingdon Street opposite the Jewel Tower.

The Jewel Tower

This inconspicuous moated tower is in fact a survival of the medieval Palace of Westminster. It was built in 1365 to house the monarch's personal treasure, and this remained its function until the death of Henry VIII. It now houses a collection of pottery and other items found during excavations in the area, and is open to the public.

Walk up the right-hand side of Abingdon and St Margaret's Streets, past the **Houses of Parliament.** *Cross Bridge Street and turn right to return to Westminster Underground Station.*

Smith Square

This square is named after Sir John Smith, who owned and developed the land. Some of the houses were rebuilt after World War II, but No 5 dates from 1726. In the centre of the square is Thomas Archer's fine church of St John. Concerts are often broadcast from the church, which has been specially adapted for the purpose. St John's also has its own orchestra, now of international repute. Other buildings in the square include the headquarters of both the Labour Party (Transport House, in the south-east corner of the square) and the Conservative Party (No 32).

Walk round the west end of the church to leave Smith Square by Dean Bradley Street. Walking up the right-hand side, cross Horseferry Road into Dean Ryle Street. Continue along John Islip Street, crossing Page Street, Marsham Street and Bulinga Street and cross the road at the back of the Tate Gallery. Turn left into Atterbury Street and at the end cross Millbank and turn right. Walk towards Vauxhall Bridge and bear left into a small garden.

Lambeth Palace

Much of this historic structure, which has been the London residence of the Archbishop of Canterbury for 700 years, was rebuilt during the 19th century. Extensive damage was caused by bombs during World War II. Of the old palace, the most interesting parts are the Lollards Tower and the Gatehouse, both of the 15th century, and the 13th-century Chapel Crypt. Parts of the palace, and its grounds, are open to the public. Adjoining the south gateway of the palace is the former church of St Mary, now being restored as a

Vauxhall Bridge Garden

A large bollard here marks the approximate site of Millbank Penitentiary from which, between 1816 and 1867, convicts sentenced to transportation embarked on their journey. The garden also contains a sculpture by Henry Moore, fountains and seats.

Return along Millbank with the river on the right, and the **Tate Gallery** *on the left. Continue along Millbank and turn right to cross Lambeth Bridge. On the other side of the bridge, follow the pedestrian subway to the Albert Embankment on the left, for a view of Lambeth Palace.*

Locking Piece, a sculpture by Henry Moore, is to be found in a small garden by Riverside House at the end of Vauxhall Bridge Road.

The Tudor brickwork of Morton's Tower, the main entrance to Lambeth Palace.

Walk 2

Start: Victoria Bus Station
Approximate distance: 2¼ miles

To Buckingham Palace and Westminster Cathedral

This walk leads past the walls of Buckingham Palace to the 18th-century elegance of Queen Anne's Gate. It makes its way to Maunsel Street – one of London's many hidden gems, finishing in the shadow of Westminster Cathedral's imposing tower.

Lord Haldane's house in Queen Anne's Gate.

Places in **bold italic** type in the route directions are described elsewhere in this book. Names shown in black on the map are described in the text.

From the west side of the Victoria Bus Station in Terminus Place follow Buckingham Palace Road northwards along the left-hand side. Cross Lower Grosvenor Place, then pass the entrance, on the left, to the Royal Mews.

The Royal Mews

Designed by John Nash and completed in 1825, the Royal Mews contain the state coaches. The Windsor Greys and Cleveland Bay carriage horses are kept in the stables. The Queen's Gallery (see page 103), a fine art gallery, may be visited by turning left into Buckingham Gate.

*At the traffic lights near **Buckingham Palace** turn right then cross the road and go through the gates into Birdcage Walk on the right-hand side.*

Birdcage Walk

Birdcage Walk owes its name to an aviary owned by Charles II which was situated here. It contained, among other rarities, a crane with a wooden leg!

*Continue along the right-hand side of Birdcage Walk, with **St James's Park** on the left, to Wellington Barracks.*

Wellington Barracks

The barracks were first built in 1833, and the Guards Chapel which stands in front of them is the latest of many additions and alterations. It was built in 1961–63 on the site of the original chapel, which was largely destroyed by bombs in World War II. The barracks serve as the regimental headquarters of the Grenadier, Coldstream, Scots, Irish, and Welsh Guards.

Take the next right into Queen Anne's Gate and follow it round to the left.

Queen Anne's Gate

This quiet close, built in 1704, is undoubtedly one of the most charming streets in London. It has been the home of several distinguished figures in British history, including Lord Palmerston (who lived at No 20), and the statesman, lawyer, and philosopher Lord Haldane (No 28). A statue of Queen Anne stands outside No 13, and No 26 still has the snuffer for extinguishing the linkman's torch after he had lighted its owner's home.

Take the next right into Carteret Street. At the end of the street cross the road into Broadway.

Broadway

No 55 Broadway is the headquarters building of London Transport. It was designed by the architect Charles Holden in 1927–29, and had to combine the functions of an underground station with a large number of offices. Holden's uncompromisingly modern building was bold for its day, and the sculptures attached to its façade were considered revolutionary. They include 'Night' and 'Day' by Jacob Epstein and horizontal figures of the winds by Eric Gill and Henry Moore.

Turn right at the post office into Caxton Street and walk up the right-hand side as far as Caxton Hall.

Caxton Hall

The name and look of this registry office were once familiar to all followers of high society doings, as until 1977 it was the most fashionable place for out-of-church weddings.

Cross to the other side of Caxton Street and walk to the Blewcoat School at the end.

The Royal Mews in Buckingham Palace Road contains royal transport.

The Blewcoat School

William Greene, founder of what is now Watney's Brewery, established this charity school in 1688. The building itself, with its charming figure of a charity boy above the doorway, dates from 1709 and now belongs to the National Trust.
By the nearside of the school turn left into Brewers Green, then join Buckingham Gate. Cross Victoria Street into Artillery Row. Take the next left into Greycoat Place. Ahead is the Greycoat Hospital.

The Greycoat Hospital

This is another old charity school, founded in 1698 as a boarding school for seventy children. The original building, which dated from 1701, was partly destroyed during World War II and has now been restored in the Queen Anne style. The figures of the Greycoat boy and girl over the door are of painted wood, and may date from the early 18th century. Since 1873 it has been a day-school for girls only, who number over 600.
Cross the pedestrian crossing in front of the school and turn left. Take the next right into Horseferry Road. Pass the Industrial Health and Safety Centre and take the second right into Maunsel Street.

Vincent Square, in the heart of London, is the playing fields for Westminster School.

The Roman Catholic cathedral at Westminster, built about the turn of the century, is based on the Byzantine style.

The Albert in Victoria Street is a fine example of London's many historic public houses.

The 'Blewcoat Boy' stands above the Blewcoat School in Caxton Street.

Maunsel Street

After the rather dingy appearance of Horseferry Road, Maunsel Street comes as a delightful surprise. It is lined with charming 19th-century cottages, several of which are enlivened by window-box gardens.
At the end of Maunsel Street turn right alongside Vincent Square.

Vincent Square

Named after William Vincent, Dean of Westminster 1802–15, the square contains playing fields for the boys of Westminster School. This continues a long tradition, for in medieval times the area was part of the old Tothill Fields, where young men practised military skills such as archery, wrestling, and tilting at the quintain.
At the end of the square cross Rochester Row

into Emery Hill Street. Take the second left into Francis Street, then the first right into Ambrosden Avenue. Walk to Westminster Cathedral at the end of the street.

Westminster Cathedral

This imposing Byzantine-style Roman Catholic cathedral, built between 1895 and 1903, used to be completely hidden from view, but as the result of recent clearance it now stands at the back of a small piazza. Its nave is the widest in England and its bell-tower (at 284 ft) is nearly 50 ft higher than the west towers of Westminster Abbey. Cleaned of its grime, it is well worth a visit, not least for the view from the top of the bell-tower, which is reached by lift.
Cross the piazza and turn left into Victoria Street. Return to Victoria Station.

Walk 3

Start: the National Gallery
Approximate distance: 2¾ miles

St James's

From the formal dignity of Trafalgar Square this walk leads to the studied elegance of Pall Mall and St James's Street. It then leads into the complex of buildings which make up St James's Palace and emerges in one of London's best-loved parks.

Places in **bold italic** type in the route directions are described elsewhere in this book. Names shown in black on the map are described in the text.

From the National Gallery walk towards St Martin-in-the-Fields, pass the statue of George Washington, and turn left into St Martin's Place. Bear left round the National Portrait Gallery into Irving Street. Continue into Leicester Square.

Leicester Square

This large square gets its name from Leicester House, a mansion built here by the Earl of Leicester in the 17th century. The open space, then known as Leicester Fields, was ideal for fighting duels. The mansion has long since disappeared, and in Victorian times the fields were laid out as a garden, with a statue of Shakespeare in the centre and busts of famous local residents at the four corners. Cinemas abound in this area. *Continue past the gardens, and on into Panton Street. Cross Whitcombe Street and continue to Haymarket. Turn left and walk down the left-hand side of Haymarket, across Orange Street, to Pall Mall.*

Pall Mall

Pall Mall takes its name from *paille maille*, a French ball game similar to croquet, introduced into England in the reign of Charles I. Numerous famous, and usually exclusive, clubs are situated in Pall Mall. Outside the entrance to the Athenaeum Club, in Waterloo Place, are two slabs of stone, placed here as a mounting-block at the request of the Duke of Wellington.
Cross at the traffic lights to the south side of Pall Mall. Turn right, then left, into Waterloo Place. Turn right below the Duke of York Column.

The Duke of York Column

This tall monument commemorates the second son of George III – the 'Grand Old Duke of York' – who marched ten thousand men up and down a hill in the nursery rhyme. The same men paid for the memorial – most of its cost was met by stopping one day's pay for every soldier in the army. The column was designed by Benjamin Wyatt in 1833.
Cross Waterloo Place. To the left are the Duke of York steps leading down to the Mall and Carlton House Terrace.

Carlton House Terrace

John Nash designed this dignified group of buildings as part of his architectural scheme for Regent Street. The terrace gets its name from Carlton House, which stood on the spot now occupied by the southern half of Waterloo Place. At No 6 is the Royal Society (formed 1660, royal charter 1662). Past members include such distinguished scientists as Sir Isaac Newton, Sir Humphry Davy, and Charles Darwin. No 12 is now the Institute of Contemporary Arts, and houses an art gallery (see page 102), and a theatre.
Turn right below the Duke of York Column and return along the west side of Waterloo Place. Cross Pall Mall at the pedestrian crossing and walk up Regent Street. Cross Charles II Street and take the next left into Jermyn Street.

Green Park is mainly green, but these brightly painted crowns add a splash of colour.

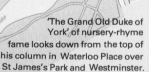

'The Grand Old Duke of York' of nursery-rhyme fame looks down from the top of his column in Waterloo Place over St James's Park and Westminster.

Buckingham Palace from the air, with the Mall, St James's Park and Westminster.

Jermyn Street

Jermyn Street is famous for its many old-established shops. One of the most interesting is the ancient premises of Paxton and Whitfield, the cheese shop. Further along is the Cavendish Hotel with its wrought-iron lamps, which although it has been rebuilt still carries memories of the eccentric hotelier Rosa Lewis, the original 'Duchess of Duke Street'.
Pass the church of St James's Piccadilly, cross Duke of York Street and Duke Street, and walk on as far as Piccadilly Arcade.

Piccadilly Arcade

This pleasant covered thoroughfare connects Jermyn Street and Piccadilly. It is adorned with hanging baskets of flowers and lined with expensive shops.

Continue along Jermyn Street, cross Bury Street, then turn left into St James's Street.

St James's Street

Many of the best known gentlemen's clubs in London are situated in this genteel street. They include Boodle's (No 28), White's (No 37), and Brook's (No 60), all of which have been established here since the 18th century. Among the old-established shops here are James Lock, hatters for more than 200 years, and Berry Bros and Rudd, wine merchants since the 17th century.

Piccadilly Arcade, lined with expensive 'gift' shops, connects Jermyn Street with Piccadilly.

The Household Cavalry ride down the Mall in the distinctive red tunics and white-plumed helmets of the Life Guards.

Cross St James's Street on the pedestrian crossing outside Rothmans, turn left and cross Pall Mall opposite the sentry outside **St James's Palace.** *Turn right along Cleveland Row then left into Stable Yard.*

Stable Yard

Stable Yard is part of the system of interlocking courts and passages which connect the different parts of St James's Palace. On the south side is Lancaster House, a fine 19th-century building adorned with cast-iron lamp standards topped by crowns. Adjoining the palace buildings is Clarence House, which was built in 1825, and is now the official residence of the Queen Mother. Virtually all that remains of the original vast Tudor palace which stood on this site is the gateway and Chapel Royal.

Cross to the right, to leave Stable Yard by the gateway into the Mall. Turn right and walk on, bear right beside the gates of **Green Park,** *and cross Constitution Hill at the traffic lights. Turn left and walk alongside* **Buckingham Palace** *gates. Bear left to circle the Victoria Memorial. Cross Buckingham Gate and Spur Road and walk up the south side of the Mall. After passing a tall stone pillar turn right into* **St James's Park.**

St James's Park

Although it is comparatively small, St James's is perhaps the most attractive of the royal parks. Pelicans, ducks, and many other kinds of water birds inhabit the lake; there are open spaces of grass, and areas shaded by trees; and fine views across to Whitehall and the towers of the Houses of Parliament.

Follow the path to the lake, turn left opposite the island, and walk on round the lake. Pass the bridge, then bear right at the fork. Pass a rockery on the left and leave the park by the gates directly ahead. Cross Horse Guards' Road and walk across Horse Guards Parade itself to the archway opposite. Go through into the courtyard and emerge into **Whitehall** *opposite the Banqueting House.*

Admiralty Arch separates Trafalgar Square from the Mall.

The Banqueting House

Inigo Jones (1573–1652), the greatest architect of his day, designed this Palladian-style building, completed in 1622 as part of the old Palace of Whitehall, which James I wanted to modernise. A fire destroyed most of it in 1698, but the House was one of the few survivals. The sumptuous interior, with its ceiling painted by Rubens, is open to the public. From here Charles I passed on to the scaffold where he was beheaded in 1649.

Turn left along Whitehall and walk up to Trafalgar Square.

Trafalgar Square

Pigeons outnumber people in the square. They perch on heads and shoulders, and are fed, photographed, and fussed over. The square itself, dominated by Nelson's Column with its four lions designed by the Victorian painter Landseer, was laid out in memory of Nelson and completed in 1841, but the fountains were added in 1948. On the parapet nearest the National Gallery the Standard British Linear Measures are let into the stonework.

Complete the walk in Trafalgar Square.

Trafalgar Square commemorates Nelson's famous victory over the French.

Walk 4

Mayfair

Mayfair's elegant shops, hotels and houses make it one of London's most exclusive areas. It has two famous squares – Berkeley and Grosvenor – and a wealth of hidden areas that retain qualities of ages past. Some of the enchanting little streets surrounding Shepherd Market still have rural names reflecting the original May Fair which took place here.

From Piccadilly Circus Underground Station follow subway 3, and take the second stairway to exit by Piccadilly House with Eros to the right. Walk up the left-hand side of Piccadilly.

Piccadilly

This famous London thoroughfare takes its name from a form of 17th-century ruff (or collar) called a 'piccadil'. At the eastern end of the street is Piccadilly Circus, always packed with shoppers and sightseers. In its centre is the statue known as Eros, erected in 1892 as a memorial to Lord Shaftesbury. The sculpture represents the Angel of Christian Charity. This is the centre of London's West End; all around are theatres, cinemas, and restaurants. Set back from the hubbub is the attractive 17th-century Church of St James. The railings around it also enclose the Garden of Remembrance given by Viscount Southwood to commemorate the courage of the people of London during World War II. Further along Piccadilly is Fortnum and Mason's shop. Figures of Mr Fortnum and Mr Mason (who founded the shop in 1707) emerge from the clock high on the wall on the hour and bow to each other as the carillon plays a tune.

*Cross the road by Fortnum and Mason, taking care to watch for buses approaching from the right as well as the main traffic stream from the left. Walk up the right-hand side past the **Royal Academy** and turn right into Burlington Arcade.*

Thomas Goode's, in South Audley Street, have been famous for their top-quality china for over 50 years.

Bond Street is the home of some of London's most exclusive and expensive shops – a paradise for those 'just looking'.

Burlington Arcade

This delightful Regency arcade is still patrolled by a beadle in traditional dress who also closes the gates at either end each night. The covered walk leads from Piccadilly to Burlington Gardens, and is lined with charming bow-windowed shops. Built in 1819, the arcade was owned by the Chesham family. Their coat of arms is still to be seen above the Piccadilly entrance.

At the end of the arcade turn left into Burlington Gardens. Cross the road, continue to the end, and turn right into Bond Street.

Bond Street

Famous as one of the world's most exclusive shopping streets, Bond Street is noted particularly for its jewellers and art dealers. It takes its name from Sir Thomas Bond, who, with John Hinde, a goldsmith, built it it 1686.

Walk up the right-hand side of Bond Street, crossing to the left at the Clifford Street junction. At the crossroads turn left into Bruton Street and cross to the right-hand side. Take the first turning right into Bruton Place.

Bruton Place

Emerging from the pavement here are several oddly-shaped bollards which were created by the simple expedient of placing redundant 19th-century cannons upright in the ground.

At the end of Bruton Place is Berkeley Square.

Berkeley Square

Beautiful plane trees almost 200 years old cast their shadows over the buildings around this famous square. Most of the Georgian houses which stood here have been demolished, but some survive on the west side, including No 45, which was the home of Clive of India. No 9, since demolished, was the home of the 18th-century poet Alexander Pope.
Walk anti-clockwise round the square, across Hill Street, and at the corner turn right into Charles Street.

Charles Street

Enormous 18th-century houses line both sides of Charles Street. Some of them have ornate ironwork on their exteriors, and all have sumptuous interiors. Also in the street is the curiously named 'I am the only Running Footman' pub. The

humorist and author, Sydney Smith, lived at No 32.
Cross Hay's Mews on the right and then cross to the left-hand side of Charles Street. Turn left into Queen Street and walk up the left-hand side, across Clarges Mews, to the end. Go over the pedestrian crossing and turn right along Curzon Street. Turn left into Trebeck Street, then left again into Shepherd Market.

Shepherd Market

Set in the heart of Mayfair, this is one of the most delightful areas in all London. Some of the original 18th century buildings survive, but it is the unique 'village' atmosphere which gives this tiny oasis its special charm. The present web of narrow streets was laid out by the builder and designer Edward Shepherd in 1735.
Turn right by Ye Grapes pub, then right again into Shepherd Street. Walk along the right-hand side of Shepherd Street, cross Trebeck Street, and continue to the junction with Hertford Street. Turn right. Cross the western end of Shepherd Market and continue along Hertford Street. Turn left into Curzon Street, pass Derby Street, then cross to the right-hand side of Curzon Street and keep on to its junction with South Audley Street. Turn right into the street.

South Audley Street

Sir Richard Westmacott (1775–1856), an outstanding sculptor of his day, lived at No 14. At No 57 is the famous gunsmiths, Purdey and Son. No 71 is an exceptionally fine Georgian house. Just after the crossroads with South Street is the blue and white Grosvenor Chapel, where American servicemen worshipped during World War II. It was built in 1730.
Continue up the left-hand side of South Audley Street. Cross Stanhope Gate and Tilney Street (where the road widens to form Audley Square) and cross Deanery Street. Cross to the right-hand side of South Audley Street (for No 14), walk on, crossing Mount Street and passing the Adams Row junction. At the end of South Audley Street cross to the left-hand side of Grosvenor Square and the United States Embassy.

In an incomprehensible piece of architectural vandalism, Nash's elegant Regent Street façades vanished forever when they were 'restored' in the 1920s.

Dogs guard the entrance of St George's Church, Hanover Square, a favourite place for society weddings until the late 1920s. Its register includes such famous names as Disraeli, Shelley and George Eliot (Mary Anne Evans).

Shepherd Market, a curious tangle of streets and alleyways

US Embassy

This huge building takes up the entire west side of Grosvenor Square. It was designed by Eero Saarinen, the Finnish-American architect, and completed in 1960. An eagle with a wingspan of 35 ft dominates the structure. Opposite the Embassy in the square's central garden stands a statue of Franklin D Roosevelt.
Walk clockwise round the square, crossing Upper Brook, North Audley and Duke Streets. Walk up the left-hand side of Brook Street.

Brook Street

The 18th-century composer Handel lived at No 25 for over thirty years. Nearly all his works were written here, including the *Messiah* (1741).
Cross Binney, Gilbert, and Davies Streets, South Molton Lane, and South Molton Street. Pass Haunch of Venison Yard, and cross to the right-hand side of Brook Street (to No 25). Cross New Bond Street and continue along Brook Street to Hanover Square.

Hanover Square

Like Berkeley Square, Hanover Square once contained elegant Georgian houses, but many of these have now been replaced by modern offices. A statue of William Pitt the Younger stands at the south end of the square facing St George's Church.
Turn right into St George Street and walk up it on the left. Turn left into Maddox Street and take the first right into Mill Street. Cross Conduit Street on the pedestrian crossing and enter Savile Row.

Savile Row

Savile Row is world-famous for its high-class tailoring establishments. No 14, the last home of the playwright Richard Brinsley Sheridan (1751–1816), is now occupied by Hardy Amies, couturier to the Queen.
Keep to the left-hand side of Savile Row, and cross New Burlington Place and New Burlington Street. At the end of Savile Row, between Sackville Street and Burlington House, is the entrance to Albany.

Albany

This secluded court dates from the early 19th century and was designed to provide exclusive apartments for gentlemen. Many famous men have lived here, including the 19th-century Prime Minister Gladstone and the poet Lord Byron (1788–1824).
Turn left into Vigo Street (to the right is the Museum of Mankind) and then right into Regent Street.

Regent Street

Regent Street owes its existence to George IV, who as Prince Regent lived at Carlton House. He wanted to build a country villa on Primrose Hill and connect it to Carlton House by a new road. The villa was never built, but Regent Street was laid out in 1813–20 by the great architect John Nash (1752–1835). The total rebuilding of Regent Street that began in 1900 has made it one of the finest shopping streets in the world, at the expense of some of the greatest architecture.
Follow the curve of the street and cross Air Street before returning to Piccadilly Circus to complete the walk.

Walk 5

Start: Holborn Underground Station
Approximate distance: 2½ miles

Bloomsbury and Holborn

Bloomsbury is dominated by the vast bulk of the British Museum and the University of London. Its squares and terraces have been the homes of countless intellectuals and members of the leisured classes. Holborn basks in the reflected glory of the Inns of Court, especially the venerable façade of the Staple Inn.

There are two memorials to Mahatma Gandhi in Tavistock Square – this contemplative statue and a tree, planted in 1953.

Places in **bold italic** type in the route directions are described elsewhere in this book. Names shown in black on the map are described in the text.

From Holborn Underground Station, cross High Holborn to the west side of Southampton Row, and bear left into Sicilian Avenue. At the end turn left into Bloomsbury Square.

Bloomsbury Square

The name 'Bloomsbury' probably derives from the medieval manor of Blemund'sbury, bought by the Earl of Southampton in 1545. Bloomsbury Square was laid out on its site by one of his descendants in 1661, and was the first open space in London to be called a 'square'. The original mansions have all disappeared, but the houses on the north side date from 1800–14. The gardens were planted in about 1800 by the celebrated landscape gardener Humphrey Repton. No 6 was the home of Isaac D'Israeli, father of Benjamin Disraeli. *Cross Southampton Place, then turn right across Bloomsbury Way, to walk along the west side of Bloomsbury Square. At the end turn left into Great Russell Street.*

Great Russell Street

Celebrated as the home of the British Museum, Great Russell Street has also had some famous residents. At No 46 lived Ralph Caldecott (1846–86), an outstanding illustrator of children's books, while No 91 was the home of George du Maurier (1834–96), who from 1860 drew for *Punch* but is probably better known for his novel *Trilby*, in which he created the character of Svengali. Bloomsbury's association with the world of books is evident in and around Great Russell Street, where there are numerous publishers' offices and small bookshops.

The British Museum

The museum's main entrance is on the north side of Great Russell Street. The imposing classical façade is 370 ft long and has 44 columns. The present structure was built in the mid-19th century to replace Montague House, which the museum previously occupied on the same site but proved too small to house the splendid library donated by George IV.

Sicilian Avenue runs between Southampton Row and Bloomsbury Way.

*Continue along Great Russell Street to the traffic lights and turn right into Bloomsbury Street. Walk up the street and along the east side of Bedford Square. Turn right into Montague Place, passing the King Edward VII Galleries of the **British Museum** on the right, with the University of London on the left. Turn left, and walk along the west side of **Russell Square.***

Russell Square

Russell Square is the largest of Bloomsbury's squares. It lies at the heart of an area dominated by the buildings of London University, which was founded in 1836 as an examining body but became a teaching university only in 1900. *Keeping forward, follow a path leading between modern university buildings to Woburn Square.*

Woburn Square

Scarcely a square at all, but rather a long, narrow strip, Woburn Square contains mainly modern buildings. Among those on the western side are the Warburg Institute and Courtauld Institute Galleries. The latter (open) contain a fine collection of modern paintings and other works of art (see p. 102).

Walk along the left-hand side of Woburn Square. At the end, turn right and cross to the south side of Gordon Square.

Gordon Square

Gordon Square is associated with the circle of 20th-century writers, critics and intellectuals known as the Bloomsbury Group. The novelist Virginia Woolf (1882–1941) lived at No 46 for a time before she married. The same house was later the home of the leading economist John Maynard Keynes (1883–1946). The critic and biographer Lytton Strachey (1880–1932) lived at No 51. At the south-west corner of the square stands the Gothic Church of Christ the King.
Walk straight on past the Percival David Institute of Chinese Art (open). Enter Tavistock Square; walk straight on along the south side, then turn left into the gardens.

Tavistock Square

To the right of the central walk through the square's garden is a copper beech tree planted by Pandit Nehru on 13 June 1953 to mark the unveiling of the statue of Mahatma Gandhi in the centre of the garden. The statue in the south-east corner of the gardens is of Dame Louisa Aldrich-Blake (1865–1925), pioneering surgeon to the Elizabeth Garrett Anderson Hospital for women. This memorial is by Sir Edwin Lutyens, who also designed the large building of the British Medical Association on the east side of the square. This building occupies the site of a house where Dickens lived for nine years, and in which several of his novels were written. On the north side of the square is Woburn House, in which is the fascinating Jewish Museum (open at certain times).

The British Museum is the largest museum in the world.

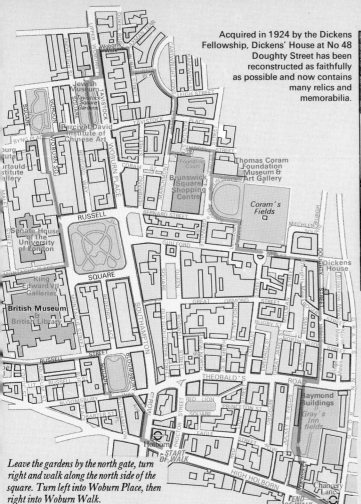

Acquired in 1924 by the Dickens Fellowship, Dickens' House at No 48 Doughty Street has been reconstructed as faithfully as possible and now contains many relics and memorabilia.

Leave the gardens by the north gate, turn right and walk along the north side of the square. Turn left into Woburn Place, then right into Woburn Walk.

Woburn Walk

This genteel little thoroughfare has a double row of early 19th-century houses, all of which have picturesque shop fronts. The Irish poet W B Yeats (1865–1939) lived at No 5 for a while.

Woburn Walk has the charm of an 18th-century village street.

At the end of Woburn Walk turn right into Burton Street, then left into Burton Place. On entering Cartwright Gardens, turn right and follow the terrace round to Marchmont Street. Turn right and walk up the left-hand side of Marchmont Street, across Tavistock Place. At the edge of the Brunswick Centre, a striking modern complex resembling a stepped pyramid, turn left into Foundling Court. A few yards along this terrace is the Brunswick Square shopping centre. Go down the steps and walk up Handel Street. Turn right into Hunter Street and cross to the far side. Walk straight down the west side of Brunswick Square. To the left, on the north side of the square, is the **Thomas Coram Foundation** Museum and Art Gallery. Bear left with the road and turn right into Lansdowne Terrace, then left into Guilford Street. Walk up the street, passing on the left the entrance to Coram's Fields.

Coram's Fields

Coram's Fields are a playground laid out on the grounds of the Foundling Hospital, which was established in 1729 by Captain Thomas Coram. Among the governors of the school were the painters William Hogarth and Sir Joshua Reynolds, and the choir was trained by Handel.
Cross over Guilford Street to continue along the south side. At the next crossroads turn right into Doughty Street.

Doughty Street

Among the pleasant Georgian buildings in this street is Dickens House (No 48). It is the only one of Charles Dickens' London homes to survive, and now contains a collection of portraits, letters, furniture and mementoes (see page 111).
Cross Roger Street and walk up John Street. Turn right into Theobalds Road, cross it and turn left through a gateway into Raymond Buildings. Skirting **Gray's Inn** (entrance in Field Court, to the left), walk straight on through an archway into Warwick Court.

Warwick Court

On the left beyond the arch into Warwick Court is a bronze plaque depicting the face of the Chinese leader Sun Yat-Sen (1866–1925), who lived in exile in a house on this site.

At the end of Warwick Court turn left into High Holborn. Continue along the left-hand side to the foot of Gray's Inn Road.

Holborn Bars

On either side of the road, stone obelisks surmounted by silver griffins mark the start of the City of London. Cross the road for the Staple Inn.

The Staple Inn

The timber-framed Inn, built in 1586, is the only surviving Elizabethan domestic building in London. It is said to have been a hostel of the wool merchants ('merchants of the staple') in the 14th century. In the reign of Henry V (1413–22) it became one of the nine Inns of Chancery in London. The others have disappeared or been rebuilt, and Staple Inn itself was restored after war damage.
Enter Chancery Lane Underground Station to complete the walk.

The Staple Inn's history as an Inn of Chancery dates back to the 15th century.

Places in **bold italic** in the route directions are described elsewhere in this book. Names shown in black on the map are described in the text.

From Piccadilly Circus walk up the left-hand side of Shaftesbury Avenue.

Shaftesbury Avenue

Laid out in 1877–86, the Avenue is named after the great Victorian social reformer and champion of the anti-slavery cause Lord Shaftesbury. It stretches from New Oxford Street to Piccadilly Circus, and is now known chiefly for its theatres.

After a short distance bear left into Great Windmill Street.

Great Windmill Street

This is the home of the Windmill Theatre, famous for its wartime slogan: 'We never close'. The area as a whole is somewhat seedy, but by way of contrast note the House of Floris, patissiers and confectioners by appointment to HM Queen Elizabeth the Queen Mother.

Turn right into Brewer Street and walk along the left-hand side as far as Rupert Street (which has a street market). At the end of Brewer Street cross over to the right to the Round House pub for a view of the Post Office Tower.

The Post Office Tower

Completed in 1964, this 619-ft-high needle of concrete and glass is one of the tallest buildings in London. It has a revolving restaurant and a viewing platform which are reached by high-speed lift. The Tower reaches such dizzy heights in order that the telecommunication signals it receives will not be affected by the surrounding buildings.

Cross Wardour Street.

Wardour Street

During the 1920s and 1930s, Wardour Street became the home of the British film industry. But while film moguls were making (and losing) fortunes here, television was being developed in nearby Frith Street.

Enter Old Compton Street.

St Anne's Soho

The remains of this 17th-century church stand at the corner of Wardour Street and Old Compton Street. It was almost totally destroyed during World War II, but the tower (added in 1801–3) survived, and the churchyard has been laid out as a garden where memorials to the essayist William Hazlitt (*d.*1830) and Theodore, King of Corsica (*d.*1756), can still be seen.

Walk down the left-hand side of Old Compton Street.

Meard Street boasts a row of exceptionally well preserved 18th-century houses.

Walk 6

A Walk round Soho

Bounded by Oxford Street, Charing Cross Road, Shaftesbury Avenue, and Regents Street, Soho still suffers from its reputation for shadiness. In fact it is an area of considerable interest, with streets of lovingly-preserved town houses, a dignified square, and several historic religious foundations. It also has lively street markets and some of the best restaurants in London.

Eros and the garish advertisements of Piccadilly Circus.

Old Compton Street

This street is famous for its exotic provision shops, the legacy of the 19th-century flood of immigrants – particularly French, Italians and Greeks – into the area.

*At the end of Old Compton Street turn left into Charing Cross Road with Centre Point on the right. Walk up the left-hand side of Charing Cross Road past St Martin's School of Art and **Foyles** bookshop. Turn left into Manette Street.*

Manette Street

This street is unusual in that it is named after a character in fiction, Dr Manette, the French émigré in Dickens' *A Tale of Two Cities.*

At the end of Manette Street pass under an

archway into Greek Street.

Greek Street

Many famous people are associated with this street. Dr Samuel Johnson, the poet and critic, and Sir Joshua Reynolds, the English portrait painter, founded a Literary Club here; Sir Thomas Lawrence, the 18th-century portrait painter, lived and worked here for 25 years; Thomas de Quincey, who wrote *Confessions of an English Opium Eater*, indulged his addiction here; and Josiah Wedgwood had his London showroom here to show off his famous Wedgwood china.

Turn right and walk along the right-hand side of Greek Street as far as No 1.

Centrepoint is one of London's most famous tower blocks.

The House Of St Barnabas

One of the finest Georgian houses in London, with richly decorated ceilings, woodcarvings, and ironwork, the House of St Barnabas was founded as a charitable institution in 1846 to help the destitute in London. It is now open to the public.

From Greek Street enter Soho Square and walk round it anti-clockwise.

Soho Square

The name 'Soho' is said to come from the cry of huntsmen unleashing dogs to chase hares, *so* meaning 'see', and *ho* 'after him'. The Duke of Monmouth, Charles II's illegitimate son, had a mansion in Soho Square, and when he and his followers made a bid for the Crown at the Battle of Sedgemoor, 'Soho!' was their battle-cry. On the east side of the square is the Roman Catholic Church of St Patrick, built in 1891–3. It has a fine Italianate interior. In the north-west corner is the French Protestant Church of London, founded in 1550 under a royal charter from Edward VI. The present building dates from 1893. Soho has been a foreign quarter since the reign of Charles II, when a great number of French Protestants fled here as the result of religious persecution. Known as 'Huguenots', they were mostly silk-weavers, and in the back gardens around Soho Square there may still be some of the mulberry trees they planted for their silkworms.

Leaving Soho Square, walk down the right-hand side of Frith Street.

Frith Street

It was in his room at No 22 Frith Street that John Logie Baird succeeded in transmitting a picture by wireless – the start of television. That was in 1926, after Baird had spent years researching and experimenting. There are several

Liberty's

At the end of Great Marlborough Street is Liberty's, built in 1924. It was first planned as a reproduction Tudor building throughout, but was then given a neo-classical façade to match its surroundings. The half-timbering on the north side is not purely decorative – the timbers are structural and come from genuine men-of-war. Every quarter hour, the St George on the clock which adorns the façade fights the dragon, slaying him on the hour.

At the end of Great Marlborough Street turn left into Regent Street and walk up the left-hand side. Take the first left into Fouberts Place, cross Kingly Street, and turn right into **Carnaby Street.**

The Liberty Clock St George slays the dragon every hour for passers-by.

Beak Street

Here, for a few poverty-stricken years, lived the Venetian painter Antonio Canaletto (1697–1768).

Take the first right into Upper James Street and walk down the left-hand side through Golden Square into Lower James Street. Continue along Lower James Street into Sherwood Street which takes you back to Piccadilly Circus.

Above: Soho Square, a welcome relief from the crowded maze of Soho's streets.

Shakespeare leans out of his window to watch the world go by at the Shakespeare pub, Great Marlborough Street.

handsome Georgian houses at the end of the street nearest to Soho Square; William Hazlitt died at No 6.

At the Dog and Duck pub turn right into Bateman Street. Turn left into Dean Street and take the first right into Meard Street.

Meard Street

For those who like old houses this short 18th-century street, named after a carpenter, John Meard, is the most rewarding in all Soho. Nos 1–21 are exceptionally well preserved.

At the end of Meard Street, cross into Peter Street and walk down the right-hand side. Turn right into Berwick Street.

Berwick Street

This is famous for its lively fruit and vegetable street market, which also extends into Rupert Street. Kemp House, a block of flats built for Westminster City Council, was the first example of 'mixed development' in central London.

Turn left into Broadwick Street, walk down the right-hand side, and take the first right into Poland Street. Cross Poland Street, take the first left into Great Marlborough Street, and walk up the left-hand side.

The exciting Carnaby Street of the '60s seems somewhat jaded now, but still has some interesting shops.

Carnaby Street

The Bard of Avon on the wall of the Shakespeare's Head pub has seen some changes in Carnaby Street. Built in the 18th century for 'poor and miserable objects of the neighbourhood', it was never fashionable. Then in the early 1960s a transformation took place, and the decrepit shops and houses were turned into 'boutiques', at first for men's clothes, later also for girls'. By the mid 1960s it was a teenagers' paradise, but the craze lost momentum as it spread to the King's Road and High Street, Kensington. Nevertheless Carnaby Street is still a must for many foreign tourists.

At the end of the pedestrian precinct turn left into Beak Street.

49

Places in **_bold italic_** type in the route directions are described elsewhere in this book. Names shown in black on the map are described in the text.

Walk 7

The Strand and Covent Garden

The rich assortment of buildings which occupy the area between the Strand and the Thames are the sites of mansions which survive in name only. Further from the river are the peaceful expanses of Lincoln's Inn Fields, and the bustling warren of streets that make up Covent Garden.

Leave Embankment Underground Station by the north exit (marked Villiers Street) and turn right. Walk up the right-hand side of Villiers Street.

Villiers Street

In this area in the 17th century stood the mansion and gardens of George Villiers, Duke of Buckingham. He sold them for redevelopment, but insisted that every word of his name and title be preserved in the new street names: George Street, Villiers Street, Duke Street, Buckingham Street, and Of Alley (now renamed York Place). East of Villiers Street, the area between the Strand and the Thames was named the Adelphi (from the Greek work for brothers, *adelphoi*) after the four Adam brothers who were responsible for laying out the streets in 1768–74. Much of the area has been rebuilt but the name survives in the Adelphi Theatre.
Opposite the Players' Theatre turn right into the Victoria Embankment Gardens.

Victoria Embankment Gardens

On the left is the old York House Water Gate, the entrance to the Duke of Buckingham's garden from the Thames. In the Duke's day (the 1620s) boats bringing guests would tie up at the Water Gate, which marks the former boundary of the River Thames. There are numerous statues and memorials in the gardens. Of special interest are the little memorial to the Imperial Camel Corps (1921), statues of the poet Robert Burns and Robert Raikes, founder (1780) of Sunday Schools, a bust of the composer Sir Arthur Sullivan (d. 1900) and the tree commemorating Queen Elizabeth II's coronation in 1953.
Leave the gardens by the Savoy Place exit. Cross Savoy Place into Carting Lane and walk past the rear of Shell-Mex House.

Shell-Mex House

Shell-Mex House was originally the Cecil Hotel, which, when it opened in 1886, was the largest hotel in Europe. The old-fashioned street lamp here is always alight, burning gases from the sewers below.
Cross to the Embankment entrance of the Savoy Theatre. Turn right along Savoy Way (at the back of the Savoy Hotel).

The Savoy Hotel

In 1884, Richard D'Oyly Carte, who had already built the Savoy Theatre as a home for Gilbert and Sullivan's comic operas, decided to build a hotel to compete with the best in America. His new Savoy was famous for its 70 bathrooms – such an unheard-of number in those days that the builder asked him if his guests were to be amphibians.

Turn left into Savoy Hill and continue on the left-hand side to the Chapel of the Savoy.

The Chapel of the Savoy

The buildings and streets with 'Savoy' in their name stand on the site of the ancient Savoy Palace, originally built in 1241, and rebuilt as a hospital by Henry VII in 1510–16. The only part of the hospital to survive is the Queen's Chapel of the Savoy, the private chapel of the reigning monarch as Duke of Lancaster, now used by the Royal Victorian Order. Most of the present building is a 19th-century reconstruction.
Cross Savoy Hill by the churchyard and turn right into Savoy Street. At the traffic lights turn left and walk along the **_Victoria Embankment_**, *passing under Waterloo Bridge. Turn left into Temple Place, then left again into Surrey Street. From there follow the sign to the Surrey Steps 'Roman Bath'.*

Surrey Steps 'Roman Bath'

The 'Roman Bath' here is in fact more likely to date from the early 17th century. A spring of cold water which bubbled up here for hundreds of years disappeared mysteriously in 1972. It is open to the public.
Walk on up Surrey Street to the Strand.

The Strand

In Elizabethan times and long afterwards, the Strand was bordered by noblemen's mansions with gardens running down to the riverside or 'strand'. It is still, as it always was, the principal route between the West End and the City, running for nearly a mile, from Charing Cross to the Temple Bar Memorial – where statues of Queen Victoria and Edward VII, and a griffin in the road mark the boundary of the City. The Temple Bar itself, a triple gateway designed by Wren, was dismantled at the end of the last century and removed to Theobald's Park in Hertfordshire. In much earlier times, the severed heads of traitors and other criminals were impaled on spikes on top of the gateway to the City.
Turn right in the Strand and cross on the pedestrian crossing to Australia House. Look right for **_St Clement Danes Church_**. *Cross to the north side of the Strand and turn right, then left into Clement's Inn. Bear right at the Mobil*

Court building, go up the steps, and bear left into Clement's Inn Passage. Walk up Clare Market and turn right into Portugal Street. Cross the road, pass the George IV pub on the left, and turn left into Portsmouth Street. Cross the street to the Old Curiosity Shop.

The Royal Courts of Justice in the Strand were designed in 1874.

The Queen's Chapel of the Savoy is the private property of the monarch.

The York House Watergate in Victoria Embankment Gardens.

...s shop in St Martin's Lane caters especially theatrical performers.

Covent Garden

Until 1974, when the famous fruit and vegetable market moved to Nine Elms, near Vauxhall, there had been a market on this site for over 300 years. In an effort to preserve the attractive old market buildings, they have been extensively renovated and many small craft shops, business premises and restaurants may now be found here.

Turn right in front of the Jubilee Hall Recreation Centre and walk along the south side of Covent Garden through the Jubilee Market. Turn right again along the east side and walk past St Paul's Church.

Old Curiosity Shop

Established in the 17th century, this is said to be the shop immortalised by Dickens in his novel of the same name.
*Bear right past the shop and turn right into **Lincoln's Inn Fields**. Walk anti-clockwise round the square.*

Lincoln's Inn Fields

Lincoln's Inn Fields were laid out in the 17th century and were a famous haunt of duellists. A tablet here marks the spot where Lord William Russell was executed in 1683. Handsome buildings, including the Sir John Soane's Museum (see page 99) and the Royal College of Surgeons, surround the fields.
*Turn right into Sardinia Street and walk up to Kingsway. Turn right, then cross Kingsway at the traffic lights, walk back down it to the left, and turn right into Kemble Street. Walk up Kemble Street, across Drury Lane, and up Russell Street. Cross Bow Street and continue on Russell Street until the left turn into **Covent Garden**.*

St Paul's, Covent Garden

In 1631, John Russell, fourth Earl of Bedford, commissioned the architect Inigo Jones to lay out a square with surrounding streets on the former monastic gardens at Covent Garden. Jones' plans included this, the first new church to be built after the Reformation, but the Earl wanted to spend as little as possible on it, and said it should not be much better than a barn. 'Well then,' replied Jones, 'you shall have the handsomest barn in England.' There are many memorials in the church.
Turn left into King Street, cross Bedford Street, walk up New Row, and turn left into St Martin's Lane.

St Martin's Lane

St Martin's Lane is easily recognised by the globe on top of the London Coliseum, now the home of the National Opera. Thomas Chippendale, the greatest furniture maker in England's history, opened his workshop at No 62 in 1753.

Continue down the left-hand side of St Martin's Lane. Opposite the Odeon Cinema is the entrance to Cecil Court.

Cecil Court

This narrow pedestrian precinct is filled with antiquarian and secondhand bookshops.
Cross William IV Street at the traffic lights opposite the Post Office. St Martin's Lane now becomes St Martin's Place.

St Martin's Place

In the middle of the road there is a statue of Nurse Edith Cavell, shot by the Germans in 1915 for helping prisoners of war to escape.
*Continue to **St Martin-in-the-Fields**.*

Since Covent Garden Market moved to its new site at Nine Elms, great efforts have been made to transform the old market buildings into an attractive and distinctive shopping area.

St Martin-in-the-Fields

George I was churchwarden in this, the parish church of Buckingham Palace, a unique instance of a reigning monarch holding such an office. A church has existed here since the 13th century, and it was the open country surrounding the medieval church which gave the present 18th-century church its name. St Martin-in-the-Fields is now famous for its lunchtime concerts. These were begun by the pianist Dame Myra Hess (1890–1965) in the National Gallery during the Blitz. The catacombs, cleared in 1938, were used during the war as an air-raid shelter. Its churchyard, where Nell Gwynne, mistress of Charles II, was buried, was cleared in 1829 to make way for Duncannon Street.
Cross Duncannon Street at the traffic lights and walk past South Africa House to finish the walk at Charing Cross Underground Station (formerly Trafalgar Square).

Walk 8

The Inns of Court and Fleet Street

From the Embankment this walk leads through the complex of open spaces, lanes and buildings which make up the Temple. It then leads past the impressive bulk of the Royal Courts of Justice to the picturesque buildings of Lincoln's Inn. It emerges into Fleet Street and continues up Ludgate Hill to St Paul's Cathedral, from where it returns, via ancient streets and modern walkways, to Blackfriars.

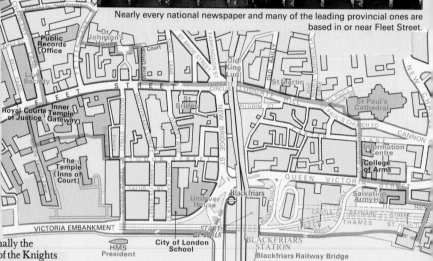

Nearly every national newspaper and many of the leading provincial ones are based in or near Fleet Street.

There are many secluded courtyards, passages and gardens in the Temple.

> Places in **bold italic** in the route directions are described elsewhere in this book. Of particular relevance to this walk is the section of the book called The City, which begins on page **28**. Names shown in black on the map are described in the text.

*Leave Blackfriars Railway Station by the main exit and turn left for the subway. Follow the sign for Blackfriars Bridge. At the bridge, turn left for the **Victoria Embankment**.*

The Victoria Embankment

Sir Joseph Bazalgette built this fine riverside parade in the latter half of the 19th century. All along it there are fine iron lamp posts with dolphins twined round their bases, and seats supported by kneeling camels. The river wall is made of granite and is eight feet thick.
Look right for the City of London School.

The City of London School

Established in 1834 as a successor to a 15th-century foundation for the education of 'four poore men's children', this school now has 780 boy pupils. The girls' school is now situated in the Barbican.
Reach HMS President, turn right at the traffic lights and cross the road into Temple Avenue. Take the next left into Tudor Street and go through the gateway into the Temple.

The Temple

The Temple was originally the English headquarters of the Knights Templars. The order was dissolved in 1312, and the Temple eventually passed to the Knights Hospitallers of St John, who leased it to a number of lawyers. From this point on, the Inner and Middle Temples began to develop into Inns of Court. The oldest building in the complex is the Temple Church, which is one of only four round churches surviving in England. The nave and porch date from the 12th century. The magnificent Middle Temple Hall dates from 1562 (it is open to the public). There are many other venerable buildings in the Temple, although considerable damage was caused during World War II.
Turn right into King's Bench Walk (which has two 17th-century buildings attributed to Sir Christopher Wren), follow it round to the left, then cross the top end of the square and take the passageway to the right of the Library. This leads to another courtyard with the Inner Temple Hall on the left and the Temple Church on the right. Go through an archway straight ahead into Pump Court (high up on the right-hand side is a 17th-century sundial inscribed 'Shadows we are and like shadows depart'), and then turn right into Middle Temple Lane, with Hare Court (the site of the chambers of Judge Jeffreys, notorious for his ruthlessness in the infamous 'Bloody Assize' of 1685) on the right. At the end, go through a gateway into Fleet Street. Across the road to the left are the Royal Courts of Justice.

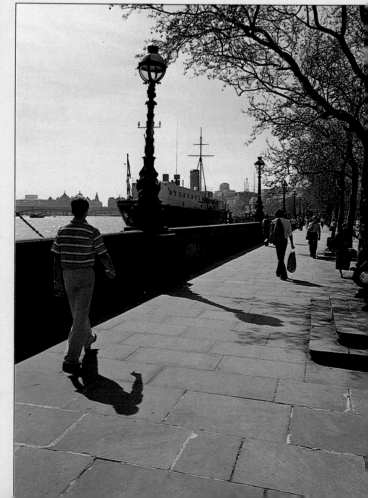

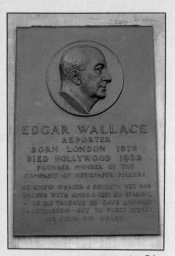

The memorial to the thriller-writer Edgar Wallace at Ludgate Circus.

Royal Courts of Justice

Generally called the Law Courts, the Royal Courts of Justice were designed in the Gothic style by the distinguished Victorian architect G E Street. The foundation stone was laid in 1874, but the building was not completed until 1882, after Street's death. The Central Hall contains a monument to him. The main entrance, in the Strand, has archways flanked by twin towers in which are stairs to the public galleries.
*Also to the left is the **Temple Bar Memorial**. Turn right to Inner Temple Gateway, almost opposite Chancery Lane.*

The Inner Temple Gateway

This picturesque half-timbered building of 1610–11 has on its first floor 'Prince Henry's Room' (open to the public), supposed to have been the council chamber of the Duchy of Cornwall under Prince Henry, the son of James I. The room retains its original plasterwork ceiling.
Cross the road into Chancery Lane and follow it past the Law Society buildings (decorated with golden lions) on the left, and the Public Records Office on the right.

The Public Records Office

This is the chief repository for the national archives. The Search Rooms, containing records from the Norman Conquest onwards, are open to the public, and there is a small museum in which may be seen famous documents such as the *Domesday Book*, William the Conqueror's survey of 1086. Also on display are letters from Cardinal Wolsey and Guy Fawkes, and Shakespeare's Will.
Pass Carey Street and turn right into Breams Buildings. Ahead, on the left-hand side of Chancery Lane, are Lincoln's Inn Old Buildings.

Left: HMS *Chrysanthemum* moored by the Victoria Embankment; in the foreground, one of the Embankment's characteristic lamp-posts.

Lincoln's Inn Old Buildings

These date mainly from the 16th and early 17th centuries. The Gatehouse, still with its original oak doors, was built in 1518 by Sir Thomas Lovell, whose arms appear above it. Lincoln's Inn was established in the 14th century as a law school. Dominating the Inn is the Victoria New Hall and Library, dating from 1843. The Old Hall dates from 1506, and was extensively restored in 1928. The chapel was rebuilt in the 17th century, and is thought to have been designed by Inigo Jones.
*At the end of Breams Buildings cross Fetter Lane, turn right, then left into West Harding Street. Bear right, then left, into Pemberton Row, and in 50 yds turn right into Gough Square. (On the right is **Dr Johnson's House**, which is open to the public.) Turn left, then walk through a second archway at the far end of the court. Turn right into Wine Office Court.*

Wine Office Court

In this narrow court is the Old Cheshire Cheese, a 17th-century tavern associated with Dr Johnson.
Go through the archway and turn left into Fleet Street.

The church of St Mary Somerset, built by Wren in 1695, was pulled down in 1871; only the tower remains.

Fleet Street

Nearly every national and provincial newspaper or periodical has an office in or near Fleet Street. It is one of the most ancient thoroughfares in London, and has had links with the printing trade since about 1500. The present building are mostly modern.
On reaching Ludgate Circus, keep straight on at the traffic lights, past the Old King Lud pub and up Ludgate Hill. The next turning on the left is Old Bailey.

The Old Bailey

The Central Criminal Court is popularly known as the Old Bailey from the name of the street on whose corner it stands. On this site, until 1902, stood the notorious Newgate Prison. On the first two days of each session the judges carry posies of flowers, and the courts are strewn with herbs, a custom dating from the time when it was necessary to do so to disguise the stench of the prison.

*Walk on up Ludgate Hill, passing on the left **St Martin-within-Ludgate**. Cross to the steps of **St Paul's Cathedral**, and turn right, then left, alongside the churchyard. Turn right and cross the road into Godliman Street. At the end, turn left into Queen Victoria Street. On the left is the College of Arms.*

The College of Arms

Sometimes called the Heralds' Office, this is the official authority in Great Britain (except Scotland) and the Commonwealth on armorial bearings and pedigrees. Its officers, who have resounding titles such as Rouge Dragon Pursuivant, also assist the Earl Marshal, an office hereditary to the Duke of Norfolk since 1672, in arranging state ceremonies such as coronations. The building itself is an imposing 17th-century structure, and stands on a site that has been occupied by the College of Arms since 1555.
Cross the road and turn right into Lambeth Hill. At the bottom turn left, and left again. Cross the footbridge across Upper Thames Street and at the bottom turn sharp right along High Timber Street. Pass several warehouses and at the end bear left for the start of a new riverside walk. Follow the walk underneath Blackfriars Railway Bridge, then turn right and go up the steps to Blackfriars (road) Bridge. Turn right on to the north end of the bridge (a plaque on the right describes the bridge's history) and return to Blackfriars Station.

Looking towards St Paul's up Ludgate Hill.

Walk 9
The Heart of the City

Start: Bank Underground Station
Approximate distance: 3 miles

From the Bank of England this walk leads past the gold-crowned pillar of the Monument to the site of public executions outside the Tower. It then returns to the Bank along some of the City's fascinating streets and alleys.

Places in **bold italic** type in the route directions are described elsewhere in this book. Of particular relevance to this walk are the sections of the book called The Tower (pages 24–27), and The City (pages 28–31). Names shown in black on the map are described in the text.

An ornate doorway to the Bank of England in Threadneedle Street.

*From Bank Underground Station (Mansion House) follow signs for Lombard Street. Walk up the north side of the street, then fork right past St Mary Woolnoth into King William Street. Take the second right into Abchurch Lane, passing **St Mary Abchurch**. Turn right at the end, then cross Cannon Street to Laurence Pountney Hill. At the end of Abchurch Lane a detour from the main walk can be made by turning right into Cannon Street for the London Stone, which is set in the front wall of the Oversea-Chinese Banking Corporation on the corner of St Swithin's Lane.*

The London Stone
This is said to be the milestone from which distances were measured on the great military roads radiating outwards from Roman London.
Cross over Cannon Street, turn left, and take the second right to rejoin the main route at Laurence Pountney Hill.

Left: The view from the Monument to Tower Bridge.

Above: The Monument.

Laurence Pountney Hill
Nos 1 and 2 were built in 1703 and are the finest early 18th-century houses in the City. Amid the rich carving of the doorways are two delightful cherubs playing marbles.
Turn left, go through the churchyard, then turn right into Laurence Pountney Lane. Turn left into Upper Thames Street, and left again into Arthur Street. For a short detour to the Old Wine Shades, take the first left into Martin Lane.

Old Wine Shades
This old tavern and wine shop was built in 1663 and was the only City hostelry to survive the Great Fire of London. It seems to have a charm over it, since it also escaped damage during the Blitz.
*Continue up Arthur Street to the traffic lights. Turn right into King William Street and walk down it past the 19th-century **Fishmongers' Hall** on to **London Bridge**. Fine views of the Pool of London may be obtained from here. Return, and use the subway at the side of Fishmongers' Hall to reach Lower Thames Street. Turn right, pass **St Magnus the Martyr**, turn left, cross Lower Thames Street, and walk up Fish Street Hill to the Monument.*

The Monument
Splendid views over the City can be obtained from the top of this famous landmark. Designed by Sir Christopher Wren and Robert Hooke, the Monument was erected in 1671–7 to commemorate the Great Fire of London which devastated the City in 1666. Its height (202 ft) is said to equal the distance from its base to the place in Pudding Lane where the fire started on 2 September, destroying nearly 90 churches and around 13,000 houses.
*Turn right into Monument Street and cross Pudding Lane. Walk downhill into Lower Thames Street, passing **Billingsgate Fish Market** on the right. Cross to the other side of the street at the **Custom House**. Walk on past the building until the Tiger Tavern is seen on the opposite side of the road.*

The façade of the Custom House in Lower Thames Street.

The Tiger Tavern

Although rebuilt in this century, this tavern's history stretches back over 400 years. Every ten years, the lord mayor, sheriffs, and aldermen of London take part in an unusual beer-testing ceremony here. A sample of beer is poured on a stool provided by the official tester, and he then sits on it. If his trousers stick to the seat (and they always do), then the beer is pronounced to be of acceptable quality.
At the bottom of Tower Hill, look left for the entry to the old Tower Subway.

The Tower Subway

All that can be seen of this revolutionary engineering work is a small cylindrical tower which bears the inscription: 'London Hydraulic Power Company Subway Constructed AD 1868'. It marks the entrance to the first underground railway tunnel under the Thames, which now carries cables.
Tower Hill runs along the west side of the **Tower of London**.

The Tower of London

Across the (now dry) moat of the Tower may be seen the western section of the inner wall with its three massive towers (Bell, Beauchamp and Devereux) built in the reign of Edward I. Princess Elizabeth was once imprisoned in the Bell Tower, from which curfew is still rung nightly, and the section of the ramparts leading up to Beauchamp Tower is known as Princess Elizabeth's Walk.
Follow the road up past Tower Gardens and the Moat, and at the top cross at the traffic lights into Trinity Square Gardens.

Trinity Square Gardens

Just inside these gardens is the Merchant Navy Memorial to the ships and men lost in the two world wars. Trinity Square was the site of public executions until the 17th century; more than 125 people were put to death here, including Sir Thomas More (1535), Thomas Cromwell (1540), and the Duke of Monmouth (1685).
Cross the gardens to the right, then turn left past Tower Hill Underground into Coopers Row. Make a detour right under Midland House to reach a large section of the old Roman Wall, then return to Coopers Row, turn left, and go back to Trinity Square. Turn right past Trinity House. At the end of the square turn right into Byward Street, then right into Seething Lane.

Seething Lane

This is the site of the Navy Office in which the diarist Samuel Pepys worked. Almost opposite, is St Olave's which Pepys calls 'myne owne Church', and where he and his wife are buried. Charles Dickens also refers to the gateway of this church with its macabre decoration of skulls in *The Uncommercial Traveller* as St Ghastly Grim (also see page 121).
At the end of Seething Lane, turn right into Crutched Friars and cross to the north side. Follow the street under the railway bridge, then take the next left into Lloyd's Avenue. At the far end cross Fenchurch Street and turn right along it to the Aldgate Pump.

Escapologists entertaining tourists on Tower Hill.

The Aldgate Pump

This disused drinking fountain stands over what was once St Michael's Well, whose water was renowned for its efficacious qualities as far back as the 15th century. For many years a 'draught (draft) on the Aldgate pump' was a facetious expression for a worthless bill.
For a short detour from the main walk, continue up Aldgate to the Sir John Cass School.

The Sir John Cass School

Founded in 1710 as a charity school, this philanthropic establishment was rebuilt in 1909. Over the doorway are two figures of school children that probably came from the original building.
Return to the main walk, and turn down Leadenhall Street. At **St Katharine Cree** *turn right into Creechurch Lane. Go down the slight hill, bear right, and at the crossroads turn left into Bevis Marks. Pass on the left the gateway to the Spanish and Portuguese Synagogue.*

The Spanish and Portuguese Synagogue

Originally founded in Creechurch Lane in 1657, this, the oldest synagogue in England, was rebuilt on this site in 1700–1 by Joseph Avis, a Quaker. One of its main beams was donated by Queen Anne. The interior of the building, which has three galleries supported on wooden Tuscan columns, contains many beautiful fittings.
Continue across St Mary Axe into Camomile Street and follow it to Bishopsgate. Turn left into Bishopsgate and pass the Magpie and Punchbowl pub. Continue down Bishopsgate past the enormous National Westminster Bank and the church of **St Ethelburga**. *In a hundred yards turn left down Great St Helen's. On the right is the entrance to St Helen's Church.*

Old and even older. From this section of the Roman wall can be glimpsed the turrets of the White Tower of the Tower of London.

St Helen's Church

St Helen's Church dates back at least to the 12th century. Since the 13th century, when it became the church of a Benedictine nunnery, it has had two naves, one used by the nuns and one by the City parishioners. It contains many tombs and monuments of City dignitaries, including the tomb of Sir John Crosby, builder of Crosby Hall (see also page 118).
Outside the church, turn right and pass the P & O building. Cross the piazza, passing on the left, on the far side of St Mary Axe, the church of **St Andrew Undershaft**. *Cross Leadenhall Street into Lime Street. Take the first right into Leadenhall Place and walk through* **Leadenhall Market**. *At the far end, bear right across Gracechurch Street and enter St Peter's Alley. Pass* **St Peter-upon-Cornhill**, *turn left into Cornhill, then left again into St Michael's Court and walk down the alley to the* **Jamaica Wine House**. *Just before an archway, turn right along Castle Court, passing two famous City chop-houses – the George and Vulture and Simpson's Tavern.*

The George and Vulture and Simpson's Tavern

The George and Vulture is one of the many hostelries mentioned in *Pickwick Papers*, Dickens' great comic novel. The unusual name derives from two separate taverns, The George and The Lively Vulture, which stood here before the Great Fire. Simpson's has been a favourite City eating place since 1757 and has remained a perfect example of its kind.
Turn right into Birchin Lane, and cross Cornhill into Finch Lane. At the end of the lane turn left into Threadneedle Street. Cross the road at the traffic lights and turn half-right into Old Broad Street, with the **Stock Exchange** *on the left. Cross the road, turn left into Throgmorton Street, and pass the 19th-century Drapers' Hall. Take the next left down Bartholomew Lane, with the eastern side of the* **Bank of England** *on the right. At the end cross Threadneedle Street and turn right past the* **Royal Exchange**. *Return to Bank Underground Station.*

Walk 10

Start: Bank Underground Station
Approximate distance: 2¼ miles

City Streets and Alleys

Despite the rebuilding of the City after the Great Fire of London, and despite the ravages caused by bombs during World War II, the timeless character of the City can still be discovered in the tiny thoroughfares around St Paul's Cathedral. Here and there ancient buildings remain, and these survivors from distant times contribute to the City's historical continuity.

From the Bank Underground Station exit next to the Waterloo and City line follow signs for Walbrook. Walk along Walbrook to St Stephen Walbrook Church. Turn right into Bucklersbury, then left into Queen Victoria Street, passing the railed enclosure of the Roman Temple of Mithras.

The Temple of Mithras

Discovered in 1956 during excavations to locate the bed of the River Walbrook, this temple dates from the 2nd century AD. The cult of Mithras, a Persian sun-god, was restricted to men and especially popular with soldiers, and the ceremonies associated with his worship were conducted in great secrecy. This temple is one of the most important Roman remains in London, and has been reconstructed near to the site where it was found.
At the traffic lights turn right across Queen Victoria Street and immediately half-left, crossing Queen Street, into Watling Street. Pass St Mary Aldermary Church and further on Ye Olde Watling pub.

Ye Olde Watling

This interesting old pub which dates from 1666 was used as an office by Sir Christopher Wren during the building of St Paul's Cathedral.
Walk on, crossing Bow Lane and Bread Street.

Bread Street

The poet John Milton was born in this street in 1608. Its name is derived from the fact that in medieval times bakers sold their bread here.

Sculpture in Paternoster Square.

The temple of Mithras, one of the most important Roman finds in London, was discovered in 1954.

At the end of Watling Street, turn right into New Change and cross the road. For a detour to St Paul's Garden turn left and cross New Change.

St Paul's Gardens

In these gardens is a plaque marking the site of Old Change, a 13th-century building where bullion was stored before being taken to the Royal Mint, and which gave its name to a street, alas destroyed by bombs in 1941. New Change, a much wider street, was built after the war a little to the east of its predecessor and the reconstructed spire of the Wren church of St Augustine, Watling Street.
On the main walk pass an office block on the left (a plaque on one of its walls marks the site of the ancient St Paul's School). Pass the rear end of St Paul's Churchyard, then turn left. Follow a sign to St Paul's Shopping Centre, cross Paternoster Row and turn left up Panyer Alley Steps.

Paternoster Row and Panyer Alley Steps

Paternoster (Our Father) is a reminder of the participants in medieval processions who told their rosaries round the precincts of Old St. Paul's. Here they recited the Lord's Prayer. For several hundred years Paternoster Row was associated with the book trade, but it was entirely destroyed during the Blitz, and only the ancient name survives. The Steps commemorate the Panyer Boy, an inn whose 17th-century sign is to be seen on the side wall. It shows a baker's boy with his pannier or basket.
Enter the St Paul's Shopping Centre and go through an archway into Paternoster Square. Bear left across the square and leave by a small opening in the wall. Go down a ramp, cross the road, and turn right into Warwick Lane. Pass on the left an entrance to Amen Court.

Amen Court

Like Paternoster Row, this name also derives from medieval religious ceremonies. By the time this court was reached they had come to the 'Amen'.
Continue along Warwick Lane to Cutlers' Hall. At the end turn left into Newgate Street (on the opposite side of the road are plaques marking the sites of the 16th-century Christ's Hospital and the 13th-century Greyfriars Monastery). At the traffic lights is the Old Bailey, and on the opposite side of the road, the Magpie and Stump pub. Turn right here across Newgate Street into Giltspur Street. To the left is St Sepulchre's Church and a watch-house. Cross the road by the watch-house and walk up the left-hand side of Giltspur Street.

Giltspur Street

At the junction of Giltspur Street and Cock Lane (first left) is 'Pye Corner', once thought to mark the point where the Great Fire of London was finally put out. High on the wall stands the gilt figure of the 'Fat Boy', formerly part of the sign of a nearby tavern called the Fortune of War.
Bear left round West Smithfield, then cross to the garden in the middle. To the left is Smithfield Meat and Poultry Market, and to the right the gate and walls of the older part of St Bartholomew's Hospital.

St Bartholomew's Hospital

'Barts' was founded in 1123 as a religious establishment and at the dissolution of the monasteries was given to the City of London by Henry VIII. It is the oldest hospital in London on its original site. Nearby, a half-timbered Elizabethan gatehouse marks the entrance to the Norman church of St Bartholomew the Great, the oldest church standing in the City.
Enter the central garden (a plaque gives the history of Smithfield). Leave the garden, cross to the wall of the hospital and turn left along it (there are various memorial plaques on it). Turn right into Little Britain. Shortly a detour can be made by keeping straight ahead for the National Postal

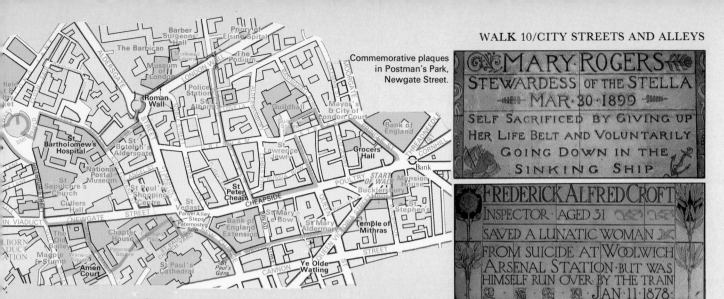

Commemorative plaques in Postman's Park, Newgate Street.

MARY ROGERS STEWARDESS OF THE STELLA MAR·30·1899 SELF SACRIFICED BY GIVING UP HER LIFE BELT AND VOLUNTARILY GOING DOWN IN THE SINKING SHIP

FREDERICK ALFRED CROFT INSPECTOR·AGED 31 SAVED A LUNATIC WOMAN FROM SUICIDE AT WOOLWICH ARSENAL STATION·BUT WAS HIMSELF RUN OVER BY THE TRAIN JAN·11·1878

Gateway to St Bartholomew the Great.

Museum in *King Edward Street*. On the main walk turn left with *Little Britain*, noting **St Botolph** Aldersgate on the right. Turn left, then left again up the stairs to the Barbican High Walk and the **Museum of London**. Turn right, then right again alongside the museum.

The Roman Wall

On the left here, at ground level, are the ruins of a wall and tower which formed part of a Roman fort. Another section of the wall is visible to the right, on the south side of London Wall alongside Noble Street.
Continue across the bridge over Wood Street, to the Podium pub. A detour from the main walk can be made here. Instead of crossing the bridge, turn left. Then cross the bridge over the entrance to Monkwell Square, and turn left again for three ages of architecture: in the foreground the Roman

The crest of the Grocers' Company on their hall. Similar marks or plaques appear on a number of City buildings, usually signifying that the place is owned by the guild whose crest appears on it.

Seen from the air, St Paul's Cathedral triumphs over the encircling anonymous office blocks.

Wall; to the right, **St Giles Cripplegate**, where Oliver Cromwell was married and the poet Milton buried; in the background, the massive modern Barbican. Return to the main route and cross the bridge to the Podium. Turn right, cross the footbridge over London Wall and at a snack bar turn right and go down the stairs to Wood Street. Pass St Alban Wood Street on the right. Continue down Wood Street, crossing Gresham Street. At the end of Wood Street pass, on the right, the small churchyard of St Peter Cheap.

St Peter Cheap

In the churchyard is to be seen a plane tree, supposed to be the one in Wordsworth's poem, *Poor Susan*. There is a story that until the tree dies nothing can be built here.
Turn left into Cheapside.

Cheapside

This was the high street of the medieval City, a great open-air market which came to be called West Chepe (as opposed to East Cheap) from the Anglo-Saxon word for 'barter'.
*Pass **St Mary-le-Bow** and at the traffic lights turn left into King Street. At the end, cross Gresham Street and pass the back of the restored **St Lawrence Jewry** to enter Guildhall Yard. Turn right into a lane known as Guildhall Buildings, and pass the Mayor's and City of London Court (1893) on the right. At the end turn right into Basinghall Street, then cross Gresham Street again and turn left. Pass Old Jewry on the right, then bear right into Prince's Street as far as the entrance leading down to the Grocers' Hall.*

The Grocers' Hall

The Grocers' Hall is the fourth building on this site. A casualty of the flying bombs in 1944, it was restored only to be gutted by fire in 1965. The Grocers' Company dates from 1428 and is second in precedence of the twelve great City livery companies. Outside the hall stands a statue of its patron, St Anthony of Coma.
Continue along Prince's Street back to the Mansion House and Bank Underground.

Walk 11

Start: Sloane Square
Approximate distance: 2¾ miles

The Highways and Byways of Chelsea

From the trend-setting boutiques and shops of the King's Road to the quiet streets by the Thames, Chelsea has an air of secure prosperity. During the 19th century it was one of the most popular of London's villages – inhabited by a host of scholars, poets, and writers, many of whose homes can still be seen.

Places in **bold italic** in the route directions are described elsewhere in this book. Names shown in black on the map are described in the text.

From the south side of Sloane Square follow the right-hand side of Lower Sloane Street. After 220 yds turn right into Turk's Row. At the end turn left into Franklin's Row along Burton's Court. Cross the main road at the pedestrian crossing and go through the gateway into the Royal Hospital.

The Royal Hospital
The Royal Hospital, Chelsea, was founded in 1682 by Charles II for veteran and invalid soldiers. Sir Christopher Wren designed most of the buildings, and his work can be seen at its finest in the Figure Court and the Chapel. Alterations and additions were subsequently made by Robert Adam and Sir John Soane. The Hospital now houses 500 army pensioners, who parade in their scarlet frock-coats on Oak Apple Day (May 29). The famous Chelsea Flower Show is held here every year.
At the end of the walk go through the gateway. Turn left into Ranelagh Gardens for a detour from the main walk.

Chelsea Pensioners on parade in their winter colours of dark blue at the Royal Hospital, Chelsea.

Ranelagh Gardens
This garden of trees and lawns is the site of the famous 18th-century Ranelagh Pleasure Gardens. The author and wit Horace Walpole, who was here on the opening night in 1742, said that it was crowded 'with much nobility and much mob'. So for a while it continued. There was music, opera, gambling, dancing, and masquerades – and the entry fee of half-a-crown included coffee and punch. But it declined in favour towards the end of the century and finally closed its gates in 1804.

Sir Thomas More looks out over the gardens of Cheyne Walk, Chelsea, where he once lived.

On the main walk take the next footpath on the right. At the end turn right and go through the gateway into the road along the west side of the Hospital. Go through another gate and turn left into Royal Hospital Road. Take the third left into Swan Walk, and at the end turn right along Chelsea Embankment. Watch for gates on the right just before Royal Hospital Road joins the Embankment.

The Physic Garden
Just before Royal Hospital Road joins the Embankment, there is a garden on the right which has handsome iron gates decorated with the sign of Apollo and a dragon. This is the Physic Garden, begun in 1673 for the study of plants used in medicine (physic) by the Society of Apothecaries. The garden was presented to the Society in 1723 by the physician, collector, and President of the Royal Society, Sir Hans Sloane. By the late 18th century it was famous throughout Europe for the rare and curious plants that were grown there. It is still a living library of plants for botanic research. The garden is not open to the public.
At the traffic signals turn right, cross the road, and turn left into Cheyne Walk.

Cheyne Walk
This fine row of 18th-century houses has been lived in by several famous persons including George Eliot (Mary Ann Evans), author of *The Mill on the Floss*, who died at No 4 in 1880. A plaque at No 23 commemorates the site of Henry VIII's manor house. Henry took a fancy to the village of Chelsea while visiting his friend and Chancellor, Sir Thomas More (who lived nearby) and decided that the fresh country air would be good for his children. Edward VI, Mary, and Elizabeth all lived here. Sir Hans Sloane bought the manor after his retirement in 1742 and intended to leave it to the nation as a home for his vast collection of treasures. But the government removed the collection (to form the nucleus of the British Museum) and demolished the manor. Many houses in Cheyne Walk have fragments of it built into their garden walls.
At the next traffic signals cross Oakley Street and bear right. At the King's Head and Eight Bells pub (which was established in 1580) turn right into Cheyne Row.

Cheyne Row
This unspoilt terrace, built in 1708, includes the home of the historian Thomas Carlyle. He lived at No 24 for 47 years, and the house now belongs to the National Trust (see page 110).
At the next crossroads turn left into Upper Cheyne Row, and then left again into Lawrence Street.

Lawrence Street

Chelsea China was manufactured at the north end of this street from 1745 to 1784. The Chelsea factory competes with Bow for the honour of being the first to make English porcelain.
*At the end turn right to rejoin Cheyne Walk and shortly reach **Chelsea Old Church**.*

Chelsea Old Church

Inside this largely rebuilt church are the only chained books remaining in a London church. These include a 'Vinegar Bible' – the edition of 1717 containing a printer's error which turned the parable of the vineyard into the parable of the vinegar.
Continue, and cross Old Church Street, then take the next right into Danvers Street to reach Crosby Hall.

Crosby Hall

This 15th-century hall once formed part of a mansion and originally stood at Bishopsgate. Fire destroyed most of the building in the 17th century, but the great hall survived, and was moved to its present site in 1911. At one time the hall was leased by Sir Thomas More, and it now stands on what was part of the gardens of the great house he built here in 1520. His house was demolished in the 1740s, but Crosby Hall still serves to remind passers-by of one of Chelsea's most famous residents. It is usually open to the public.
Enter Paulton's Square, turn right down Paulton's Street, then left into Old Church Street. Walk to the Rectory on the right.

The Rectory

Charles Kingsley (1819–75), the author of *The Water Babies*, once lived in this otherwise undistinguished house.
*At the next crossroads turn right into the **King's Road**.*

Below: Charles II wanted the Royal Avenue to link the Royal Hospital with Kensington, but only a part of it was ever completed.

The King's Road

It is hard to believe that this bustling thoroughfare was once a quiet country footpath. During the 17th century it was enlarged to become Charles II's private carriage route between St James's and Hampton Court, but did not become a public highway until the beginning of the 19th century. Mary Quant, the designer who revolutionised women's clothing, opened a boutique here in the 1950s, and the whole road promptly achieved a fashionable reputation which it has never lost.
Continue along the King's Road as far as Royal Avenue.

Royal Avenue

The Avenue is part of a road designed by Sir Christopher Wren to link the Royal Hospital with Kensington Palace. The road was never finished but the section that remains was completed in 1694. The terraces are 19th-century.
Continue past the Royal Signals Regimental Headquarters and return to Sloane Square.

Above: The essayist Leigh Hunt's house in Upper Cheyne Row.

Below: The ornate gateway of Rossetti's house in Cheyne Walk.

Hampstead

Streets of 17th- and 18th-century houses, historic inns, and the wild glories of the Heath, combine to give Hampstead its unique village-like atmosphere. It is an atmosphere that has attracted distinguished men of letters and the arts for many generations, as is evidenced by the number of commemorative plaques to be seen throughout this walk.

Church Row, with its elegant 18th-century terraces leading down to the church, is often described as the 'finest street in Hampstead'.

Places in **bold italic** in the route directions are described elsewhere in this book. Names shown in black on the map are described in the text.

Leave Hampstead Underground Station, cross and turn left along Heath Street, past the Everyman Cinema on the right. Turn right into Church Row.

Church Row

Church Row is Hampstead's finest street. On the south side its 18th-century terraces lead down to the church, while the houses opposite show an attractive variety of styles. *Continue to St John's Church at the end of Church Row.*

St John's Church

St John's is the parish church of Hampstead, rebuilt 1745–7, and subsequently added to and altered in the 19th century. The handsome wrought-iron gates to the churchyard date from the 18th century, and were brought from the mansion of the Duke of Chandos in Edgware when it was demolished. Many famous local residents are buried in the churchyard. In the south-east corner lies the painter John Constable (1776–1837), in the newer part north of the road the actor-manager Sir Herbert Beerbohm Tree (1853–1917), the historian of London, Sir Walter Besant (1836–1901), and George du Maurier (see Hampstead Grove below).
Leave the church and turn right along Holly Walk, passing Prospect Place, Benham's Place, and Holly Place, with St Mary's Catholic Church near the top. At the end of Holly Walk, turn right into Mount Vernon, then take the second left down a path into Holly Bush Hill. Turn left, then immediately right up the hill past the house once lived in by the 18th-century painter George Romney. Walk straight on into Hampstead Grove.

Another of London's eccentricities, the Admiral's House was supposed to resemble a ship and its owner would fire cannons from the roof at news of a naval victory.

George du Maurier's house in The Grove.

Hampstead Grove

This is a street of pleasant houses of various dates set back from the road. On the left is Fenton House, a mansion of about 1693 with a walled garden. It contains a collection of furniture, porcelain, and early keyboard instruments, including a harpsichord of 1612 played by Handel. The house belongs to the National Trust and is open to the public. Further along on the right, at No 28, is New Grove House, from 1874 to 1895 the home of George du Maurier, the *Punch* cartoonist better known for his novel *Trilby* (1894) in which he created the character of Svengali.
A short detour can be made here by turning left into Admiral's Walk.

Admiral's Walk

Two of the houses in Admiral's Walk are especially interesting because of their former residents: Admiral's House, the home (1856–64) of the architect Sir George Gilbert Scott, and Grove Lodge, where the novelist John Galsworthy, author of *The Forsyte Saga*, lived from 1918 until his death in 1933.

Return to Hampstead Grove. Walk straight on and at the end of Hampstead Grove cross by the pedestrian crossing to Whitestone Pond, from which it is said ten counties can be seen. Turn left and follow the edge of the pond to the far side. Crossing a minor road, walk straight on into North End Way, past the Old Court House and Jack Straw's Castle on the left.

Jack Straw's Castle

This old inn was well known to the novelists Dickens and Thackeray. Badly damaged during World War II, it was restored in 1963.

Cross by the pedestrian crossing to Heath House, in front of which stands a war memorial. Cross on the second pedestrian crossing to the far side of Spaniards Road. Walk north along Spaniards Road for about half a mile with **Hampstead Heath** on either side until the **Spaniards Inn** and the Old Toll House are reached.

The Spaniards Inn and Old Toll House

This historic 15th-century inn was once a haunt of the highwayman Dick Turpin. The Toll House was originally built in the 17th century, but has been extensively restored.

Pass the Spaniards Inn on the left and after 200 yds turn right and enter Ken Wood.

Ken Wood

Ken Wood's wooded grounds now form the most beautiful part of Hampstead Heath. They were laid out in the 18th century by William Murray, first Earl of Mansfield, and Lord Chief Justice under George III, when the mansion of Kenwood came into his possession. The house was enlarged for Lord Mansfield in 1767–9 by Robert Adam, who is responsible for the orangery, the library, and the portico over the north entrance, the north and east wings being added later in the century. It was bequeathed to the nation in 1927 by the first Earl of Iveagh, who had bought it in 1925, together with his magnificent collection of paintings, which includes many fine 18th- and 19th-century portraits by Gainsborough, Reynolds, Romney, Raeburn and Lawrence, as well as other important works by Rembrandt, Vermeer, Van Dyck and Turner (see also page 102).

Highgate Ponds are the source of the Fleet River

Parliament Hill, at the southern extremity of Hampstead Heath, is supposed to have been the burial place of Queen Boadicea (or Boudicca)

Dr Johnson's summerhouse in the beautifully landscaped grounds of Kenwood House

Facing the rose garden to the west is Dr Johnson's Summer-house, which originally stood in the grounds of Thrale Place, Streatham, where Dr Johnson was a frequent visitor during many years of friendship with Mr and Mrs Thrale. The Summer-house was originally moved from Streatham sometime in the 1820s to Knockholt in Kent, and it was transferred to its present position in 1967.

From the rose garden, walk west to east along the front of Kenwood House and follow the path round to the right leading down to the lake. Pass the white bridge and follow a wide track through woodland for two hundred yards. Leave the woods through low iron gates and follow the path straight downhill and then to the left to Highgate Ponds. Turn right alongside the ponds to reach a four-path junction just after the last pond. Take the path on the right to the top of Parliament Hill.

Parliament Hill

Situated at the southern tip of Hampstead Heath, this large expanse of grass and trees is famous for its panoramic views across London. Walk down the other side of the hill and at its foot keep straight on across the causeway between Hampstead Ponds, the source of the Fleet River. Follow the path to the left along the edge of the ponds, down past a wooded green to Hampstead Heath BR Station. Cross South End Road by the pedestrian crossing opposite the station and turn right. After 50 yds turn left into Keats Grove (**Keats' House** is the first white house on the left and is open to the public). Continue to the top of Keats Grove and St John's Church. Turn right into Downshire Hill.

Downshire Hill

This attractive thoroughfare, which has some good Regency period houses, has been the home of several distinguished figures. They include the painter John Constable, who stayed at Nos 25–6, the poet Edwin Muir (1889–1959), who lived at No 7, and the famous art historian, Roland Penrose, who lived at No 21. Walk past the Freemasons' Inn and turn left into Willow Road. Bear left at the fork (noting the colourful Willow Cottages on the left). Cross Gayton Road and turn left into Flask Walk, taking the raised path on the right.

Flask Walk

Flask Walk runs out of Well Walk, which takes its name from the wells which made Hampstead a fashionable spa in the 18th century. In Flask Walk itself are the Victorian Flask Walk Baths (now closed). Next to them is an attractive group of restored Georgian artisans' cottages. Walk on past the Flask Inn to Hampstead High Street.

Hampstead High Street

The High Street still has some of its original 18th-century houses hidden behind modern shop fronts. Turn right to return to Hampstead Underground Station.

A London History

The Birth of London

Julius Caesar invaded Britain in 55 BC, and although he did little more than survey the ground and exact tribute from the native Celts, the future of the country was set. At the time of Caesar's invasion there was no permanent settlement on the site of what is now London. The Thames, much wider than it is today, flowed through an extensive and unhealthy marsh in which the only dry land was a few hillocks of gravel. The inhabitants of this forbidding swamp were a few tribesmen, water birds, fish, and mosquitoes.

Nearly 100 years later one of Caesar's successors, the Emperor Claudius, landed on the Kent coast and began the full-scale conquest of south-eastern England. The commander of his troops, Aulus Plautius, pressed forward to reach Colchester, then the most important settlement in Britain. He was halted by the Thames, however, and was obliged to build a bridge across it. This is thought to have been in AD 43, and recent excavations in South London suggest that the bridge was sited only a few yards downstream of the present London Bridge.

At first the crossing had only military importance for the Romans, but the bridge provided a focal point both for traffic on the newly-built Roman roads which fanned out across the country, and for the boats which were able to sail up the Thames. London, or *Londinium* as it was known to the Romans, soon became an important trading-post.

When Queen Boudicca (Boadicea) and her Iceni tribesmen attacked London in AD 61 it was already full of traders. Many thousands were killed and the town was razed to the ground. Within months London was rebuilt, with a hotchpotch of timber-framed houses and shops clustered round the more imposing official Roman buildings.

Over the next century London became the administrative centre of Roman Britain and developed into a substantial town with many fine buildings, including the largest *basilica*, or town hall, this side of the Alps, an enormous palace for the governor, bath-houses, a temple, and at Cripplegate, a fort for the London troops. About AD 200 a wall was built round the town as a defence. It was to dictate London's size and shape until the middle ages. London prospered in trade, and at the peak of Roman times the population was about 45,000.

As the Roman Empire began to collapse, at the end of the 4th century, Roman troops were recalled across the Channel, leaving the trade routes, which were London's lifeblood, undefended. The population gradually dispersed, and the town fell into ruins.

London Re-born

Trade began to recover during the 7th century, and by the 9th century London was once again a prospering town increasing its trade links with the rest of Europe. Its wealth was such that it attracted the Vikings, who repeatedly raided it during the 9th century. In one of these attacks, in 851, the Danes sailed some 350 longships up the Thames and burned the city to the ground, just as Queen Boudicca had done nearly 800 years before. A series of power struggles followed with control of London passing between Danish, English and Norman kings. By 1017 the Danish King Canute ruled, and under him Danish traders were allowed to settle in

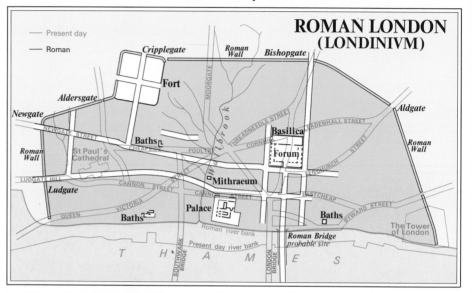

London. Under his successor, Edward the Confessor, who was Norman by descent, French influence came to the town.

The Capital of England

By now London was the largest, most prosperous and most important city in the land – but it was not yet the capital. It had become the usual place of residence for the reigning monarch, but it was not the place where kings were crowned. Edward the Confessor restored the ancient monastery at Westminster, which had been founded in the 8th century, and the Abbey Church was consecrated on the 28th December, 1065. Edward died a week later, and his successor, Harold, was crowned in the abbey soon afterwards. London was truly the capital of England. It was a capital with two centres – the City, ruled by the merchants and the guilds, and Westminster, where the monarch had his palace.

On Christmas Day, 1066, William the Conqueror was crowned in Westminster Abbey, three months after his momentous victory at The Battle of Hastings. He granted special privileges to the citizens of London, but built the Tower to remind them of his overwhelming power. It was in the Tower that Richard II took refuge from the angry Kent and Essex mobs in the Peasant's Revolt of 1381, but it could not prevent the rabble from entering, seizing and beheading his ministers, including Simon of Sudbury, the Archbishop of Canterbury.

Two relics from Roman London. Above: a medallion commemorating the submission of London after the Diocletian rebellion. Below: A carving of four Celtic mother goddesses dating from the late 2nd century AD.

Setbacks and Advances

In 1348 the Black Death, or bubonic plague, which had already swept across Europe, struck London. Between the first outbreak and the last, in 1665, London suffered 16 major outbreaks of the plague, with an astonishing number of deaths. The noble and the rich took to building their houses outside London wherever possible, and left the city at the slightest suspicion of an outbreak.

Despite these crushing disasters, London expanded at an extraordinary pace. The Strand, which ran towards the king's palace at Westminster, was the home for many of the rich landowners. Lawyers took up residence along Fleet Street (at the Temple), and it was here also that the first printers in London, Caxton and Wynkyn de Worde, set up shop. The River Fleet, then called the Holbourne, was at that time navigable by boats, and along its banks houses, shops and docks developed on what is now Farringdon Street (the river was covered over in the 18th century).

When Henry VIII came to the throne in 1509, London's population was about 50,000. By the end of the century it had risen to about 200,000. Southwark, populated since Roman times, grew also.

South Bank Revels

The south side of the river had always had a special significance for Londoners, for it was outside the jurisdiction of the City of London authorities. It became a centre for brothels, cheap drinking houses and shady activities of all sorts. In Elizabethan times it was the place for London's favourite sports – bear-baiting and bull-baiting.

It is not surprising, therefore, that Elizabethan London's newest and most famous amusement – the theatre – found a home in Southwark. London was no stranger to plays, but they were usually performed in inns. The City authorities discouraged them – not because of their content, but because they wasted workmen's time. The first special playhouse was built outside the City limits in Finsbury Fields by James Burbage in 1576. It was called 'the Theatre' and a year later another, 'the Curtain', was built nearby. Shakespeare's *Romeo and Juliet* was first performed here. More famous, however, were the theatres on the south bank, such as 'the Swan', 'the Bear Garden' and 'the Globe' which was opened in 1599. That the present day regards the plays, not only of Shakespeare, but also of others such as Ben Jonson, or Beaumont and Fletcher, as almost unsurpassed in the heritage of the English language might well have seemed odd to Elizabethan Londoners. After all, these plays were then performed on what was the seamy side of town, and their spectators may well have heartily partaken of the other pastimes nearby.

Right: The trial, imprisonment and eventual release from the Tower of Charles, Duke of Orleans who was captured at the Battle of Agincourt. This view of the Tower, with London Bridge in the background, dates from about 1485.

Below: London in the 1570s had not grown much outside the Roman and medieval walls. The south bank was however well known as a place of revelry and sport for the citizens – and as a refuge for felons.

LONDINVM FERACISSIMI ANGLIAE REGNI METROPOLIS

A Phoenix from the Flames

Plagues, civil war and a devastating fire mark the 17th century as the most dramatic era of London's history. Yet in the late 1600s London emerged stronger than ever, a sound platform of parliamentary democracy and financial strength on which, in the 18th century, London could develop in arts, science and business, as well as in actual size.

In the eyes of the citizens of London Elizabeth I could do no wrong, but their feelings towards her successor, James I, were entirely different. It was not that they resented a Scottish king (he was also James VI of Scotland) – it was James's debauched behaviour and unconcealed hatred of the people of London which sowed the seeds of discontent and was eventually to lose James's successor his head.

James did, however, bestow on London two great achievements. One was the architecture of Inigo Jones, and the other was Middleton's New River Project. London's growing population badly needed new sources of fresh water, and Hugh Middleton's great engineering venture to bring fresh water to London from Hertfordshire would have failed but for James's financial backing. Inigo Jones was appointed Surveyor of the Royal Buildings in 1615 by the King, who had great plans for London but little money to carry them out. Jones was undoubtedly the greatest architect of his day, and his influence on building design was enormous. The Banqueting House in Whitehall, and the Queen's House at Greenwich both display his absolute mastery of proportion.

With a father like James I, Charles I stood little chance of gaining popularity, and his continual defiance of Parliament made civil war virtually inevitable. In 1642 the King left London, which by then was in a state of rebellion, and the war escalated into open

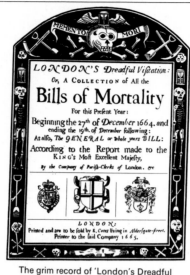

The grim record of 'London's Dreadful Visitation' of 1665 when almost 70,000 people died of Bubonic plague.

conflict. London's financial support of the Parliamentary forces was probably the decisive factor in the King's defeat, and in 1649 Charles returned to the capital to be tried and finally executed outside his father's greatest monument, the Banqueting House.

The 11-year Commonwealth which followed was a dismal time for Londoners. Not only were they forced to pay for the Civil War, but also the Puritans stripped London

of its amusements. Playhouses were closed and anything that was considered to be frivolous, which included maypoles, dances, music, and bright clothes, was violently suppressed. Churches were emptied of organs, choirs and everything remotely 'papist'. In 1652 the House of Commons even succeeded in abolishing Christmas Day. The Commonwealth had begun in a spirit of genuine idealism, but ended as a repressive dictatorship.

The Restoration and The Fire

It was no wonder that the streets of London rang with rejoicing in May 1660 at King Charles II's return from exile. As the 'Merry Monarch', Charles symbolised the end of austerity and the return of previous pleasures. Theatres were allowed to re-open and restrictions on building were eased allowing developers to build new houses in the rapidly-expanding and increasingly-fashionable West End.

In the city itself gaiety was soon to turn to grief. In 1665 London experienced its last and worst plague, and the following year a small fire in the house of the King's baker in Pudding Lane was fanned by an east wind and became the Great Fire of London. For four days the fire raged through the tightly-packed wooden buildings until the wind slackened and the fire was halted. Few died, but four-fifths of the city, some 436 acres in all, was completely destroyed. This included 13,000 houses, 89 churches, 52 Companies' halls, and St Paul's Cathedral.

Within days the citizens were discussing how to rebuild the city and in less than a week Christopher Wren had produced plans for a new London which would have been made up of great piazzas, and wide, straight boulevards. More plans quickly followed but none were adopted because the speed needed to reconstruct the city meant that rebuilding went ahead on the old street-plan. Wren's designs, however, set the style and to him London owes the beauties of St Paul's Cathedral and many fine churches.

In this contemporary painting of the Great Fire of London, the old St Paul's Cathedral is seen silhouetted against the flames. The City was devastated, but the fire also wiped out the plague.

This view of London before the Great Fire, painted by Visscher in 1650, shows, on the right, the Tower of London, and in the centre, London Bridge, on which until 1750 stood houses and shops.

London's Renaissance

The end of the 17th century saw London grow in three ways – in size, in thinking and in business. The new Royal Society, with such distinguished Fellows as the scientists Robert Boyle and Isaac Newton, was patronished by Charles II and brought scientific and philosophical thinking into the age of reason.

The non-conformists who set up communities in the New World were adventurers as well as moralists, and may have inspired London businessmen, who had also been studying the trade success the Dutch were having with their colonies in the East Indies, to found large companies which undertook expensive but profitable overseas voyages. London began to build an empire.

London in the 18th century was a mixture of sophistication and squalor, of elegance and lawlessness. The crowded slums of the city contrasted sharply with the newly laid-out and finely-built squares of Bloomsbury and Mayfair. While lawyers reached new peaks of eloquence and learning – their wigs and dress are still imitated today – crime and corruption flourished. Penalties for offenders were savage and severe – public executions at Tyburn and Newgate were common and popular events.

Increased trade with the rest of the world changed the lifestyle of many Londoners. Luxury shops opened selling Indian cotton and Chinese silk, Oriental lacquer furniture and porcelain. Tobacco became cheap enough for the ordinary man and imports of tea, chocolate and coffee changed society's habits. Taking tea became very fashionable and the newly-formed coffee houses were places where businessmen could meet to talk. Lloyds of London, the great insurance house, is an example of one of the many coffee houses that grew to become financial institutions.

Novelists like Defoe and Fielding, and artists such as Hogarth and Rowlandson have left vivid records of life in 18th-century London. The bustling streets shook with the clatter of carriages and the clamour of street vendors, while the opera houses resounded with the music of Handel, who came to London from Germany in 1711. For amusement Londoners liked to visit the Vauxhall and Ranelagh Gardens which, on either side of the river, vied with each other to present the most spectacular attractions, pavilions, lodges, groves, grottos, lawns, temples, fountains, cascades, fireworks and light shows. For many Londoners the 18th century was a time of great opportunity, increasing wealth, and tremendous enjoyment.

A rich assortment of street sellers and itinerant craftsmen were once a familiar sight in London.
Above: an ink-seller.
Below: a chair- mender.

One of the earliest-known paintings of a London coffee-house, dating from about 1700. Coffee-houses became great social gathering places, where men met to talk politics or business.

67

London's development and achievement in the 19th century was phenomenal. In population alone its expansion was enormous. The first official census of 1801 showed that London's population was about 959,000 and by 1901 this figure had risen to nearly 4½ million.

Many Londoners enjoyed a good standard of living, at least when compared to other parts of the country. Dicken's pictures of London were, however, correct, for there were sweat-shops, and the exploitation of women and child labour was iniquitous – but with shipping, commerce, banking, insurance, public administration, retail trade, services and entertainment, Londoners enjoyed a far wider choice of employment than anywhere else.

Regency London

The first 30 years of the 19th century, loosely called 'Regency', were in character very similar to the 18th century. The changes to London were mostly in looks, perhaps the most famous being the works of the architect John Nash. The landscaping of Regent's Park and the beautiful terraces around it, the expansive Portland Place and the stately Regent Street, Marble Arch, and the landscaping of St James's Park are just a few of the more famous surviving examples of this genius's work.

Having more direct importance to Regency Londoners, perhaps, than Nash's great schemes were the enlargement and development of London's docks and the building of new Thames bridges. London's second bridge, Westminster Bridge, had only been built in 1750, and Blackfriars Bridge had been completed in 1769, but in the early 1800s a spate of bridge-building took place so that by 1850 nearly all of London's bridges had been constructed.

The Hub of an Empire

From the elegance of the Georgian period London quickly grew in the age of steam and industry. The Great Exhibition of 1851 was as successful as London itself, and despite the social problems of the day, Victorian Londoners stood proud. For them London led Britain and Britain led the world.

Nash designed Regent Street (above) for the Prince Regent as the route from the Prince's home, Carlton House, to Regent's Park. The design was never completed, partly because funds ran short and partly because the Regent, when he became George IV, declared that Carlton House was 'no better than a slum' and told Nash to convert Buckingham House into a palace.

Below: A Frost Fair on the Thames. Before Sir Joseph Bazalgette built the embankments in the 1840s the Thames was wider, shallower and flowed more slowly. Thus, it sometimes froze over in cold winters and quite large fairs could be held on the ice.

The Coming of the Railways

London's biggest problem at this time was that people had to live near their work. Transport was poor and working hours long. The rich could afford to live further away and travel in their own coaches, but the poor had to live in cramped and squalid slums. Sanitation was inadequate and there was always a danger from disease. In fact a number of cholera epidemics occurred – in 1849, for example, 14,000 died and in 1854 further epidemics claimed 10,000 lives. The introduction of the horse-drawn omnibus eased the problem, but it was the coming of the railways which had the most impact. By 1848 Paddington, Euston, King's Cross, Fenchurch Street, London Bridge and Waterloo Stations had all been completed. Victoria, St Pancras, Charing Cross, Blackfriars, Broad Street and Holborn Viaduct Stations were all built in the 1860s. A more complex technical achievement was the opening, in 1863, of the world's first underground railway from Paddington to Farringdon Street.

The coming of the railways coincided with the beginning of Queen Victoria's 64-year reign and it must have seemed the beginning of a new age for London. The steam revolution enabled people to escape the unhealthy slums, and suburbs began to spread out from London along the routes of the railway tracks. The age of commuting had begun.

Above: The Great Exhibition of 1851 celebrated Victorian achievement. Paxton's masterpiece, the Crystal Palace, stood in Hyde Park. It was later moved and burnt down in the 1930s.

Reforms and Social Achievements

London, remained, as it had always done, a place of great contrasts. The capital of an empire which encompassed most of the known world, it still had sickening poverty, blatant social injustice, and an often corrupt bureaucracy. Social change was slow, but it followed hard on the heels of material advancement and a growing awareness of the plight of the poor. The Metropolitan Police were formed in 1829. The Great Reform Bill, which almost doubled the electorate, was made law in 1832, and a series of Factory Acts, which improved working conditions and shortened working hours, were passed between 1819 and 1895.

It was a time of great success and achievement for Britain as a whole, and London was at its centre. It was marked in 1851 by the Great Exhibition, sponsored by Prince Albert and held in Hyde Park in the architect Joseph Paxton's specially-built Crystal Palace, a revolutionary building of glass and cast iron, three times the length of St Paul's. Later the Crystal Palace was moved to its permanent site at Sydenham Hill (it burned down in 1936). Health and sanitation were problems that had been with London virtually since its foundation, but during Victorian times they became so pressing that something had to be done. Despite Dickens' picture of an administration of idle and ineffectual bureaucrats, there were men who did much to improve the city. Some measures, such as purifying London's water supply, took many years. Sewers were extensively laid throughout the 1840s but they emptied straight into the river. In the 1860s great sewers which ran alongside the Thames collecting the effluent before it entered the river were ingeniously incorporated into the Victoria Embankment on the north bank, and the Albert Embankment on the south

bank, which not only tidied up the unsightly riverbank, but also gave a wide processional route from Westminster to the City and facilitated the building of further underground railways.

The second half of the 19th century was as much a time of destruction as of construction. It has been estimated that for every five buildings standing in the City in 1855, only one remained in 1905. Little country villages on the outskirts of London, such as Hampstead and Highgate to the north, and Streatham in the south, were soon to be swallowed up by the growing sprawl. As London expanded ever outwards, so the population of the City dwindled. The more offices, factories, warehouses and railway lines that went up in the City, the less room there was for people to live. In 1801 over 120,000 people lived there. In 1901 only about 30,000 actually lived in the City and today only a few thousand are residents although it is estimated that there is a daytime population of over 400,000.

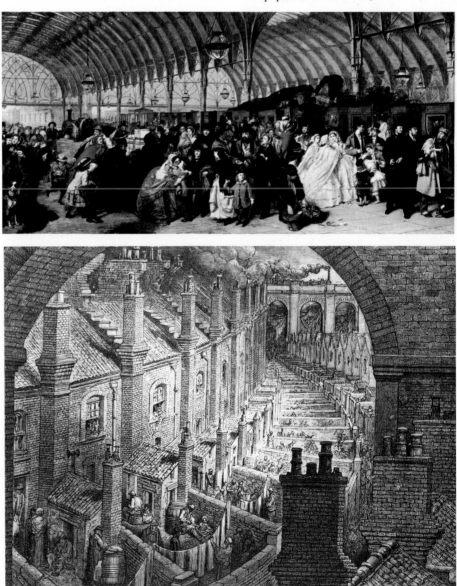

Two sides of the age of steam: travel made easy for some; for others, lives overshadowed by monstrous viaducts.

A Capital for a New Age

From the ravages of two world wars London emerged battered but unshaken. London welcomed the 20th century with open arms – redevelopment in the centre of the city has destroyed more than bombs ever did, and the urban sprawl is so great that it is hard to say where London begins and ends – but the capital still retains its ancient heritage, and its character, though constantly evolving, remains unique.

Changing times during World War I, a woman drives a luggage trolley at Liverpool Street Station

Queen Victoria's death in 1901 in fact marked the end of an era, but Edwardian London showed few outward signs of it. All the glory, standards, tastes and values of the previous reign lived on. The 'high life', however, of the Edwardian era could not hide the social problems of the day. Whether at home, with the advent of the motor-car and the protest of the Women's Suffragette movement, or abroad with the build-up of the German Navy, change was inevitable. What precipitated those changes and hurled London into the 20th century was the First World War. It was a time of great personal tragedy for London's rich and poor alike, for while the West End was full of an abnormal gaiety as troops on leave took what pleasures they could, many more were unwittingly saying their last farewells at London's stations before boarding a train to the Continent and almost certain death.

London itself suffered little material damage – but the German zeppelins and aeroplanes did come. In all there were about 25 bombing raids, mostly in eastern London and in the City.

Peace but not prosperity came in 1918. Food queues became dole queues and the victory parades were followed by hunger marches. Throughout the country industrial discontent grew, culminating in the General Strike of 1926.

London continued to expand through the austere days of the '30s. A number of new suburban developments were being built, either along the arterial roads which led into London, or as planned estates. Today these rows upon rows of pebble-dashed mock-Tudor or mock-Georgian houses may look monotonous, but a small house with a garden was welcome enough to families who had been used to living in dingy Victorian brick-built terraces.

London at War

Tension grew in the late '30s, and while the abdication of Edward VIII in 1936 took most Londoners' minds off international problems for a while, the threat of war with Hitler's Germany loomed large. London prepared itself and on the 3rd September, 1939, war was declared on Germany.

Londoners expected to be in the front line of attack and began to evacuate their children to safer parts of the country, dig trenches and build air-raid shelters. All seemed quiet at first, but it was the lull before the storm.

In September 1940 the onslaught began. Hitler, unable to gain supremacy in the skies during the Battle of Britain, unleashed his fury on London with the Blitz. For months on end, hundreds of German bombers raided London every night in a determined attempt to bring the capital to its knees. The threat was not only from high explosives but also from small incendiary bombs which could be put out without too much trouble – if detected. If not, they could set a building

Their finest hour. Volunteers of the Civil Defence worked ceaselessly during the Blitz in 1940–1.

alight. The overstretched police, fire, and ambulance teams were helped by ordinary Londoners taking turns at fire-watching duty, who when their duties had finished, as often as not had to spend the night in air-raid shelters in their gardens, in public shelters, or in Underground stations.

The docks, the East End, and the City were the worst-hit areas. On one night after Christmas, 28 incendiary bombs fell on St Paul's but somehow the cathedral was saved. Out of the City's 460 acres, 164 were reduced to rubble. But though the Germans could destroy the bricks and mortar, they could not break the Londoners' will. 'London can take it' became their motto and by early 1941 the worst of the Blitz was over. On May 8th 1945 London celebrated V-E Day, the end of war in Europe.

A mass of hats and open-topped omnibuses at the junction of Oxford Street and Tottenham Court Road, 1912.

The New Elizabethan Age

London began to re-emerge almost before the ashes were cold. The most immediate problem was that of housing the homeless. The planners can hardly be blamed for the proliferation of pre-fabricated houses and high-rise blocks of flats that were to cause such social problems in years to come as they seemed the ideal solution at the time. The 'pre-fabs' were only supposed to be temporary, yet 30 years later a number are still being lived in. The rise of the Welfare State at this time was a mark of the social changes that were needed to get Britain back on its feet, and though rationing and shortage still continued after the war, they could not dampen the country's spirit.

This optimism was displayed in the Festival of Britain, held on the South Bank in 1951, exactly 100 years after Prince Albert's Great Exhibition in Hyde Park. That exhibition was staged to display Britain's achievements and connections with the rest of the world – the Festival of Britain seemed to mark the end of wartime austerity and to show what Britain might accomplish in the future.

The succession of Queen Elizabeth II in 1952 seemed to herald a 'new age', and while statistics may show that it was not a time of plenty, the '50s certainly saw a great improvement in most people's standards of living, particularly in London and the south-east. Towards the end of the '50s and in the early '60s, young people, too, found themselves with money to spend, and London quickly catered for them. Its boutiques, pop music industry, and Carnaby Street soon earned the nickname 'swinging London'.

Present-day London continues to grow, though decentralisation policies and the development of 'new towns' well outside the London area have tried to curb expansion within Greater London itself. The building of new road and motorway schemes and the increasing number of office blocks gives parts of London a concrete jungle look known in so many cities. Yet, considering the effect of fires, wars and centuries of planners and developers, it is remarkable how much ancient character London has managed to retain. And despite the economic problems of the day, London is still thriving. Problems have always been a part of London's history, but, somehow, it always overcomes them.

The pageantry of the coronation of Queen Elizabeth II as the procession moved along Oxford Street on 2nd June 1953.

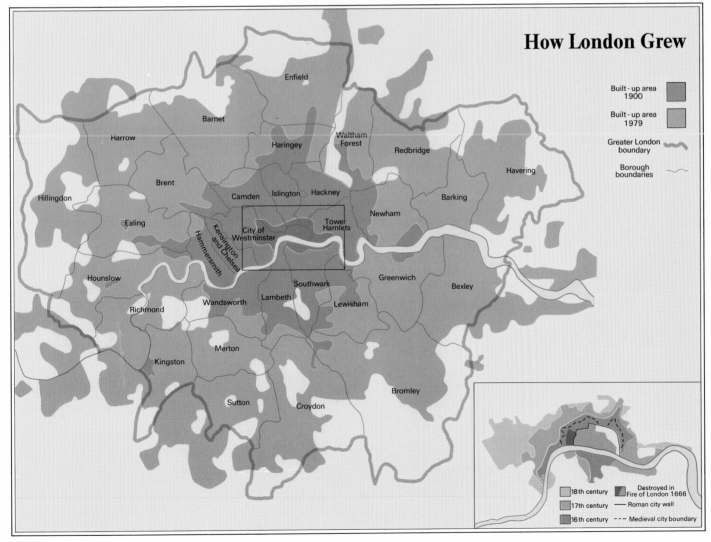

How London Grew

Built-up area 1900

Built-up area 1979

Greater London boundary

Borough boundaries

18th century

17th century

16th century

Destroyed in Fire of London 1666

Roman city wall

Medieval city boundary

Curious London

There is much about London that is unexplained and mysterious. Alleys lead nowhere, rivers disappear, and bumps are heard in the night. Rumours of discovered treasure have attracted flocks of Londoners for centuries. Many aspects of curious London are taken seriously by enthusiasts. Ghost hunters stalk their prey with sophisticated electronic devices, and earnest-looking men can be seen combing the banks of the Thames with metal detectors at low tide.

Unusual street furniture is much more easily found. There are cannons, converted into bollards, in many London streets and alleys. Street lamps appear in almost every conceivable shape and size; there is even one near the Temple that is fuelled by sewer gas. Curious London is everywhere, but it needs to be looked for.

Ghostly Encounters

London is said to be the most haunted city in the world. Considering that the capital's history is soaked with blood and liberally splashed with acts of human cruelty almost to the point of nightmare, perhaps this is not surprising. Many of London's dark and secret places are ideal locations for unexplained manifestations of all sorts.

Not all ghosts are as sinister as the evil presence that is said to haunt a small top room at 50 Berkeley Square. It so frightened a girl during the 19th century that she went insane and was never able to tell what she had seen, and a man who spent the night in the room was mysteriously found dead the next day. Far more benevolent is 'The Man in Grey' who haunts the Theatre Royal, Drury Lane. He is often seen in the Upper Circle, dressed in 18th-century clothes, and actors welcome his appearance at a matinee as it means that the show will be a success.

The Tower of London is undoubtedly the most haunted place in London. Spectral occupants of its walkways and greens include kings, queens, knights and nameless shapes. Needless to say, many of these eerie manifestations appear without their heads, or with them tucked under their arms. The guards who patrol the Tower at night have become immune to the successions of bumps, creaks, groans, and whispers which accompany their lonely vigils.

Swords at Dawn

London's secluded courtyards made ideal spots for duels, and it is said that the clash and clatter of swords can still be heard in a few of these usually quiet places. One such courtyard is Raquet Court, which is north of Fleet Street, where Dennis Connel killed Thomas Wicks in 1721. Pickering Place, which is situated up an alleyway next to Berry Bros in St James's Street, is said to have been the scene of the last duel ever fought in London.

A famous 17th-century duel resulted in a strange phenomenon in Tavistock Square, Bloomsbury. Known as Southampton Fields before being built over, it was here, in 1685, that two brothers fought a prolonged duel over a woman they both wanted to marry. As she sat watching they charged back and forth at each other until they both fell, mortally wounded. It was said that where they stepped the grass would never grow again, and indeed, long after the battle their footprints could be seen. It became known as the Field of Forty Footsteps, and today in one corner of the gardens in Tavistock Square faint dips and depressions can still be seen.

Underneath London

Few Londoners, driving from King's Cross to Blackfriars along King's Cross Road and Farringdon Road, realise that to have taken this journey in Pepys's time would have

Left: The mummified remains of the philosopher Jeremy Bentham who was one of the founders of University College in Gower Street, the oldest of the colleges that make up the University of London. Bentham (1748–1832) held that the bodies of great men should be preserved and put on general display. Accordingly, he had himself embalmed when he died and now sits in his old chair and wearing his own clothes in a glass case near the entrance hall of his College. In this way, he hoped to preserve his influence on its affairs. His presence is felt in another way, however, for his ghost is said to haunt the building and has been seen and heard tap-tapping its way round the passageways. Books known to have been left on shelves are often found lying open next morning.

Below: The operating theatre at Old St Thomas's Hospital in Southwark is a grim reminder of the early days of surgery. Operations were carried out here on women patients from 1822 when the theatre was opened, until 1862 when the hospital moved to Lambeth. Antiseptic methods were unknown in London until the 1870s, and operations were frequently carried out without anaesthetic – including amputations, when strong assistants would hold the patient down. The old operating theatre has now been restored and includes such authentic details as the box of sawdust to catch the blood from the operating table.

The smallest police station in Britain, and quite possibly in the world, is contained inside this lamp-post in Trafalgar Square. It has a direct telephone link with New Scotland Yard.

required a boat. For this is the course of one of London's most famous old rivers, the Fleet. At one time there were a number of rivers running through London and into the Thames. Most are now completely covered over and flow, unseen and largely unknown, beneath London's buildings and streets.

The Fleet, whose source is on Hampstead Heath, flows under Camden Town, the Regent's Canal, King's Cross Station and eventually enters the Thames just west of Blackfriars Bridge. Below King's Cross it was also known as the Holbourne, and Holborn Viaduct clearly indicates where the Fleet valley lies. The Fleet was used by river craft of all sorts up until the end of the 18th century. By that time it had become an unwholesome open sewer known as Fleet Ditch and few local residents mourned its passing when it was covered over.

The Walbrook was an important river in Roman times and it now runs under the heart of the City. Its source was in the marshes to the north of the city, in the area that is now called Moorfields, and on its banks were many fashionable Roman houses. It runs right under the Bank of England and during building work carried out in the 19th century it was found still to be flowing through the foundations. From here it flows just west of the street called Walbrook and into the Thames near Southwark Bridge.

The source of the famous Tyburn River is marked by a fountain at the corner of Lyndhurst Road and Fitzjohn's Avenue in Hampstead. It still supplies the water for the lakes in Regent's Park and St James's Park. Before running into the Thames it divided to form Thorney Island – on which Westminster Abbey was built. Oxford Street

used to be called Tyburn Road, and the infamous gallows known as 'Tyburn Tree' was sited at the corner of Oxford Street and Edgware Road. The Serpentine in Hyde Park was formed by damming another river which is now underground, the Westbourne.

Rivers are not the only things which run unknown beneath London's surface. Some 70 feet below ground level is the 6½-mile long tunnel of the Post Office railway. It runs between Whitechapel and Paddington Station and has 8 stops, one of which is the giant sorting office at Mount Pleasant.

Buried Treasure

It was once common practice to bury valuables in times of uncertainty or danger. Many of these hoards were never recovered by the people that secreted them, and have subsequently been accidentally discovered.

The oldest treasure to have been recovered is that of the worshippers of the cult of Mithras, who lived in Roman times and hid their precious religious objects when they were persecuted. These were found centuries later and are now on display in the Museum of London. Similarly, during the dissolution of the monasteries under Henry VIII, the monks of London buried many of their valuable jewels and religious treasures, and a number of these hoardes were later unearthed. One discovery was a large iron-bound chest full of jewels, gold and silver coins from the time of Henry VIII which was found in a deep cellar under Long Acre.

Somewhere in the vicinity of Trafalgar Square lie the Crown Jewels of France. Louis XV's mistress brought them to London in 1793 and is supposed to have buried them in

The lion on Westminster Bridge came from the Lion Brewery, Southwark. He is of artificial stone made to a secret formula, since lost, by the now defunct Coade Factory.

the Royal Mews which were later demolished when Trafalgar Square was built in the 1820s. The unfortunate lady died on the guillotine without telling anyone where the jewels were.

The Thames is said to hold much treasure, either at the sites of old fords or where valuables may have been thrown overboard by dockers who hoped to recover them at low tide. In the late 1800s a silver casket filled with thousands of Spanish gold coins was found near Execution Dock at Wapping.

The blue plaques denoting houses where famous people have lived are well known. There are a number of other curious plaques to be seen, particularly in the older parts of London. Rare now, though some are preserved in the Museum of London, are Fire Marks. Before a regular fire-fighting service was introduced in the 1860s, it was left to insurance companies – one of the plaques meant that the building was entitled to their service. Other plaques were used as property marks and illustrate the crest of the company or institution to whom the building belonged. Right, and below right, are two of Christ's Hospital's marks. Most common of all are parish boundary marks; below left and centre are those of St John the Baptist, Walbrook, and St Mary-le-Strand.

London's River

LONDON'S RIVER

Father Thames

The Thames has been used as a highway ever since prehistoric times, when rivers provided the safest and most direct way of travel. It takes its name from the latin *Tamesis*, an amalgamation of two ancient words, *tam* and *isis*. *Tam* is thought to mean 'wide', and *isis* (by which name the river is still known at Oxford) is derived from *uisge*, the Celtic word for water.

It is to the Thames, and the Romans, that London owes its existence. There was no permanent settlement where London now stands until the Romans built the first bridge across the river. From that beginning London grew to become the heart of an empire that encompassed a quarter of the world, and its life-giving artery was the Thames. Today some 12 million people depend on Thames water for their domestic requirements. It has been calculated that each drop of water is used seven times between the source and the mouth of the river. It is fitting, therefore, that the Thames, like the Tiber which nourished Rome, has been called 'Father'.

To travel on the Thames is to make a voyage through a nation's history. From the magnificent Tudor palace at Hampton Court the river winds in great loops into the heart of London. It flows beneath the walls of the Houses of Parliament and reflects the forbidding outline of the Tower of London in its waters. From the Pool of London it descends through Dockland and passes Greenwich, the site of another royal palace.

This statue of Old Father Thames marks the source of the river.

At Chelsea picturesque painted houseboats lie almost in the shadow of a power station. The launches of the river police skim up and down the river at all times, and sometimes a tug boat pulling a string of barges can be seen making progress of a more laboured kind.

The Thames is once more a clean river. It is hard to believe that as late as the 1950s the river was so filthy that it was unable to support fish life of any kind. Tremendous efforts to clean up the river were made in the '60s and '70s, and now nearly 100 fish species have been recorded in the Tideway, though salmon, which used to be common in the Thames, have not yet returned in any numbers; however, one or two sickly-looking specimens have been found recently.

Each time a river trip is undertaken there will be something new to see. The Thames has many moods, some of them dictated by the state of the tide, and some by the weather. This changing character has inspired painters and poets for centuries, and continues to enchant those content simply to look and enjoy.

Key to River Maps

Thames Ditton stands on the opposite bank of the river to Hampton Court Park and its few old-world houses and pubs contrast sharply with the suburban developments in the surrounding areas. Thames Ditton Island is covered with private houses and is connected to Thames Ditton by a charming suspension bridge.

On the Water

The most relaxed way to see many of London's most important monuments is from the deck of one of the boats that make their unhurried way up and down the Thames.

Palaces, parks, ancient pubs, and old-world villages are passed between Hampton Court and Chiswick, and as the river enters Westminster impressive government buildings and monolithic skyscrapers dominate the view. St Paul's Cathedral can be seen amongst the glass and concrete mountains of the City, and beyond Tower Bridge the riversides are lined with industrial buildings. Gaunt warehouses, many of which are empty and neglected, glower over the water. This sombre prospect is enlivened by riverside pubs and the architectural glories of Greenwich.

There is a constant coming and going of river craft of all sorts, although the big ships now have their moorings miles downstream. Elegant yachts cruise on the upper reaches, and at Mortlake tireless crews pull at their oars in faultless unison.

Details of ferry services and boat tours are given on page 13, in the section of this book called A London Compass. The temperature over water is usually several degrees lower than it is over land, and passengers travelling on the river are advised not to embark without some form of wind proof clothing.

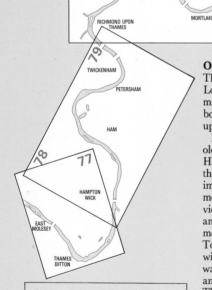

Royal elegance by the Thames

The Long Water at Hampton Court. Charles II ordered this mile-long lake in emulation of the splendours of Versailles.

Hampton Court Palace

No description will prepare the first-time visitor for the magnificence and sheer size of Hampton Court Palace. Built of red brick, it is nearly 700 ft long by 400 ft wide and contains over a thousand rooms. Cardinal Wolsey began the palace in 1514 during a phenomenal rise to power which had begun when he was made Chaplain to Henry VII. After Henry VIII had come to the throne Wolsey's ascent became meteoric and he decided to build for himself a home that was to be the finest private dwelling in the Kingdom. By this time the Cardinal's vast wealth was attracting suspicion and jealousy, and in 1529 he attempted to regain Henry's favour by presenting the palace and its contents to the King as a gift. Henry, however, had made up his mind, and the following year Wolsey was imprisoned for high treason. Hampton Court became Henry's favourite palace and he spent large sums of money improving and enlarging it. Subsequent monarchs used the palace regularly, but no extensive changes were made to the fabric of the building until the reign of William and Mary. They did not like the palace at Whitehall and commissioned Sir Christopher Wren to rebuild Hampton Court, which they intended to be their equivalent of the great French palace at Versailles. The plans to completely rebuild the palace never came to fruition. The western part of Wolsey's original palace was left virtually untouched, and Wren's work consisted of adapting and rebuilding the eastern part of the building. It is Wren's South Front which is so conspicuous from the river. George II was the last monarch to use the palace, and since that time many of the apartments have been lived in by servants of the Crown. In 1838 Queen Victoria opened the State Apartments to the public. The palace contains an enormous collection of treasures, ranging from domestic utensils to great works of art by such masters as Mantegna and Verrio. Complementing the palace's superb architecture are the grounds which surround it. *For further details of Hampton Court and its grounds see the sections of this book called Royal London (page 16) and Green London (page 140).*

Hampton Court Bridge

Built in 1933 to the designs of Sir Edwin Lutyens, this elegant bridge connects Hampton Court with East Molesley. The River Mole flows through East Molesley to enter the Thames just below the bridge. To the north of the bridge is Hampton Green, where there is a splendid group of mainly 18th-century buildings. Amongst these is Old Court House, which was the home of Sir Christopher Wren for a while, and the Royal Mews, which comprise a 16th-century barn and an earlier building. On the other side of the Green is Hampton Court House, an imposing structure dating from the middle of the 18th century.

Thames Ditton

Tucked away near the suspension bridge that connects this unspoilt riverside village with Thames Ditton Island are a number of picturesque old houses. The village's charm is emphasised by the contrast of the featureless modern suburbs that flank it on both sides.

The Great Gatehouse of the Tudor parts of Hampton Court date from Henry VIII's time. The 'King's Beasts' guarding it, however, are 20th-century additions.

From Kingston to Richmond

This obelisk at Teddington marks the boundary of the Port of London Authority.

Kingston Bridge

Kingston owes its origins to the fact that here was one of two safe fords across the Thames above Westminster. A bridge had been built here by the 12th century, and for centuries the only bridge below it was London Bridge. The present bridge was built between 1825 and 1828. An excellent tow path leads upstream from it to Hampton Court.

Kingston upon Thames

Originally called *Cyningestun*, Kingston's written records go back to the 9th century when it was the coronation place of Saxon kings. The stone upon which they were crowned is preserved outside the Guildhall. Kingston is still an important market centre, as it has been since the days when it grew up near the ford across the Thames, and it has managed, despite modern traffic, to keep its character. Many old buildings have been preserved. Of special note are the parish church and the Lovekyn Chapel, both of which date from the 14th century, and the imposing 19th-century town hall. Kingston's attractive river frontage, centred round the bridge, is unspoilt.

Teddington Weir

This is the point at which the tidal Thames is separated from the non-tidal waters. The weir was built in 1811, and fully mechanized in 1912. The fresh water flow of the Thames is measured and controlled from here, the average daily flow of water passing over the weir being about 1500 million gallons. It was bombed during World War II, and the tidal waters reached much further upstream.

Teddington Lock

On the east bank of the river, 300 yds downstream of the lock, is an obelisk which marks the official boundary between that part of the river controlled by the Thames Conservancy, and the tidal river, which is controlled by the Port of London Authority. Teddington Lock is the largest on the river, and is capable of taking a tug and a string of barges. The large building on the Teddington side of the river is occupied by the studios of Thames Television.

An important river-crossing since the earliest times, Kingston has been a busy market town for centuries.

Strawberry Hill

In 1747 Horace Walpole, the son of the then prime minister, bought at Twickenham a riverside house which he called 'a little plaything'. The changes that Walpole subsequently made to Strawberry Hill were to have a momentous effect on British architecture, for he converted it into what resembled a Gothic castle, complete with battlements and towers. It was the first Gothic Revival building in the country to have any real influence over contemporary architects, who until that time had regarded the Classical style as being the ideal. Perhaps the single most important thing about the design of the house is that it is asymmetrical, with parts of the building protruding from the main block in a way that seems quite arbitrary. The exterior can be enjoyed from the river, but the ornate interior of the building, which is used as a training college, can only be viewed on application.

Teddington Weir is the upper limit of tidal water on the Thames.

Eel Pie Island

One of the largest islands in the Thames, Eel Pie Island is approached from Twickenham over a charming iron bridge. During the 1960s the island was famous for the Eel Pie Hotel, which was a venue for jazz bands and beat groups. It was demolished several years ago. During the 18th century the island was renowned, as its name suggests, for its eels, and for its lampreys, primitive water-living creatures which resemble eels. Numerous archaeological finds discovered in the river bed around the island suggest that it was occupied in prehistoric times.

Hammerton's Ferry. A number of small ferries exist (or used to exist) on the Thames. Often there is just a man and a punt or rowboat operating for the most part on a casual basis.

York House

Footpath

Eel Pie Island

Ferry

Orleans Park

Playing Fields

Ham House

Petersham

Hammerton's Ferry

Marble Hill House and Park

RICHMOND

Glover Island

Petersham Lodge

River Lane

Petersham Meadows

Richmond Hill

Richmond Lock

St Mary's Ferry

Obelisks Old Deer Park Recreation Ground

Twickenham Bridge

Richmond Ait

Richmond Bridge

Ferry Departure Point

Footpath

York House
This 17th-century house is now used as offices by Richmond upon Thames Council, and throughout its history the building has been tenanted by distinguished people, among them the Earl of Clarendon and the Duke of York. The peculiar group of statuary which embellishes the spacious grounds of the house was installed by an Indian merchant prince, Sir Ratan Tata.

Petersham
Set below the slopes of Richmond Hill, Petersham is a riverside village of considerable character. Its best buildings are not visible from the Thames, but are situated close to it. River Lane has two exceptional houses – 18th-century Petersham Lodge, and Rutland Lodge, which was built in 1666. Charles Dickens rented a house in the village, and John Gay, the author of *The Beggar's Opera*, lived at Douglas House during the 18th century.

Ham House, dating from the 17th century, is now a branch of the Victoria and Albert Museum.

Richmond Hill
The most famous of all views of the Thames is gained from Richmond Hill. It is also, incorrectly, associated with the folk song *Sweet Lass of Richmond Hill*. The song actually refers to the Richmond in Yorkshire. Many handsome 18th-century buildings cluster on the slopes of the hill. They are overshadowed by the grandiose bulk of the Royal Star and Garter Home for disabled servicemen.

Richmond Bridge
Excellent views up and down the Thames may be obtained from this majestic bridge. It was built in 1777 to the designs of James Paine in a pleasing Classical style.

Ham House
Sir James Vavasour, a courtier of James I, built this superb riverside mansion in 1610. In 1672 it came by marriage to the Duke of Lauderdale, who lavished such attentions on it that its name became a by-word for luxurious living, and equally luxurious spending. He commissioned artists and craftsmen from Germany, Holland and Italy to decorate and furnish its many rooms and galleries. The poet William Cowper lived in the house for some time during the 18th century. It was presented to the National Trust in 1948, and now houses many treasures from the Victoria and Albert Museum.

Marble Hill House and Park
Elegantly manicured lawns run up from the Thames to the charming Palladian-style house that is Marble Hill. It was built for Henrietta Howard, the mistress of George II, and it was here that she entertained the great and fashionable figures of the time. Mrs Fitzherbert, mistress and secret wife of the Prince Regent (later to become George IV), was a later occupant of the house. In the early 20th century William Cunard purchased the whole site, with the intention of building on it. Prompt action by several local councils saved the house and its grounds, and the view from Richmond Hill.

From Richmond to Chiswick

Richmond upon Thames

Standing as it does between two large areas of parkland and being set on an exceptionally attractive reach of the Thames, Richmond has one of the best positions of any of London's towns. It makes good use of this setting, for it has a multitude of beautiful buildings, many of which were built in the 18th century when Richmond was a fashionable resort. The town probably owes its origins to Henry I, who established a royal palace here in 1125. It was then called Shene Palace, and when Richard II came to the throne he had considerable improvements made, including the installation of toilets and hot and cold running water, conveniences that had not been known in England since the departure of the Romans. After Richard's wife died in 1394 he ordered the demolition of the palace. Henry VII rebuilt it when he came to the throne and renamed it Richmond after his estates in Yorkshire. He died here, as did Elizabeth I. During the Commonwealth it was neglected and partly dismantled, but was subsequently restored and remained a royal residence until 1689. After that time it fell into ruins, and all that now remains is a Tudor gateway situated on Richmond Green, a beautiful area surrounded by superb 17th- and 18th-century buildings. Of special note here are Trumpeter's House, Old Palace Place of 1687, and Asgill House, which overlooks the river and was built in 1758 for a former lord mayor of London. It is open on application during the summer. Richmond is particularly rich in old terraced houses, notably Maids of Honour Row, Old Palace Terrace, and The Wardrobe. Richmond's parish church is partly Georgian and contains a large number of excellent memorials.

Virginia and Leonard Woolf moved to Hogarth House in Paradise Road, in 1915 and it was here that they set up the famous Hogarth Press, which published, amongst much else, T S Eliot's poem *The Waste Land*. To the north-east of Richmond is the Old Deer Park, once a royal hunting ground and now used for a variety of sporting purposes. In the park is an observatory built by William Chambers in 1729 for George II. *For Richmond Park see the section of this book called Green London (page 140).*

Isleworth

From the Thames, Isleworth, with its houses clustered round its church tower, looks like a sleepy country village. This impression is reinforced by the wooded greenery of Isleworth Ait. In fact the tower is all that remains of a 15th-century church that was accidentally burnt down in 1950, and away from the river Isleworth looks much like any other London suburb. The body of the church has been rebuilt in a bold modern style. Near to it is the London Apprentice pub, a handsome 18th-century building that is reputed to have been much frequented by smugglers.

Syon Park

The ornamental grounds of Syon Park, which stretch down to the banks of the Thames here, were laid out by the great landscape artist Capability Brown. An elegant boathouse, said to have been designed by Brown, stands on the riverside. *For further details of Syon Park see the section of this book called Green London (page 140).*

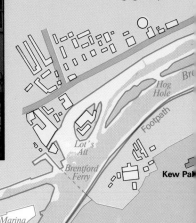

Neo-Gothic architecture in Church Street, Isleworth.

science of botany. To this end some thirty thousand plants are identified each year and over seven million dried specimens are preserved in the Herbarium. Behind-the-scenes research work is carried out by a large staff of botanists and new discoveries are constantly being made. *For further details of the gardens see the section of this book called Green London (page 140).*

Syon House

In 1431 a convent founded by Henry V was moved to this site. After the dissolution of the monasteries in 1547 the building and its grounds were granted to Protector Somerset (regent to the infant King Edward VI). The house that he built here still forms the core of the present building. In 1766 the first Duke of Northumberland commissioned the architect Robert Adam to convert the house into a great mansion. It is the interior of the house, particularly the Great Hall, which displays Adam's brilliant craftsmanship at its finest.

Royal Botanic Gardens, Kew

Kew Gardens are undoubtedly the most famous of their kind in the world. It is not often realized, however, that the primary function of the gardens is not to give pleasure to the thousands of people who visit them each year, but to serve the

Right: The severely functional shapes of a gas holder and several high-rise flats silhouetted against the sky at Brentford.

Below: Rowers passing Strand-on-the-Green's picturesque riverside houses.

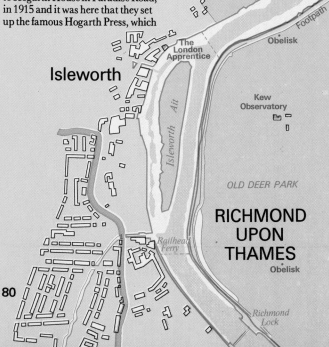

Isleworth

The London Apprentice

Isleworth Ait

Obelisk

Kew Observatory

OLD DEER PARK

RICHMOND UPON THAMES

Obelisk

Railhead Ferry

Richmond Lock

Syon Park

Syon House and remains of Abbey

Footpath

Aboretum

Marina

Lot's Ait

Brentford Ferry

Kew Park

Hog Hole

Footpath

Royal Botanic Gardens

Kew Palace

A sundial near Kew Palace marks the site of the White House, which from 1731 onwards was the home of Frederick, Prince of Wales, and his wife Augusta. It was Augusta who laid out the nucleus of Kew Gardens by planting a small botanical garden near the Orangery. In 1802 the White House was demolished and George III moved into Kew Palace, which had previously served as an annexe to the White House. Kew Palace, or the Dutch House, as it is sometimes known, was built in 1631 for a London merchant, and is a fairly modest red brick building typical of the period. George III came here to escape the Court life that he detested, but when his wife, Queen Charlotte, died in 1818 the house was abandoned. It is now in the care of the Department of the Environment and contains mementoes of George III as well as an excellent collection of 18th-century furniture.

Syon House, set in lovely grounds laid out by Capability Brown, displays Robert Adam's work at its best.

Kew

The centre of old Kew is formed by the Green, a wide expanse of tree-shaded grass on which cricket has been played for over 200 years. Overlooking the Green are a large number of splendid Georgian buildings, several of which were built for royal servants who worked at Kew Palace. Set beside the Green is St Anne's Church, a rather odd-looking building that dates partly from the 18th century. A number of seemingly haphazard additions and extensions have been made to the church, and it is these which give it its singular appearance. Kew Bridge was originally built in 1759 to replace a ferry, but the present structure was opened in 1903 by Edward VII.

Strand-on-the-Green

Strand-on-the-Green, which is part of the Borough of Hounslow, forms one of the most delightful groups of buildings on the Thames. Many of the houses were originally fishermen's cottages and date from the 18th century. As a precaution against high tides and flood waters, the front doors of many of the houses are approached by steps.

Chiswick Bridge

This concrete bridge was built in 1933 to the designs of the architect Sir Herbert Baker. Just downstream from it, opposite the Ship Inn, is the finishing point of the Oxford and Cambridge Boat Race. Between the bridge and the inn is an attractive group of houses of varying dates, and beyond them, on the south bank, is the huge Mortlake Brewery.

Chiswick

Chiswick's river frontage stretches from Strand-on-the-Green to Chiswick Mall, near Hammersmith Bridge. Downstream from Chiswick Bridge the riverbank is lined with poplars and willows, and behind these is Duke's Meadow, which is part of the grounds of Chiswick House. The house is the only survivor of three mansions whose grounds used to come down to the river here. It dates from the early 18th century, and is considered to be one of the finest Palladian-style buildings in Britain. It is open throughout the year.

From Barnes to Battersea

Behind the busy thoroughfare of Barnes Terrace are these elegant Regency houses, some with elegant wrought-iron balconies.

The Bull's Head, Barnes
On boat-race days this pub, and the terrace in front of it, is packed with spectators. The building itself, which is famous for its jazz evenings, has a Victorian exterior, but parts of it date from the 18th century. Attached to it is another old pub, the Waterman's Arms. Upstream is The Terrace, a delightful row of Regency houses, some with intricate wrought-iron balconies. The terrace is divided in two by the ironwork of Barnes Railway Bridge.

Chiswick Mall
Chiswick Eyot, the small island by Chiswick Mall, was once famous for its osiers, a type of willow that is used in basket weaving. Old willows can still be seen on the island. Fuller's Brewery, some of whose beer is still delivered by horse-drawn drays, stands behind the island. The Mall itself contains an exceptionally fine group of Georgian houses. Walpole House, which has a handsome gateway facing the river, was once the home of the Victorian actor-manager Sir Herbert Beerbohm Tree.

The Dove, Hammersmith
This old-world pub is situated in Upper Mall. Charles II and Nell Gwynne are said to have met here on numerous occasions, and James Thomson is reputed to have composed *Rule Britannia* in one of the upstairs rooms. William Morris lived just down the road at Kelmscott House, and he and his Pre-Raphaelite friends were frequent patrons. Sir A P Herbert described The Dove in *The Water Gipsies*, calling it 'The Pilgrim'. Upper Mall and adjacent Lower Mall are collectively known as Hammersmith Mall, and both have fine 18th-century houses dotted between ancient pubs and less attractive Victorian buildings.

Hammersmith Bridge
Sir Joseph Bazalgette, the architect who did so much to change the appearance of the Thames in central London, designed this fanciful suspension bridge in 1887. Just downstream from the bridge, on the north bank, is the converted warehouse used by Riverside Studios, a flourishing arts centre. On the opposite bank is Harrods Furniture Depository, an imposing building decorated in *art-nouveau* style. Below this is Barn Elms Park, which once comprised the grounds of a mansion that was demolished in 1954. The history of the mansion goes back to Tudor times, when it was the home of Sir Francis Walsingham, Secretary of State to Elizabeth I. The park is now used for recreational activities.

Fulham
The ranks of empty and decaying warehouses which line the north bank of the river from Hammersmith Bridge to Fulham Palace Park belie the fact that until the 19th century the land here was occupied by market gardens that supplied many of London's vegetable needs. Many of the old warehouses are now being demolished, and some of them have been replaced by modern houses and flats built in a pleasing tiered style. Craven Cottage, the home of Fulham Football Club, stands on the riverbank opposite Barn Elms Park.

An artist's impression of Hammersmith Bridge on Boat Race Day.

Fulham Palace

Between the river and the grounds of Fulham Palace is Bishop's Park, a public open space whose mature trees give this stretch of the Thames a very attractive appearance. The palace itself is set in beautiful gardens and is the official residence of the Bishop of London. The manor of Fulham has belonged to the bishopric since the 7th century. Most of the buildings which make up the palace today date from the 18th and 19th centuries, but the great quadrangle was built by Bishop Fitzjames in the early 16th century.

Putney Bridge

Graceful Putney Bridge is a 19th-century replacement of an earlier wooden toll bridge. It marks the starting point of the Oxford and Cambridge boat race, and all along the riverside there are well-kept boat- and clubhouses. North of the bridge is All Saints Church, which was largely rebuilt in 1880. The 15th-century tower has survived, however, as have many excellent memorials. These range in date from the 16th to the 19th century. Behind the churchyard, which contains the graves of ten bishops of London, is a charming group of 19th-century almshouses.

Impressive and starkly functional, Fulham power station broods over the south bank.

Hurlingham House

The elegant outlines of this 18th-century house can be seen through the trees of the park which stands between it and the river.

Wandsworth

There are a number of attractive houses between Fulham Railway Bridge, which carries tube trains, and Wandsworth Park. Wandsworth grew up round the River Wandle, and remained a quiet country village until it was swallowed up during London's dramatic 19th-century expansion. The mouth of the Wandle can be seen between Wandsworth Park and Wandsworth Bridge.

Fulham Power Station

Thriving industry may once have given this reach of the river a busy, if not very attractive, character. Now, however, the area has an air of decay and neglect, with disused railway sidings running amongst blocks of battered concrete and rusting iron frames. Dominating the scene is the vast bulk of Fulham Power Station, a grey monster that fits well in this desolate scene. In 1965 fish were found in the filter screens of the water intake here, and since that time the Central Electricity Generating Board has collected all fish that are captured in this way. The increasing numbers of fish trapped indicates the success that has been achieved in clearing the Thames of pollution.

The Old Swan, Battersea

Although the strikingly-designed pub which stands here dates only from 1969, the site is an ancient one. It was first mentioned in 1215, when the hostelry that occupied the site in those days was frequented by the watermen who rowed the knights and barons to meet King John at Runnymede. Enormous timbers from old Thames sailing barges were used in the construction of the new building. One or two barges are usually moored against the bank in front of the pub. Overlooking the pub is 18th-century St Mary's Church. The painter J M W Turner viewed the river from its chancel windows, and subsequently transferred what he had seen to canvas. Another painter, William Blake, was married here. From St Mary's to Battersea Bridge the riverside is dominated by warehouses, the largest of which belongs to Hovis, the flour manufacturers.

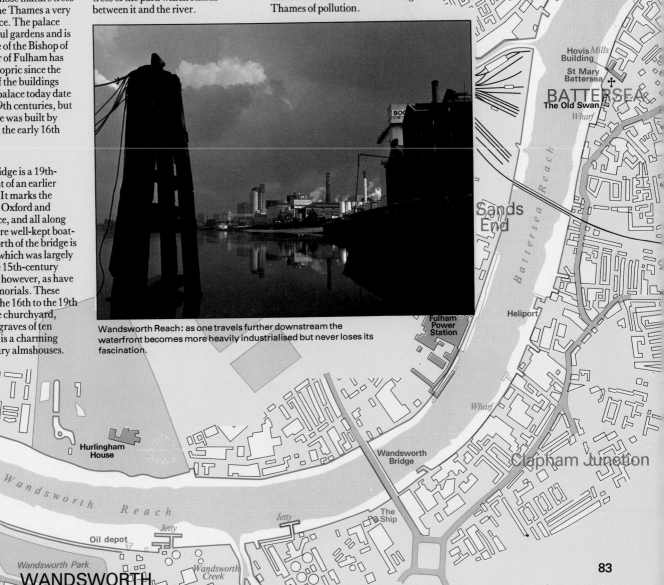

Wandsworth Reach: as one travels further downstream the waterfront becomes more heavily industrialised but never loses its fascination.

From Chelsea to Somerset House

Albert Bridge
This combined cantilever and suspension structure resembles a gigantic iron cobweb and is one of the most distinctive of all London's bridges. It was designed by R M Ordish and opened in 1873.

Chelsea
Houseboats of all sizes, shapes and conditions are moored on the Chelsea side of the river near Battersea Bridge. Above them is Cheyne Walk, one of the most desirable residential areas in London. Rows of attractive Georgian houses face the river and preserve the village atmosphere that made Chelsea popular during the 18th and 19th centuries.

Chelsea Embankment
Away from the embankment, which was built in 1871 and stretches from the Albert Bridge to Chelsea Bridge, are the grounds and buildings of Chelsea Royal Hospital, home of the famous Chelsea Pensioners.

Battersea
Until the middle of the 19th century much of Battersea's riverside was undrained marshland. In 1856 soil that had been excavated during the construction of the Royal Victoria Docks was dumped here and landscaped by Sir James Pennethorne to form Battersea Park. It was officially opened by Queen Victoria in 1858. Today the park, which is one of the least known in London, has a boating lake, a small herd of deer, and a fine river frontage. Sculpture by Henry Moore, Barbara Hepworth and Jacob Epstein graces the park, and every third year an exhibition of modern sculpture is held here.

The Albert Bridge, an eloquent example of Victorian craft.

Chelsea Bridge
This handsome suspension bridge was opened in 1937 and replaced a similar structure of 1858. The river here is the widest reach west of London Bridge and was once the scene of extravagant aquatic displays. During the reign of Charles II it was so popular that it became known as 'Hyde Park on the Thames' or 'Pall Mall afloat'. Between Chelsea Bridge and Grosvenor Bridge the entry to the now disused Grosvenor Canal can be seen. A large pumping station dominates the scene here.

Battersea Power Station
Totally uncompromising in its appearance, Battersea Power Station is a huge oblong building with chimneys at each corner. When it was built, to the designs of Sir G G Scott in 1933, this bold approach caused quite a sensation. Today most Londoners view it with grudging affection.

Nine Elms
Occupying the site of Nine Elms railway goods yard are the buildings of the new Covent Garden Market, which was transferred from its original site in 1974.

Vauxhall Bridge
Dating from 1900, this bridge is decorated with several enormous figures, one of them holding a model of St Paul's Cathedral. A sculpture by Henry Moore called 'Locking Piece' stands in a garden at the Pimlico end of the bridge.

The Albert Embankment
Sir Joseph Bazalgette designed this wide promenade, which stretches between Vauxhall Bridge and Westminster Bridge, during the second half of the 19th century.

The Tate Gallery
This imposing Classical-style building was designed by Sidney Smith and opened to the public in 1897. It stands on the site of the former Millbank Penitentiary.

The Vickers Building
Properly called Millbank Tower, the 387-ft Vickers Building was constructed in 1963 and dominates the entire north bank of the river.

Lambeth Palace
Lambeth Palace has been the residence of the archbishops of Canterbury for 700 years. Its oldest part is the 13th-century crypt. The brick gatehouse dates from 1495, and the Great Hall, with its fine hammerbeam roof, from about 1660.

St Thomas's Hospital
The new buildings of this hospital have replaced those which were built on this site in the mid 19th century. St Thomas's was founded in Southwark in 1213 and is not only a teaching hospital and the centre of the Nightingale Training Scheme for Nurses, which Florence Nightingale founded here, but also a district hospital serving a large area.

The Houses of Parliament
Big Ben and the other buildings of this grandiose pile are so familiar that some effort is needed to view them as the brilliant architectural achievement that they undoubtedly are. With luck, honourable members may be seen on the river terrace – perhaps entertaining constituents, or simply taking the air.

The Houses of Parliament occupy the site of the old Palace of Westminster, from where the river gave convenient access to the City.

Westminster Bridge
At the western end of this 19th-century bridge stands Thorneycroft's statue of Queen Boadicea. Westminster Pier is situated just north of the bridge and is one of the principal starting places for trips up and down the river.

'Little St Paul's on the Water' is the name Thames Watermen give to this model of the cathedral on Vauxhall Bridge.

The South Bank Complex

County Hall, at the south end of Westminster Bridge, was completed in 1932 and is the administrative headquarters of the Greater London Council. It was the first component part of the projected South Bank scheme. When the scheme is completed there will be an uninterrupted riverside parade from Westminster Bridge to London Bridge. Also forming part of the complex, between Hungerford Railway Bridge and Waterloo Bridge, are the Festival Hall, Queen Elizabeth Hall, the Purcell Room, Hayward Gallery, National Film Theatre, and National Theatre. Overlooking the whole South Bank area is the enormous Shell Centre, which has a 351-ft high tower and is one of the largest office blocks in Europe.

RAF Memorial

A golden eagle crowns the Royal Air Force Memorial, which was erected in 1923 and stands on the embankment in front of the colossal Ministry of Defence building.

Cleopatra's Needle

Mehemet Ali, a viceroy of Egypt, presented this famous landmark to Great Britain in 1819. It was not erected in its present position until 1879, after an eventful sea journey which cost the lives of six seamen.

Originally the Needle stood in Heliopolis, where it was one of a pair erected 3,500 years ago. Its twin now stands in Central Park, New York, and neither of them has any connections with Cleopatra.

The Victoria Embankment

Stretching from Westminster Bridge to Blackfriars Bridge, the Victoria Embankment forms one of the most interesting and attractive riverside promenades in London. The principal reason for its construction was not, however, to provide a walkway, but to help solve London's pollution problem. By 1855 the river was little more than an open sewer, and the famous scientist Michael Faraday, in a letter to *The Times*, described its appearance as 'an opaque brown fluid . . . near the bridges the feculence rolled up in clouds so dense that they were visible at the surface'. The following year, 1856, became known as the Year of the Big Stink because the stench had become so overpoweringly awful. Sir Joseph Bazalgette had drawn up plans for a comprehensive sewage system by 1856, and it was decided to

County Hall, the 6½-acre 'town hall' of London, floodlit at night. The first part of the South Bank scheme to be completed, it is the headquarters of the Council of Greater London, a county in its own right.

put these into practice. The system was designed to capture the sewage before it reached the Thames and direct it to outfalls at Barking and Crossness. The Victoria Embankment was constructed to accommodate one of the huge pipes that ran along the north bank. The York Water Gate in Victoria Embankment Gardens marks the position of the original riverbank.

Waterloo Bridge

John Rennie's beautiful Waterloo Bridge, which had been built in the early part of the 19th century, began to show signs of structural weakness in 1923. In 1934 demolition work began, and the old bridge was replaced by the present structure in 1939. It was designed by the architect Sir G G Scott and is considered to be the most graceful bridge in London.

Somerset House

This magnificent building was constructed in 1776 and stands on the site of the 16th-century palace of Protector Somerset. It was built to the designs of Sir Willliam Chambers specifically to accommodate various public bodies.

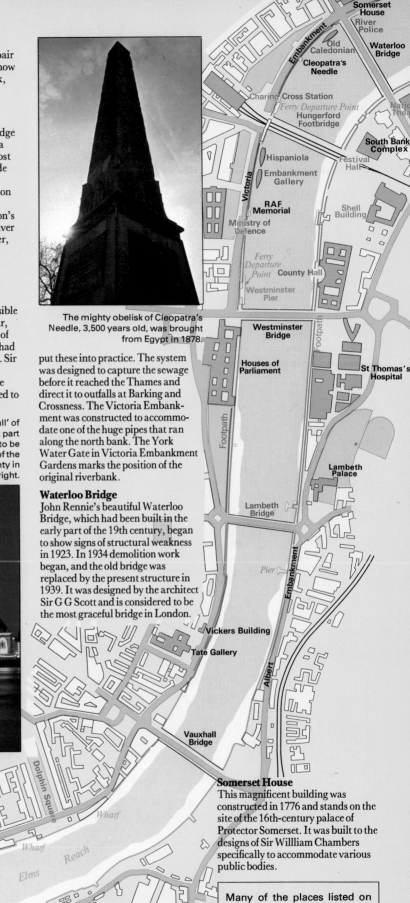

The mighty obelisk of Cleopatra's Needle, 3,500 years old, was brought from Egypt in 1878.

Many of the places listed on these two pages are described in greater detail elsewhere in this book. For further information see the index.

From The Temple to Limehouse

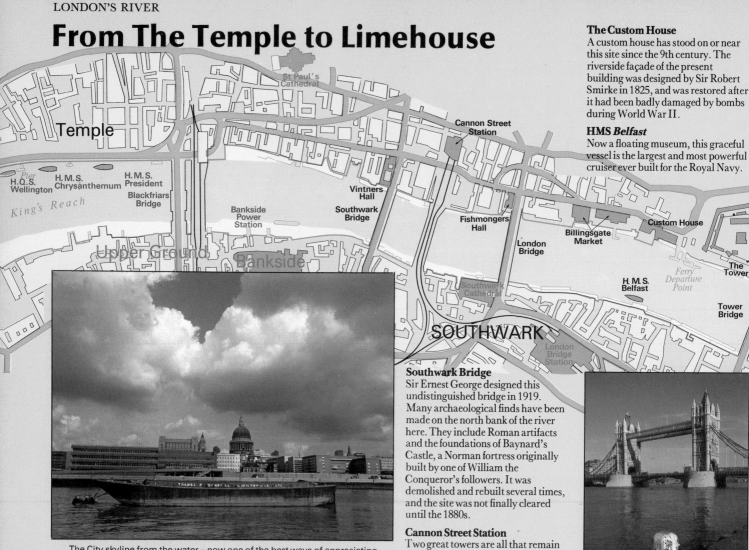

The City skyline from the water – now one of the best ways of appreciating St Paul's despite the surrounding cohorts of office blocks.

The Custom House
A custom house has stood on or near this site since the 9th century. The riverside façade of the present building was designed by Sir Robert Smirke in 1825, and was restored after it had been badly damaged by bombs during World War II.

HMS *Belfast*
Now a floating museum, this graceful vessel is the largest and most powerful cruiser ever built for the Royal Navy.

The Temple
From 1160 to 1308 this site was occupied by the Order of Knights Templars, from which it takes its name. On the embankment Sir Joseph Bazalgette's arch and stairs mark the 19th-century access to the Temple, and the point at which Westminster ends and the City of London begins. Moored against the embankment here are three vessels: HQS *Wellington*, which is the floating livery hall of the Honourable Company of Master Mariners; and HMS *President* and HMS *Chrysanthemum*, two World War I sloops which now serve as the headquarters of the London division of the Royal Naval Reserve. Captain Scott's HMS *Discovery*, which was moored here for many years, has been moved downstream to be completely refitted and overhauled.

Southwark
Southwark is divided into two parts, Upper Ground and Bankside, by Blackfriars Bridge. Upper Ground is dominated by rank on rank of warehouses and industrial buildings, many now disused and awaiting redevelopment. The most distinctive of these is the tower of the Oxo Warehouse. Beyond Blackfriars Bridge is Bankside, where, in Tudor times, were situated the Bear Garden and the Globe Theatre, places of riotous entertainment. The whole area had an evil reputation, as, being outside the jurisdiction of the City, it became the centre for the darker side of London life. Sir Christopher Wren lived at 49 Bankside during the building of St Paul's Cathedral. The house can be seen from the river – it is the white one next to the warehouse occupied by Wilcox Hoses. Bankside Power Station dominates the riverside here. It was designed in 1935 by Sir Giles Gilbert Scott, who also designed Battersea Power Station.

Vintners Hall
This partly 17th-century guild hall is hidden from the Thames by a warehouse. The entrance bears two swans, which reflect the ancient privilege the Vintners Company shares with the Dyers Company of possessing a 'game' of swans on the river. Each July the swans are collected and marked in 'Swan Upping' ceremonies.

Southwark Bridge
Sir Ernest George designed this undistinguished bridge in 1919. Many archaeological finds have been made on the north bank of the river here. They include Roman artifacts and the foundations of Baynard's Castle, a Norman fortress originally built by one of William the Conqueror's followers. It was demolished and rebuilt several times, and the site was not finally cleared until the 1880s.

Cannon Street Station
Two great towers are all that remain of this once majestic Victorian railway station. A modern replacement has been built further from the Thames.

Fishmongers Hall
Although badly damaged during the Blitz, this guild hall retains its fine riverside façade.

London Bridge
London Bridge was first built in stone between 1176 and 1209. It became almost a town on its own, having houses, shops, a chapel, fortified gates, and even water mills built upon it. All the buildings were pulled down in 1760, and the bridge itself was replaced in 1832 as it was rapidly being eroded away. The present structure dates from 1968, and its predecessor was sold to the USA. Almost hidden by buildings at the south end of the bridge is Southwark Cathedral, which, after Westminster Abbey, is the most important Gothic building in London.

Billingsgate Market
The first known reference to a market at Billingsgate goes back to AD 870. A free fish market was established here by statute in 1699, but until the 18th century coal, corn, and provisions were also sold.

Tower Bridge is a fine example of Victorian engineering. The 1,000 ton bascules of the drawbridge have never once failed.

The Tower of London
With the sun shining on it, the White Tower, or keep, of the Tower presents an unforgettable sight from the river. Although greatly restored and altered through the centuries, the Tower is probably the most important work of Norman and medieval military architecture in Britain. It has been used as a palace, a fortress and a prison since William the Conqueror built the White Tower in 1078. The entrance to the infamous Traitors' Gate can be seen from the river.

Tower Bridge
This fairy-tale structure was built in 1894. All the original machinery for raising and lowering the bridge is still in place, though the steam engines were replaced by electric motors in 1975 as they had become uneconomic.

The Town of Ramsgate, Wapping
This riverside pub was originally called the Red Cow. Its name was changed in order to attract the Ramsgate fishermen who used to sell their fish at Old Wapping Steps. Nearby are some of the few remaining Regency houses left along this stretch of the Thames.

Fishing for eels in the Thames, with the Tower as backdrop.

The Mayflower, Rotherhithe
Named after the famous ship (which had its moorings nearby) that carried settlers to the Americas, the Mayflower has the rare distinction among pubs of being licensed to sell postage stamps.

The Prospect of Whitby, Wapping
Samuel Pepys was a frequent visitor to this pub. Dating partly from 1520, it is probably the oldest pub on the river. On the riverside nearby is the site of Execution Dock, where sailors found guilty of crimes on the high seas were hung in chains to be washed over by three tides.

Rotherhithe Tunnel
Connecting Shadwell and Rotherhithe, this road tunnel was opened in 1908. Its circular air vents can be seen on either side of the river. At the Shadwell end of the tunnel is the King Edward Memorial Park, which is on the site of the ancient Shadwell Fish Market.

Surrey Commercial Docks
This is the only dock complex on the south side of the river and was built in 1807. At the top of the loop in the river in which the docks are situated is Cuckold's Point. Several unlikely explanations have been put forward to explain this odd name. One tells of a miller who was given the land here after he had come home unexpectedly to find his wife and King John in an intimate embrace. The whole of this area is scheduled for redevelopment.

The Grapes, Limehouse
Near this 16th-century pub the Regent's Canal enters the Thames. It was a branch of the Grand Union Canal and when it was fully operational, during the 19th century, it enabled goods to be shipped by barge all the way from Birmingham to the Thames.

St Katherine Dock
Thomas Telford, one of the greatest engineers of the 19th century, designed this superb group of warehouses and basins. They were built in 1828 and the warehouses were used mostly for the storage of wool and wine. Since the dock was closed in 1968 the buildings have been restored and adapted for a variety of uses. The dock basins have been transformed into yachting marinas, and there is also a floating museum of unusual water craft. Between the dock and Tower Bridge is the strikingly modern Tower Hotel.

Wapping
Behind the warehouses here are the vast London Docks. They date from 1805 and are currently being redeveloped for residential use. Thames Tunnel, the first tunnel ever to be driven under a river, runs from Wapping Station. It was engineered by Isambard Brunel and was originally built for pedestrians. In 1865 it was converted for use as a railway tunnel, and in 1913 made a part of the underground system.

Left: The entrance to St Katherine Dock.
Below: One of the oldest pubs on the river, the Prospect of Whitby was once a notorious haunt of thieves, called the Devil's Tavern.

Many of the places listed on these two pages are described in greater detail elsewhere in this book. For further information see the index.

The Isle of Dogs and Greenwich

The Royal Naval Victualling Yard

Henry VIII founded the dockyard here in 1513 and it remained an important naval centre until the 19th century. Sir Francis Drake's ship, the *Golden Hind*, was kept in dry dock here until it disintegrated. The yard was closed in the 1960s and little of it now remains.

From this site, near the Millwall Docks, was launched Brunel's great steamship, *The Great Eastern*.

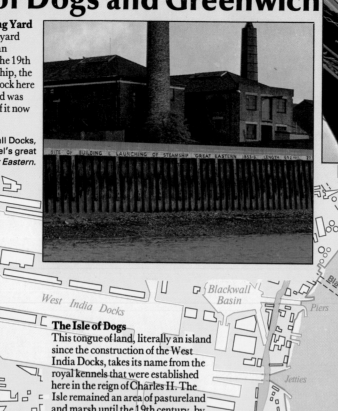

The Isle of Dogs

This tongue of land, literally an island since the construction of the West India Docks, takes its name from the royal kennels that were established here in the reign of Charles II. The Isle remained an area of pastureland and marsh until the 19th century, by which time the Port of London had become so overcrowded that Parliament authorized the construction of a new dock complex here. The West India Docks were completed by 1802, and the South Dock was added to the complex in 1870. The Millwall Docks were completed in 1864. Near the entrance to Millwall Docks, and clearly seen from the river, is the site of the launching of Brunel's steamship the *Great Eastern*. Island Gardens, at the tip of the Isle, give an incomparable view across the river to Greenwich.

Beginnings and Endings

Left: *Cutty Sark,* last of the tea clippers, is preserved in dry dock at Greenwich.
Right: Charles II founded the Royal Observatory at Greenwich in 1675 'for perfecting navigation and astronomy'. Therefore the zero meridian longitude was established here – the origin of Greenwich Mean Time.

Greenwich

The full splendour of Greenwich's superb group of royal buildings is revealed from the river. Here are the Royal Naval College, the magnificent 17th-century Queen's House, and crowning Flamsteed Hill, the Old Royal Observatory. Also at Greenwich are the *Cutty Sark,* the only surviving tea-clipper, and *Gipsy Moth IV,* in which Sir Francis Chichester sailed round the world in 1967. *For full details of Greenwich see the index.*

The Upper Reaches

The official source of the Thames is at Thames Head, three miles south of Cheltenham in Gloucestershire. There is some dispute as to the actual length of the river (which is dependent on deciding the exact location of the initial spring), but the figure usually given is 215 miles. For much of this length the Thames is a quiet country river, flowing through lush meadows and under ancient bridges. Oxford is the first large town on its banks, after which it wanders once more past lonely hamlets and church spires before reaching Reading. It then passes through Henley, Marlow and Maidenhead until it eventually reaches Windsor, where it is overlooked by the largest and most splendid castle in England. From Windsor the river occasionally touches London's outer suburbs before reaching Hampton Court. The river's journey through London has been described on the preceding pages.

From Greenwich to the Sea

Beyond Greenwich the river resumes the industrial character that had

Left: Greenwich Reach, looking upstream.
Below: Wren's scheme for the naval hospital at Greenwich used the Queen's House (designed by Inigo Jones for Anne, the consort of James I) as the focal point. In 1873 the hospital became the Royal Naval College.

typified its passage through Dockland. It sweeps up to Blackwall, where the entrance to the 19th-century East India Docks is dominated by Brunswick Wharf Generating Station.

The Royal Docks are situated east of Bow Creek and form the largest impounded dock complex in the world. They consist of Royal Victoria Dock, opened in 1855, the Royal Albert Dock, built in 1880, and the George V Dock, which was added to the group in 1921. Together these docks have a water area of 237 acres and extend for three miles parallel to the river. On the opposite bank of the river is the Royal Naval Dockyard. It was founded in the 15th century, and was the building place of many of the navy's finest warships until Devonport replaced it during the 19th century. A flood barrier is being built at Woolwich in order to protect London from the increasingly high tides that have threatened it in recent years. It is hoped that the barrier will be completed by 1982.

Beyond the Royal Docks are the sewage works which were the salvation of the Thames, and prevented the further outbreak of epidemics to which London had been subjected for centuries. Sir Joseph Bazalgette's plans to by-pass the Thames in Central London (described on page 85 under the Victoria Embankment) meant that sewage previously debouched all along the river was released in huge quantities at Barking and Crossness. Although this meant that the Thames in central London became cleaner it made the situation at Barking Reach worse. This point is horribly illustrated by the tragic wreck of the pleasure steamer *Princess Alice.* It was cut in two by a collier in September 1878 and sank near Barking. Of the 640 people lost in the disaster a number were found not to have drowned but to have been poisoned by the noxious waters. In the 1880s considerable advances were made in the treatment of sewage, and the subsequent sophistication of these techniques has meant that the water now leaving the outfalls at Barking and Crossness is probably as clear as the spring waters of the upper Thames.

Between Barking and Tilbury the river flows through marshes that are rapidly disappearing under new industrial estates and houses. One of these developments is the new town of Thamesmead on the Plumstead and Erith marshes. Tilbury is situated 26 miles beyond London Bridge by river and its huge docks cover over 3,500 acres. The Thames now becomes an estuary on which are situated Canvey Island and Southend on Sea. Beyond is Barrow Deep and the North Sea.

Cultural London

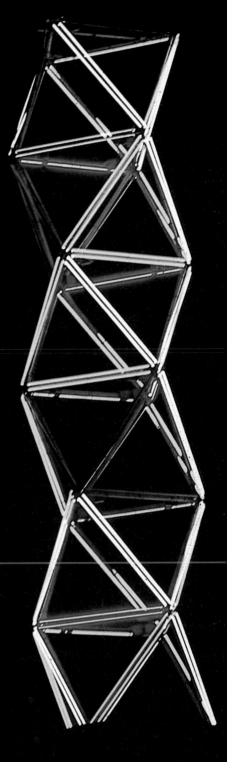

Making the Museum

In 1826 the Corporation of London established the Guildhall Museum as an addition to its library. A municipal museum with a concern for archaeology, the City, and the Corporation, it was founded specifically to accommodate the antiquities of the locality. New exhibits poured in at such a rate that the museum was soon full to the brim, and in 1876 new premises were provided under the Guildhall Library. The museum remained in the precincts of the Guildhall until the outbreak of World War II in 1939 forced its closure. Some considerable time after the war it was re-opened in temporary premises, first in the Royal Exchange, and later at Bassishaw High Walk, where it remained until 1976.

The London Museum had very different origins. It was founded in 1912 and was set up with the much broader objectives of interpreting and recreating past life rather than the preservation of antiquities. Initially the museum was set up at Kensington Palace in apartments provided by George V. It was moved to Lancaster House in the Mall in 1914, and remained there until it was closed in 1939. The museum remained closed until 1951 when it was re-opened in temporary accommodation at Kensington Palace where it stayed until 1976.

The maintenance of two museums devoted to the history of London became increasingly uneconomic and confusing, especially to visitors and students, and during the 1960s it was decided in principle to unite the collections of the London Museum and the Guildhall Museum under one roof. The planning for this undertaking took a great deal of time and effort, but the Museum of London Act eventually came into effect on 1st June 1975. It merged the two organisations, but not their various and scattered premises.

This situation was soon rectified. On 2nd December 1976 Her Majesty The Queen officially opened the specially-designed building housing the joint collections of the former London and Guildhall museums. The new venture was called the Museum of London.

The Barbican Site

Located in the south-west corner of the ultra-modern Barbican development, the museum

The main entrance hall of the museum opens directly on to the pedestrian walk-way which connects the Barbican with the rest of the City. The nearest underground stations are Barbican (closed on Sundays), St Paul's, Moorgate, and Mansion House. The nearest British Rail stations are Moorgate, Liverpool Street, Holborn Viaduct (closed on Sundays), Cannon Street, and Blackfriars (closed on Saturdays and Sundays).

The Museum of London

This is the Capital's newest and most visually exciting large museum. Its exhibits, some of which are accompanied by dramatic sound effects and suitable period music, illustrate London's fascinating and continually evolving story.

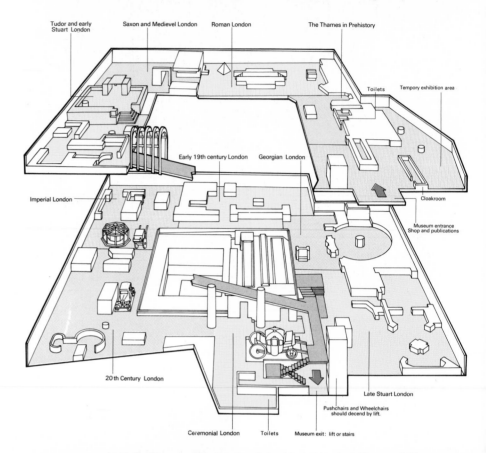

Inside the Museum of London, the whole tableau of London's history unfolds.

London after the Great Fire. Georgian London, which follows, is contained in a circular gallery, and a glazed corridor incorporating two contemporary shop fronts connects it with the Nineteenth Century Hall. Here are displayed the Woolsack from the old House of Lords and relics from the Great Exhibition of 1851. Imperial London follows with its displays of Victorian commercial units which include a chemist's, a tailor's and a cooper's. The units are treated individually and are not arranged in any form of artificial street.

The exhibition moves on to the 20th century with a 1930 Ford motor car and a collection of suffragette material inherited from the old London Museum. The exhibition culminates with Ceremonial London. The centre-piece of this display is the Lord Mayor's State Coach. It is used in the annual Lord Mayor's Show and was built in 1757. A magnificent example of the coach-builder's craft, it is lavishly decorated with gilt ornaments and allegorical scenes painted by the Italian artist Cipriani.

Set apart from the public displays are special departments which specialise in Prints, Drawings and Paintings of London, and Costumes and Textiles. There is also a research library containing a vast amount of material relating to London.

stands at the junction of Aldersgate Street and London Wall. It adjoins a stretch of historic City wall that was built c AD 200. The presence of the Ironmongers' Hall, lying at an awkward angle on an otherwise open site, presented the architects with a problem which they overcame by arranging the museum round two courts; one enclosing a garden, the other open to the north and Ironmongers' Hall.

A Hansom cab and a costermonger's barrow standing in front of a beautifully preserved Victorian pub façade.

magnet on all those who visit the museum.

A gently sloping ramp enclosed in a steel-ribbed, glass-lined tunnel leads to the lower floor. The story is then continued with Late Stuart London and the reconstruction of

The forbidding 'Bull and Mouth' pub sign and two immaculate Georgian shopfronts.

The Exhibits

The museum is devoted entirely to London and its people, presenting by way of exhibitions and tableaux the story of its development and life. Open plan and arranged in chronological order, the museum affords a continuous view from prehistoric times to the 20th century.

The main public entrance, one of whose walls is constructed entirely of glass, leads into galleries built around the inner courtyard. The exhibition begins with the Thames in Prehistory and deals with the natural site of the City and the pre-Roman settlements upon it. Archaeological levels are demonstrated by a relief model of the Thames Valley. Roman London follows and displays exhibits which formed a distinguished element in both the old museums.

Next comes Saxon and Medieval London. Superb models of William the Conqueror's White Tower and Old St Paul's make the medieval gallery especially fascinating. Tudor and early Stuart London completes the remainder of the upper floor and ends with a graphic audio-visual reconstruction of the Great Fire of 1666. This exhibit, with its realistically-crackling flames, acts like a

The Exhibition Road Museums

The tremendous collection of museums that stand on or near Exhibition Road owe their existence to the energy and enthusiasm of Prince Albert, Consort to Queen Victoria. It was his tireless persistence that resulted in the Great Exhibition being opened in Hyde Park in 1851. It was an unqualified success, and the Prince proposed that the profits made from it should be used to purchase land on which would be built an array of educational establishments. In 1856 the Gore Estate, on which the museums now stand, was purchased and building work, which continues to the present day, began.

The Victoria and Albert Museum

This is the national museum of fine and applied art, and covers all countries, periods and styles. It is a vast box of delights, with exhibits ranging from great works of art to items whose function is simply to entertain and amuse.

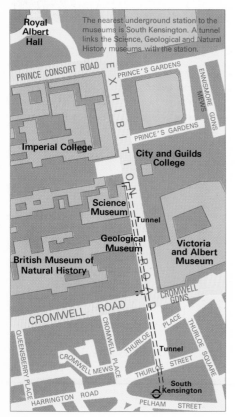

The nearest underground station to the museums is South Kensington. A tunnel links the Science, Geological and Natural History museums with the station.

A Legacy of the Exhibition

In 1857 the museum was moved to its present site, having been founded at Marlborough House after the Great Exhibition as the Museum of Manufactures, and its name was changed to the South Kensington Museum. An avalanche of new exhibits, gifts, and bequests rapidly pushed the museum far beyond its original theme, and it became apparent that a reorganisation was required and that larger premises would have to be built. A competition for the design of additional buildings facing Cromwell Road and Exhibition Road was held in 1891 and won by the distinguished architect Sir Aston Webb. The foundation stone was laid by Queen Victoria in 1899 and the museum re-opened in 1909 as the Victoria and Albert.

The Exhibits

The museum has a maze-like interior with approximately seven miles of galleries. Excellent guide books can be purchased in the museum, and visitors are advised to work out their route, and the galleries to be seen, before they begin their explorations.

There are two types of galleries: the primary ones, which display a variety of exhibits giving a comprehensive picture of a period or civilisation; and subject galleries, which contain the specialised collections.

In the primary British galleries, on the upper ground and upper first floors, there is a series of rooms decorated and equipped with the paintings, furniture and household accessories of particular periods. Amongst the exhibits on display are the enormous 16th-century *Great Bed of Ware*, an exquisite portrait miniature by Nicholas Hilliard called *Young Man leaning against a Tree*, and furniture by Chippendale. There are also primary galleries devoted to Continental arts and crafts, medieval gothic and renaissance art, Oriental art, and Islamic arts and crafts.

The subject galleries on the ground floor take in English and Continental sculpture, architecture, and costumes. The costumes, mostly English and dating from the 16th to 20th centuries, are displayed in the *Octagon Court*.

On the first floor are subject galleries covering ironwork, textiles, prints and drawings, and paintings. John Constable's brilliant evocations of the English landscape are the outstanding works of the painting galleries.

The Science Museum

The collections in the Science Museum cover the application of science to technology and the development of engineering and industry from their beginnings to the present day. Of all London museums this is the one most loved by children and their fathers. There are knobs to press, handles to turn, and all sorts of exhibit that variously light up, rotate, and make noises.

Housed in a handsome building that was completed in 1928 and added to in 1963, the collections originally formed part of the old South Kensington Museum.

The Apollo 10 space capsule in the Science Museum.

The Exhibits

In the main entrance hall is the *Foucault Pendulum*, the gentle movement of which visibly demonstrates the rotation of the earth on its own axis. The lower ground floor contains exhibits illustrating the development of lighting and mining, and includes a reconstruction of a modern coal mine. Here also is the delightful *Children's Gallery*, which provides an introduction to scientific ideas through the medium of dioramas and working models.

The ground floor galleries explain the development of motive power and contain most of the museum's larger exhibits, including an 18th-century atmospheric beam engine from a colliery in Derbyshire. Gallery 6 houses an exhibition on exploration which is due to run until the end of 1980. All aspects of exploration are covered and exhibits include the *Apollo 10 Space Capsule* and a simulated moon base. The huge new wing of the ground floor is devoted to road and rail transport. Here may be seen *Puffing Billy*, the world's first locomotive, and George Stephenson's *Rocket*.

On the first, second and third floors there are galleries dealing with astronomy, printing, chemistry, nuclear physics, navigation, photography, electricity, magnetism, and communications, etc. The exhibits range from a superb collection of model ships to the first television transmitter.

The Geological Museum

This is the national museum of earth sciences. It illustrates the general principles of geological science together with earth history, the regional geology of Britain and the economic geology and minerology of the world. It is most famous for its stunningly beautiful collection of gem stones.

The Origins of the Museum

Established in 1837 as a direct result of the Geological Survey of Great Britain, the museum originally occupied a house in Whitehall, to which specimens collected during the survey were taken for inspection. In 1851 the collection was moved to new premises in Jermyn Street, and in 1935 – the centenary of the Geological Survey – the collection was moved into its present building.

The Exhibits

The main hall contains exhibitions entitled *The Story of the Earth* and *Britain before Man*. Also on the ground floor are the precious and ornamental stones, shown in their original form and after cutting. The first floor galleries give a detailed regional geology of Britain, and the second floor is devoted to economic geology and contains the largest display of metalliferous ores and useful non-metallic ores in the world.

The central hall of the Natural History Museum.

The Natural History Museum

The collections of the Natural History Museum are divided into five departments covering botany, entomology, minerology, palaeontology and zoology.

From small beginnings

The museum's collections were built up round the specimens collected by Sir Hans Sloane. These formed a part of the nucleus of the British Museum, which was founded in 1753. Later additions to the museum included the large botanical collection bequethed by Sir Joseph Banks in 1820. By 1860, the continued expansion of the collections in the British Museum meant that a separate natural history museum was required. The necessary land was available at Kensington, but it was not until 1881 that the new museum – officially called the British Museum (Natural History) – was opened.

Covering a total of four acres, the museum is housed in a vast and elaborate 19th-century Romanesque-style building faced with terracotta slabs bearing animals, birds and fishes moulded in relief.

The Exhibits

The central hall houses stuffed examples of the larger mammals, including an African elephant over 11 ft tall. Also on display, by way of contrast, is one of the tiniest mammals, a white-toothed shrew from Spain. Bays on either side of the hall illustrate the principles of evolution by natural selection, and the evolution of man.

The west wing houses galleries devoted to birds, corals and sponges, insects (including butterflies), starfish, and fish. Also in the west wing are the *Hall of Human Biology* and the *Whale Hall*, which has models or skeletons of many types of whale suspended from its ceiling. An extensive and zoologically-arranged fossil collection is located in the east wing. It is here that the dinosaurs will be found.

On the first floor is the *Mammal Gallery*, where many rare species may be seen, and the *Mineral Gallery*. The second floor contains the *Botanical Gallery* and has beautifully-made dioramas which illustrate many different types of habitat and landscape.

The British Museum

Behind the stern façade of the British Museum is the richest and most varied collection of treasures in the world. A detailed study of the items on display would take several lifetimes, and these are only a selection of the vast number of objects that the museum holds in its vaults and store rooms.

Treasures for the Nation

The museum was founded in 1753 by an act of Parliament which set up a body of Trustees. Its nucleus was formed by the priceless collections of Sir Robert Cotton, whose manuscripts had been acquired at the end of the 17th century and stored away in vaults at Westminster, and Sir Hans Sloane, who left his enormously varied collection to the nation upon his death in 1753. To this diverse collection of manuscripts, works of art, antiquities, and natural history items the Trustees added the extensive library accumulated by the Harleys, earls of Oxford. Subsequently the old Royal Library, which had been founded by Henry VII, was presented to the Trustees by George II and incorporated in the museum in 1757. With this library came the privilege of compulsory copyright, which means that a copy of every book published in the country has to be presented free to the museum.

The act of Parliament setting up the museum provided for a public lottery to be held to raise funds for housing and maintaining these collections. The lottery raised enough cash for the Trustees to purchase a 17th-century building called

The visitor cannot possibly take in the vast wealth of treasures displayed in the British Museum at a single visit and must be content to see only a fraction.
Above and right: The Duveen Gallery which houses the Elgin Marbles, brought from Greece by Lord Elgin, and (below) the Egyptian Galleries with their ancient mummies.

Montagu House and in 1759 the museum was opened to the public. Montagu House proved woefully inadequate for the museum's constantly expanding collections, and by the early 19th century temporary buildings had been erected to accommodate many of the larger exhibits.

In 1823 Sir Robert Smirke was commissioned to design a permanent extension and produced plans for the complete replacement of Montagu House. Between 1823 and 1852 the old structure was pulled down and the present museum took its place. In 1857 the famous domed Reading Room was built in what had been the interior courtyard. Later additions to the structure included the King Edward VII Building and a gallery presented by Lord Duveen to house the sculptures of the Parthenon. The natural history collection was transferred to South Kensington in 1881, and the ethnographical collection to the new Museum of Mankind in 1970 (see page 99).

The Exhibits

It is impossible to list here more than a tiny fraction of the wealth of objects that the museum contains. Visitors are advised to equip themselves with a guide book and select a number of specific exhibits that can be comfortably looked at in the time available.

The superb *Elgin Marbles* are housed in the *Duveen Gallery* and should not be missed. The collection is named after the seventh Earl of Elgin, who sold it to the nation at a considerable loss. It includes brilliantly executed statues, friezes, and stonework from temples and other buildings in Athens.

In the centre of the *Egyptian Sculpture Gallery* is the *Rosetta Stone*, which dates from 195 BC and is inscribed with the texts which enabled scholars to decipher Egyptian hieroglyphics. The *Grenville Library* and the *Manuscript Saloon* contain some of the museum's most famous treasures, including two of the four existing original copies of the *Magna Carta*, William Shakespeare's signature, and Nelson's sketch plan of the Battle of Trafalgar.

On the upper floor is the *Mildenhall Treasure*, a collection of 4th-century silver discovered in a ploughed field in Suffolk in 1942, and the beautiful 7th-century *Sutton Hoo Treasure*, also discovered in Suffolk. Also on the upper floor are the Egyptian mummies, the exquisite 12th-century *Lewis Chessmen*, and part of the museum's vast collection of coins and medals.

> The main entrance to the museum is in Great Russell Street, and there is a further entrance in Montagu Place. The nearest underground stations are Tottenham Court Road, Holborn, and Russell Square.

London's Museums

Apart from the museums described on the preceding pages, there are over a hundred other museums in Greater London. Listed on this and the next two pages is a selection of the most interesting of them. Intending visitors are advised to check opening times before setting out, as several are not regularly open.

Military Museums

Artillery Museum
The Rotunda, Woolwich Common, SE18
This museum was originally housed in a huge tent, which was later sheathed in lead to preserve it. An exact replica replaced it in 1974, and it contains a collection of guns, muskets, rifles, and artillery.

Imperial War Museum
Lambeth Road, SE1
Founded in 1917 and established by act of Parliament in 1920, this museum illustrates and records all aspects of the two world wars and other military operations involving Britain and the Commonwealth since 1914. An extremely varied collection of exhibits is on display, ranging from tanks and aeroplanes to weapons and uniforms, as well as paintings by official war artists.

National Army Museum
Royal Hospital Road, SW3
A chronological display of the history of British, Indian and Colonial forces from 1485 onwards is housed in this museum.

Royal Air Force Museum
Aerodrome Road, Hendon, NW9
Over 40 historic aircraft, all restored in RAF workshops, are on display here in the main exhibition hall.

Regimental Museum of the Royal Fusiliers (City of London Regiment)
Tower of London, EC3
The history of the Regiment is followed from 1685, and uniforms, silver, and ten Victoria Crosses are displayed.

The two 15-inch guns in front of the Imperial War Museum, Lambeth, come from HMS *Ramillies* and HMS *Resolution*. Each weighs about 100 tons. Below: The Royal Air Force Museum at Hendon displays aircraft and equipment from the Royal Flying Corps and the RAF.

London's Nautical Heritage

HMS Belfast, *Symons Wharf, Vine Lane, SE1*
At 11,000 tons this is the largest cruiser ever built for the Royal Navy. She was built in 1939 and saved from a breaker's yard to be opened to the public in 1971.

The Cutty Sark, *Greenwich Pier, SE10*
The graceful lines of this famous clipper dominate the riverside at Greenwich. She was built in 1869 and has been preserved in dry dock since 1957.

National Maritime Museum
Romney Road, Greenwich, SE10
Part of this collection is housed in the 17th-century Queen's House, which was designed by Inigo Jones. Exhibits include some of the finest seascapes ever painted, and galleries devoted to Lord Nelson and Captain Cook.

Maritime Trusts Museum, Historic Ships Collection
St Katherine Dock, E1
The collection comprises a number of British sailing and steam-powered vessels of the 19th and early 20th centuries.

Musical Museums

Horniman Museum
London Road, Forest Hill, SE23
An extensive collection of musical instruments from all over the world is on display here. This museum also has a tremendous variety of other exhibits.

National Musical Museum
368 High Street, Brentford
Located in an old church near Kew Bridge, this museum is devoted to 'automatic' pianos and other old instruments.

Royal College of Music Museum of Instruments *Prince Consort Road, SW7*
Some of the rare and beautiful instruments housed here date from the 15th century.

Local History Museums

Bexley London Borough Museum
Hall Place, Bourne Road, Bexley
This general interest museum occupies a 16th- and 17th-century house which is set in beautiful ornamental gardens.

Broomfield Museum
Broomfield Park, Palmers Green, N13
Natural history exhibits, paintings, and pottery are displayed in this ancient mansion.

Cuming Museum
155–157 Walworth Road, SE17
Although this museum is primarily devoted to the history of Southwark, it also houses a fascinating collection of items related to London's superstitions.

The Royal Navy's largest cruiser, HMS *Belfast* is now a floating museum permanently moored at Symons Wharf.

Epping Forest Museum
Queen Elizabeth's Hunting Lodge, Rangers Road, Chingford, E4
The story of Epping Forest and its inhabitants is told by the displays in this historic 16th-century hunting lodge.

Gunnersbury Park Museum
Gunnersbury Park, W3
Located in an early 19th-century mansion that was once the home of the Rothschild family, this museum includes archaeology and transport items among its displays.

Livesey Museum
682 Old Kent Road, SE15
Southwark's history is explained by twice-yearly exhibitions here.

Passmore Edwards Museum
Romford Road, Stratford, E15
Exhibits devoted to the story of Essex and Greater London are displayed in this Victorian building.

Vestry House Museum
Vestry Road, Walthamstow, E17
This small museum is located in an early 18th-century workhouse, which stands in the conservation area of 'Walthamstow Village' Exhibits include the *Bremer*, Britain's first internal combustion engine car.

Sporting Museums

Cricket Memorial Gallery
Marylebone Cricket Club, Lord's Ground, NW8
A collection of pictures and the first urn to contain the 'Ashes' are among the mementoes displayed here.

The Wimbledon Lawn Tennis Museum
The All England Club, Church Road, SW19
Located in the grounds of the All England Club, this unique museum traces the development of lawn tennis over the last century and gives a background to the game.

A Miscellany of Museums and Experiences

Bear Gardens Museum
Bear Gardens, SE1
This museum stands on the site of the last bear-baiting ring on Bankside, close to the site of the Hope Theatre and Shakespeare's Globe. It occupies a 19th-century warehouse and consists of a permanent exhibition relating to Elizabethan theatre.

Bethnal Green Museum of Childhood
Cambridge Heath Road, E2
Located in a prefabricated Victorian hall, this museum's exhibits include toys, dolls' houses and model soldiers.

Bible House
146 Queen Victoria Street, EC4
The headquarters of the Bible Society, this imposing building houses the London Bible Gallery, a fascinating collection of scriptures from all over the world.

Geffrye Museum
Kingsland Road, Shoreditch, E2
Occupying the former almshouses of the Ironmongers' Company, this museum consists of a series of period rooms arranged in chronological order.

Guildhall Clock Museum
Guildhall, EC2
The collection here contains over 700 old clocks, watches, and chronometers belonging to the Clockmakers' Company.

The London Dungeon
28–34 Tooley Street, SE1
Appropriately set in slimy vaults, this exhibition recreates horrific scenes of medieval torture and murder.

The London Experience
Coventry Street, Piccadilly Circus, W1
By using a wide variety of mixed-media techniques the life and times of London are vividly illustrated here.

Madame Tussaud's
Marylebone Road, NW1
This famous collection of waxworks was founded in Paris in 1770, moved to England in 1802, and found a permanent home in London in 1835. The exhibits include historical figures, politicians, entertainers, and in the Chamber of Horrors, reconstructions of hideous crimes.

Museum of Mankind
6 Burlington Gardens, W1
This superb and endlessly fascinating collection embraces the art and material culture of tribal, village, and other pre-industrial societies from most areas of the world excluding Western Europe. It is a department of the British Museum.

Above: Pollock's Toy Museum in Scala Street has a charming collection of toys and dolls from many countries and periods.

Left: The masters of suspense, Alfred Hitchcock and Agatha Christie, at Madame Tussaud's wax museum in Marylebone Road. Madame Tussaud's is a perennial favourite for its wax portraits of the famous and infamous from past and present, and particularly for the gruesome Chamber of Horrors.

National Postal Museum
King Edward Building,
King Edward Street, EC1
Established in 1965, this museum contains one of the finest and most comprehensive collections of postage stamps in the world.

The Planetarium
Marylebone Road, NW1
Spectacular representations of the heavens are projected on to the inside of the Planetarium's great copper dome and are accompanied by an instructive commentary.

Pollock's Toy Museum
1 Scala Street, W1
This museum occupies two delightful interconnected houses, and its exhibits include dolls, teddy bears, board games, and toy theatres.

Public Records Office Museum
Chancery Lane, WC2
A copy of the *Domesday Book*, and many other historical documents are displayed in this museum.

Sir John Soane's Museum
13 Lincoln's Inn Fields, WC2
The character of a 19th-century private house has been preserved at this museum, which contains a collection of antiquities and works of art. Sir John Soane was a distinguished architect, and he designed this house for himself.

Art Galleries –
The National Collections

London's three national art galleries contain an enormously rich selection of works from all periods and styles of art. They range from acknowledged masterpieces in the National Gallery to contemporary works in the Tate whose place in the development of art cannot yet be fully appreciated.

Above: The National Gallery in Trafalgar Square opened in 1838.

Below: One of the many priceless exhibits in the Gallery, this cartoon of the Virgin and Child with St Anne and the infant John the Baptist was drawn by Leonardo da Vinci between 1497 and 1499. It is widely held to be one of his finest works.

The National Gallery

The National Gallery houses one of the finest and most extensive collections of masterpieces in the world. All the great periods of European painting are represented, although only a choice selection of British work is on display as the national collection of this is housed in the Tate Gallery. Built on the site of a royal mews, the National Gallery is a Classical-style building from whose majestic portico a panoramic view of Trafalgar Square may be obtained.

Masterpieces for the Nation

In 1824 the government bought the collection of pictures which had been accumulated by John Julius Angerstein, a London underwriter, and exhibited them at his former town residence in Pall Mall. These pictures formed the nucleus of the National Gallery. By 1831 space had become a problem following further bequests and purchases, and plans were made to erect a building to house the collections. The specially built gallery in Trafalgar Square was opened in 1838 and was visited by the newly crowned Queen Victoria. At first the premises were shared with the Royal Academy, but in 1869 that august institution moved to Burlington House. Space was still at a premium in the National, however, and over the years various extensions have been added to minimise overcrowding.

The Exhibits

The vestibules of the National Gallery usually contain a selection of works, including recent acquisitions. The main collection is arranged chronologically, but changes are made in the arrangement of the rooms from time to time.

Italian paintings occupy the west rooms and include the Florentine and Venetian schools, with paintings by such artists as Botticelli and Bellini. Leonardo da Vinci's cartoon *The Virgin and Child with St Anne and St John the Baptist* is one of the most outstanding works in this section. Paintings of the Dutch and Flemish schools occupy the rooms of the north-west extension and include the works of Rembrandt, Rubens, Vermeer and Van Dyck. The German and Netherlandish schools are also located here. French and Spanish paintings occupy the

east rooms of the gallery and include works by Velazquez and Goya, Manet and Renoir. British paintings, which are located on the east side of the gallery, include a selection from Hogarth to Turner. Exhibited here are Gainsborough's superb *Mr and Mrs Andrews* and Constable's famous *Haywain*.

Above: John Constable's *View of Hampstead*, from the Tate Gallery, was painted in 1836, the year before his death. Hampstead was in open countryside then, and windmills were well known landmarks on the Heath.
Left: The National Portrait Gallery.

The National Portrait Gallery

The collection of the National Portrait Gallery constitutes the world's most comprehensive survey of historical personalities. In addition to paintings the collection includes sculpture, miniatures, engravings and photographs.

An Illustrated History

Established in 1856 with the aim of illustrating British history by means of a collection of portraits of famous men and women, the gallery's first home was at 29 George Street, Westminster. After having been moved first to South Kensington and later Bethnal Green, the collection was finally housed in its present accommodation in 1896. The building was the gift of a wealthy benefactor and was designed in the style of an Italian *palazzo*. A wing financed by Lord Duveen was added in 1933, and a new annex in nearby Carlton House Terrace contains part of the reserve collection and houses temporary exhibitions.

The gallery does not usually display portraits of living persons, apart from members of the royal family. The portraits, arranged more or less in chronological order, are accompanied by furnishings, maps, weapons and other items to set them in their historical context. Beginning in medieval times, they range in quality from masterpieces to works of a mundane nature.

The National Gallery is situated on the north side of Trafalgar Square, and the National Portrait Gallery is immediately behind it in St Martin's Place. The most convenient Underground stations are Charing Cross, Leicester Square, and Embankment.

The Tate Gallery

The Tate Gallery houses the national collection of British works from the 16th century to the beginning of the 20th. It also contains modern works by British artists born after 1850, together with foreign works from the Impressionists to the present day, and traces the development of art from Impressionism to post-war European and American art. The Tate is especially renowned for its modern works of art, some of which have aroused great controversy.

Establishing the Collection

Sir Francis Chantrey, a prominent 19th-century sculptor, first put forward the idea of a national collection of British art, and bequeathed his fortune to the Royal Academy for the purchase of works by living artists as well as earlier masters. The collection was increased by the steady accumulation of pictures from the Chantrey Bequest and many further bequests. This growing collection, which was at first shuffled ignominiously between the South Kensington Museum (a forerunner of the Victoria and Albert Museum), the National Gallery and Burlington House, made the building of a special gallery essential. Eventually Sir Henry Tate, the sugar magnate, offered to finance the building of a new gallery, and to donate his own collection of 64 paintings, on condition that the government provided a suitable site. Millbank was offered and accepted, and the gallery, designed by S R J Smith in a fine Classical style, was opened to the public in 1897. New galleries and a sculpture hall were added by Tate in 1899, and in 1910 Sir Joseph Duveen financed further additions to house the multitudenous works of J M W Turner, many of them given by the artist. At this time further bequests enlarged the scope of the gallery to include foreign paintings. The most recent extension, opened on the north-east side of the building, has resulted in a re-arrangement of the gallery layout, and has enabled many more exhibits to be displayed.

The Exhibits

British works of art occupy the west of the building, whilst modern and foreign paintings and sculpture are housed in the galleries on the east side. A selection of paintings and sculpture is displayed in the Central Hall and the Sculpture Hall, and beyond these are the galleries which are set aside for special exhibitions.

The British works are arranged mainly in chronological order; they begin with *Man in a Black Cap*, which was painted by John Bettes in 1545. Thereafter the development of British painting up until 1920 is followed. Hogarth, Blake, Turner, Constable and the Pre-Raphaelites are particularly well represented, and the English mastery of landscape painting is superbly illustrated.

All schools of painting and sculpture from Impressionism onwards are represented in the modern and foreign collections. They include paintings by Cezanne, Matisse, Picasso, Braque, Chagall, and Paul Klee. There are also abstract paintings by such artists as Mondrian, Jackson Pollock, and Frank Stella. Sculpture by Henry Moore, Barbara Hepworth, and Alberto Giacometti, among others, is displayed, and there is a collection of kinetic and optical art. The Tate buys works almost before they are finished, and is therefore able to reflect the constantly changing emphasis of contemporary art.

The Tate Gallery is situated on Millbank between Lambeth and Vauxhall bridges, and the nearest Underground stations to it are Westminster and Pimlico.

Art Galleries – Smaller Collections and Exhibition Galleries

Many of London's smaller galleries house masterpieces which could happily hang beside the works in the three great national galleries. Some of the smaller collections have been presented to the nation, and some are privately owned. Several of the galleries mentioned on these two pages are used only for temporary exhibitions and are not regularly open to the public.

Courtauld Institute Galleries
Woburn Square, WC1
This superb collection of paintings was begun by Samuel Courtauld in the 1930s and presented to the University of London in memory of his wife. It is most famous for its Impressionist and Post Impressionist pictures, but there is also a collection of Old Master drawings and Italian primitive paintings, as well as works by the Bloomsbury Group, which were presented to the university by the art critic Roger Fry.

Dulwich College Picture Gallery
College Road, SE21
Housed in a building designed by the distinguished architect Sir John Soane in 1811, this is one of the most beautiful galleries in London. It is the oldest public picture gallery in England and displays works by Rembrandt, Rubens, Poussin, Gainsborough, and Reynolds.

Embankment Gallery PS Tattershall Castle,
Victoria Embankment, SW1
This unique gallery is housed in a paddle steamer which was commissioned in 1934 and was used to ferry passengers across the River Humber in Yorkshire. It has been restored to its original appearance and displays temporary exhibitions by established, aspiring, and unknown artists.

Hayward Gallery
The South Bank Complex, SE1
Opened in 1968, this purpose-built, ultra-modern building houses brilliantly-arranged temporary exhibitions which are put on by the Arts Council.

Institute of Contemporary Arts
Nash House, 12 Carlton House Terrace, SW1
The institute fosters contemporary art of all kinds. Its exhibitions are open to the public and frequently display works of an obscure and controversial nature.

The Iveagh Bequest
Kenwood, Hampstead Lane, NW3
In 1764 the great architect Robert Adam was commissioned by the Earl of Mansfield to transform the house at Kenwood into a mansion. This he did and the building has remained largely unaltered since that time. It is a magnificent Classical-style structure set in beautiful grounds. Lord Iveagh, who purchased the mansion in 1925, bequeathed it to the nation in 1928, together with his collection of paintings by Frans Hals, Vermeer, Reynolds, Gainsborough, and Rembrandt.

Kenwood House, Hampstead, makes a superb setting for the Iveagh collection of English and Dutch masterpieces.

Leighton House Art Gallery

Holland Park Road, W14

Lord Leighton had this house specially built for himself in 1866. It has an exotic interior, complete with an Arab Hall decorated with ancient tiles from Rhodes, Damascus and Cairo. Leighton was one of the great artists of the Victorian era, and many of his paintings and sculptures are displayed here, along with works by Burne-Jones and other late 19th-century artists and craftsmen. Temporary exhibitions are held throughout the year in the Winter Studio and Perrin Gallery.

The Queen's Gallery

Buckingham Palace,
Buckingham Palace Road, SW1

Housed in a building which was originally designed as a conservatory by John Nash in 1831, this gallery displays a constantly changing collection of art treasures from the Royal Collection.

Ranger's House

Chesterfield Walk, Blackheath, SE10

The Suffolk Collection of Jacobean and Stuart portraits is housed in this beautiful 17th-century mansion.

Royal Academy of Arts

Burlington House, Piccadilly, W1

George III founded the Royal Academy in 1768, and it was moved to Burlington House from the National Gallery in 1869. The famous Summer Exhibition is held here from May to August and promotes the works of living artists. The Academy owns a splendid collection of masterpieces by such artists as Michelangelo and Constable which is occasionally open to public view.

Serpentine Gallery

Kensington Gardens, W2

Monthly exhibitions of contemporary art are held here under the auspicies of the Arts Council.

The Thomas Coram Foundation for Children

40 Brunswick Square, WC1

The Foundation was formed in 1739 with the granting of a royal charter to Captain Thomas Coram to open a Foundling Hospital for destitute children. At the instigation of William Hogarth various works of art were presented to the Foundation for display in the Court Room to attract the public and raise funds. The present building, which was built in 1937 on the site of the old one, houses the vast number of exhibits which have been presented to the Foundation over the years. Of particular interest is the portrait of Coram, by Hogarth, which was the first gift.

The Arts Council chose an old tea-house near the Albert Memorial for the premises of the Serpentine Gallery, where many new artists get their first showing.

The Wallace Collection

Hertford House, Manchester Square, W1

This superb collection of works of art is housed in an elegant 18th-century town house. The collection was founded by the 1st Marquis of Hertford, and was greatly enlarged by the 4th Marquis, who spent a lifetime amassing French works of art. Richard Wallace, natural son of the 4th Marquis, brought the collection to England in the second half of the 19th century (it had previously been housed in Paris) and made further additions to it. Richard's widow presented the collection to the nation and it was opened to the public in 1900. The collection is world famous for its 18th-century paintings and furniture by French artists and craftsmen. Other paintings include *The Laughing Cavalier* by Frans Hals and works by Rubens, Holbein, and Titian. An immense variety of armour, porcelain, clocks, miniatures, and other decorative arts is also displayed.

The Whitechapel Art Gallery, owned by a charitable trust, has the dual role both of staging exhibitions of contemporary art from all over the world and of encouraging the work of local artists.

Whitechapel Art Gallery

Whitechapel High Street, E1

Opened to contribute to the cultural life of the East End, this gallery has achieved widespread fame for the excellence of its temporary exhibitions. The building has an ornate *art nouveau* façade.

William Morris Gallery

Lloyd Park, Forest Road, Walthamstow, E17

Devoted to the life and work of the great Victorian artist-craftsman, poet and free thinker, William Morris, this gallery contains many designs and articles produced by the Morris Company. Also displayed is the Brangwyn collection of pictures. The artist Frank Brangwyn worked for Morris at one time, and presented the gallery with many of his own works as well as work by his contemporaries.

Retail Galleries and Auction Houses

London is regarded as the art centre of the world, and quite apart from public art galleries it has a large number of retail galleries and auction houses where great (and not-so-great) works of art can be bought, sold, or just seen. Most of the important galleries are in Mayfair, predominantly in the Old and New Bond Street, Cork Street and Duke Street areas, but many important galleries are to be found elsewhere. There are over 140 retail art galleries in the capital and listed here are the more important and more famous ones. They are classified here according to their specialities, though in most cases galleries exhibit a wide range of material. The public is welcome to view in all of them and most are open during usual office hours and on Saturday mornings, but many close on Saturdays during the summer.

Old Masters

Thos Agnew & Sons Ltd
43 Old Bond Street, W1
Agnew's worldwide reputation is for stocking and exhibiting some of the finest Old Master paintings and drawings in London, ranging from the 14th to the 19th centuries. They also show some work by 20th-century and contemporary English artists and in January and February hold an exhibition of 18th- and 19th-century English watercolours and drawings.

P & D Colnaghi & Co Ltd
14 Old Bond Street, W1
Colnaghi's, established in 1760, is one of the oldest galleries in London. It deals mainly in Old Masters, particularly Italian, but also carries considerable stocks of drawings and prints, as well as specialising in Indian and Islamic art.

Heim Gallery
59 Jermyn Street, SW1
Specialising in 17th- and 18th-century French and Italian paintings, Heim's also deals in sculpture, ranging from Renaissance to 19th-century. Exhibitions are usually held two or three times a year.

Wildenstein & Co Ltd
147 New Bond Street, W1
Wildenstein's was founded in 1875 as part of a world-wide organisation with galleries in Buenos Aires, New York and Tokyo. The gallery is renowned for its stock of French Masters as well as Italian primitives and other European schools of art. Wildenstein's also shows sculpture by Henry Moore and holds regular exhibitions of old and modern masters and sculpture.

18th- & 19th-century Art

Frost & Reed Ltd
41 New Bond Street, W1
Founded in 1808, Frost & Reed specialise in 18th- and 19th-century British and Continental paintings and watercolours. In addition the gallery features work by selected 20th-century artists. There are a number of exhibitions throughout the year.

J S Maas & Co Ltd
15a Clifford Street, W1
Maas's gallery is particularly noted for works by Victorian artists, especially Pre-Raphaelites, in addition to English pictures from 1800 to 1920.

Early 20th-century Art

Anthony D'Offay
9 Dering Street, New Bond Street, W1
Between four and six exhibitions are held each year at the Anthony D'Offay gallery, which deals mainly in 20th-century British art and has a long list of artists in which it specialises.

Wildenstein's in New Bond Street. The building in which the gallery is housed was Lord Nelson's home for a while.

The Fine Art Society Ltd
148 New Bond Street, W1
Established in 1876, The Fine Art Society is one of the best places in London to see and buy 19th- and 20th-century British Art. In earlier days the society's name was associated with Whistler and Ruskin and it holds about 10 exhibitions a year.

The Lefevre Gallery
30 Bruton Street, W1
The Lefevre Gallery specialises in important 19th- and 20th-century European paintings and drawings and also exhibits work by contemporary British artists.

Theo Waddington
25 Cork Street, W1
Exhibiting about once a month, Theo Waddington specialises in famous 20th-century artists, including Bonnard, Hayden, Matisse and Moore.

The Leger Galleries in Old Bond Street specialise in Old Masters and usually hold two or three exhibitions a year.

Contemporary Art

Annely Juda Fine Art
11 Tottenham Mews (off Tottenham St), W1
In addition to contemporary English and foreign artists, Annely Juda specialises in the Russian Constructivism and Suprematism schools. Exhibitions are held monthly.

Christie's Contemporary Art
8 Dover Street, W1
This subsidiary of Christie's International specialises in contemporary etchings, lithographs and sculpture, and the work of over 50 artists is represented, including Moore, Frink, Piper and Hockney. Christie's Contemporary Art holds mixed exhibitions every month.

Marlborough Fine Art (London) Ltd

6 Albermarle Street, W1

Marlborough Fine Art specialises mainly in
19th- and 20th-century paintings, drawings
and sculpture, particularly Impressionists,
Post-Impressionists, Cubists and Modern.
The gallery is also noted for its exhibitions,
held about once a month, of living artists,
and for the mixed exhibition held in July and
August.

Sporting Art and Natural History Art

Arthur Ackermann & Son Ltd

3 Old Bond Street, W1

Established in 1783, Ackermann's played a
leading role in the development of art
printing techniques, particularly aquatint
and lithography. The gallery was also
responsible for the introduction of sporting,
military and topographical art, especially in
the form of works by Stubbs and Marshall.
Today it specialises in British sporting art,
fine paintings and old engravings, and holds
exhibitions three or four times a year.

The Tryon Gallery Ltd

41/42 Dover Street, W1

One of the more famous natural history
artists which the Tryon Gallery features is
David Shepherd, and the gallery has about
six exhibitions throughout the year.

Crafts and Jewellery

The British Crafts Centre

43 Earlham Street, WC2

The best of contemporary craft-work can be seen at
the British Crafts Centre.

Crafts Advisory Committee Gallery

12 and 8 Waterloo Place, SW1

The revival of interest in age-old crafts and
techniques has seen a rise all over Britain in
the number of individual craftsmen
producing hand-made pottery, textiles,
furniture and other objects. A selection of
contemporary British craft-work can be seen
in London at the above galleries with
continuously changing exhibitions of
individuals' work.

Electrum Gallery

21 South Molton Street, W1

The Electrum Gallery aims to show the best
contemporary jewellery from all over the
world, and in addition to special exhibitions
held about 10 times a year, the work of nearly
40 individual jewellery artists is on
permanent display.

Photographic Galleries

The Photographers' Gallery Ltd

8 Great Newport Street, WC2

The Photographers' Gallery is a registered
non-profit organisation funded by, amongst
others, the Arts Council of Great Britain. As
well as monthly exhibitions, the gallery aims
to show the best of the many types of
professional photography – from reportage
and advertising to the purely creative.

Robert Self Ltd

9 Cork Street, W1

The Robert Self Gallery specialises solely in
early photographic work and its particular
interest is in the first masters of photography
from 1840 to 1880, though it prefers to deal in
pre-1860 photographs. The collection
includes photographs by Cameron, Fox
Talbot and Sutcliffe, as well as early cameras
and Daguerreotypes.

The Photographers' Gallery exhibits a wide range of
professional photography by both young and
established photographers. It also has a well-stocked
bookshop.

Fine Art Auctioneers

**London has been an important art centre
ever since the French Revolution, but
particularly since the mid-1950s it has
dominated the international art market,
attracting experts in many different fields
of specialisation from all over the world.
The three big names in London are
Sotheby's, Christie's and Phillips, all of
which have international connections
and hold sales all over the world. The
public is admitted to previews and sales
except on very rare occasions when
admission is by ticket only, and all three
auction houses welcome people bringing
objects for free inspection and
estimation of value.**

Christie, Manson & Woods Ltd

8 King Street, W1

Founded in 1766, Christie's holds as many as
three or four sales a day in its King Street
salerooms. Over 150,000 pictures, pieces of
furniture, silver, porcelain, jewellery, books,
arms and armour, and *objets d'art* are sold
each year, two-thirds of them for less than
£300. There are a number of specialist sales,
and sales in the lower price range are held at
Christie's South Kensington.

Phillips

7 Blenheim Street (off New Bond Street), W1

Phillips was founded in 1796, and today up to
15 regular sales a week are held for antiques
of all sorts and works of art. In addition there
are a great number of specialist sales ranging
from coins and stamps to musical
instruments and suits of armour.

Sotheby, Parke, Bernet & Co

34 New Bond Street, W1

Sotheby's, founded in 1744, has over the last
few years seen some of the most important art
sales ever – Mentmore House, Wildenstein
and the collection of Robert von Hirsch
(which in total realised a record £18,457,000)
all fell under a Sotheby hammer. Apart from
its London offices, Sotheby's has 36 other
auction rooms, representative offices in 19
countries, and their overall turnover in
1977–78 was a staggering £162,500,000 – yet
62% of their sales went for less than £200
each and 84% were less than £500. Sotheby's
can claim a number of firsts which have
become standard practice in many
international auction houses, for instance the
introduction of specialised sales, the use of
closed-circuit television and TV satellite for
transatlantic bidding, and the use of a
computer to convert the bids instantly into
six different currencies.

The Performing Arts

London, one of the greatest cultural centres of the world, provides a kaleidoscope of live art of unrivalled variety and quality. International stars of ballet, drama, opera, and music have long been drawn to the footlights of London's theatres. The selection here is only a sample of the many venues where classical, traditional, contemporary, and experimental performances may be enjoyed.

Albery

St Martin's Lane, WC2

This theatre was formerly known as the New Theatre and was renamed in 1973 as a tribute to the late Sir Bronson Albery who presided over its fortunes for many years. The present manager is Donald Albery (son of Sir Bronson) who also controls the Criterion, the Piccadilly, and Wyndham's.

Aldwych

Aldwych, WC2

This theatre became famous between the wars as the venue of Ben Travers' hilarious 'Aldwych' farces starring Ralph Lynn and Tom Walls. Today it is the London headquarters of the Royal Shakespeare Company.

Cambridge

Cambridge Circus, WC2

The Cambridge opened in 1930 and thus qualifies as one of London's youngest theatres. The opening night was a glittering occasion and the theatre was acclaimed as the most beautiful in London. Long-running popular shows including pantomimes, operas and musicals have been the trademark of the Cambridge. The recent trend for rock musicals has not passed it by either, the most successful production being *Jesus Christ Superstar*.

Drury Lane, Theatre Royal

Catherine Street, WC2

The Theatre Royal is situated on one of the oldest theatre sites in London. The first building, dating from 1663, was destroyed by fire and replaced by one designed by Sir Christopher Wren. Here David Garrick produced plays starring John Kemble and Mrs Siddons. A third building opened in 1794 under the management of Richard Sheridan, but this too was burnt down. The present theatre is the largest in London, with sumptuous furnishings, a portico and Ionic colonnade at the rear, and numerous monuments to former exponents of the dramatic art, such as Edmund Kean and David Garrick. Henry Irving, Ellen Terry and Forbes Robertson are among those who have played in the present theatre, and more recently it has become the venue of many successful musicals such as *Oklahoma*, *Carousel*, *My Fair Lady* and *A Chorus Line*.

Her Majesty's

Haymarket, SW1

Founded by Sir Herbert Beerbohm Tree in 1887, the year of Queen Victoria's Diamond Jubilee, this pavilioned theatre is crowned by a Baroque copper dome. Sir Herbert, one of the first actors to be knighted, was also founder of the Royal Academy of Dramatic Art (RADA). He retained the management of Her Majesty's until his death in 1917.

National Theatre

South Bank, SE1

The National Theatre is part of the South Bank Arts Centre and was opened in 1976. The building in fact houses three theatres: the Olivier, which is open-staged and was named after Lord Olivier, who was the first director of the National Theatre Company (the present director is Sir Peter Hall); the smaller Lyttleton; and the even smaller Cottesloe, which specialises in experimental productions.

The National Theatre has, in the very few years that it has been in operation, won for itself a high reputation, both for the quality of its productions and for the enthusiasm with which it encourages new playwrights, as well as staging works by more established writers such as Harold Pinter.

Left: Sir Ralph Richardson and Sir John Gielgud, two of our most acclaimed actors, in a scene from Pinter's play *No Man's Land*. Below: A stage set from the same play showing the minute attention to period detail which is so characteristic of National Theatre productions. Sir Ralph Richardson is seated, foreground, with Sir John Gielgud behind him on his right, leaning against a table.

Royal Albert Hall
Kensington, SW7

Queen Victoria laid the foundation stone of the building named after her beloved Prince Albert in 1867, and it was subsequently opened to the public in 1871. The huge circular wall is composed of red brick, adorned with terracotta and a mosaic frieze illustrating Triumphs of Art and Science, and is surmounted by a huge glass dome. The auditorium has a seating capacity of 5,600 and contains one of the world's largest organs, made by 'Father' Willis. Though the Albert Hall is particularly famous for the Sir Henry Wood Promenade Concerts, performed daily between mid-July and mid-September and entailing the services of some 15 orchestras, 30 conductors, and almost 200 soloists or singers, it is also the venue of concerts ranging from classical to pop throughout the year.

Right: The Albert Hall, home of one of London's major musical events, the Promenade Concerts.
Below: Colin Davies, conducting the Last Night of the Proms on 14th September 1968. The Proms are deservedly popular with young people because they hear the best performers at relatively low prices.

Jeannetta Cochrane Theatre
Theobalds Road, WC1

Opened in 1963, the theatre is housed in an extension to the Central School of Art and Design and is named in honour of Jeannetta Cochrane, who taught at the school from 1914 to 1957. There are occasional productions by students of experimental plays as well as a number of productions for children.

Kings Head Theatre Club
Upper Street, Islington, N1

Set in the village atmosphere of Islington, the Kings Head pub houses London's first pub theatre. Now established as one of the city's best fringe theatres, plays are performed at lunchtimes as well as in the evenings.

The London Coliseum
St Martin's Lane, WC2

The Coliseum was built in 1904, and was at first used primarily as a music hall. It is easily identified by the giant electrical globe on the roof which twinkles into the sky each evening. One of the largest theatres in London, it was the first to install a revolving stage, and Sarah Bernhardt, Lillie Langtry, and Ellen Terry have all trodden its boards. Since 1968 the Coliseum has been the home of the English National Opera Company (formerly at Sadler's Wells).

The London Palladium
Argyll Street, W1

This famous music hall opened on Boxing Day 1910 with a variety bill featuring Nellie Wallace, Ella Shields, and Ella Retford. At that time such shows included farce, melodrama, and operatic scenes. Such 'variety', however, was not to last forever, and in 1912 spectacular revues took over. Christmas entertainment has always been a speciality here and *Peter Pan* held pride of place for eight years. The famous Crazy Gang Shows then enjoyed permanent residency until after the War. In 1946 the Palladium returned to a policy of top-name variety and great stars such as Judy Garland, Danny Kaye, and Frank Sinatra have been among those to appear here.

The Old Vic
Waterloo Road, SE1

Also known as the Royal Victoria Hall, this theatre was built during the early 19th century. It was noted for lurid melodramas until 1880 when Emma Cons acquired the premises and made them the home of classical plays and opera – a tradition which was carried on by her niece Lilian Baylis. For many years famous for its Shakespearian productions, the Old Vic was the headquarters of the National Theatre Company until it transferred to the South Bank in 1976.

Open Air Theatre

Queen Mary's Gardens, Regent's Park, NW1

This theatre has been in operation since 1932, braving the rigours of the British climate with the aid of a wet-weather marquee to stage summer performances of Shakespeare. The present auditorium was constructed in 1975, and the wooded surroundings provide an ideal setting for such plays as *A Midsummer Night's Dream* and *As You Like It*.

Round House

Chalk Farm Road, NW1

A massive engine-turning shed, designed by Robert Stephenson and built in 1847, was converted in 1967 into the Round House, an arts centre with a theatre, cinema, library and art gallery. The theatre proved to be an ideal place for experimental performances, and the Round House has now become very popular for the staging of new works and unconventional productions of established plays.

Royal Court

Sloane Square, SW1

Ever since its opening in 1870 the Royal Court has specialised in innovative plays. The farces of Arthur Pinero were performed here in the 1890s, followed by premiere performances of some of the plays of George Bernard Shaw (whose bust stands in the foyer) in the early years of the 20th century, when the theatre was under the management of the playwright, actor and critic Harley Granville-Barker. Some of Somerset Maughams's early work was first produced here, and probably the most famous and controversial of recent *avant-garde* plays, the English Stage Company's production of John Osborne's *Look Back in Anger*, ran here in 1956. The Royal Court still maintains its reputation as a pioneer of the London theatre, and since 1969 the small Theatre Upstairs, above the main auditorium, has specialised in particularly new and experimental work.

Royal Festival Hall

South Bank, SE1

This was the only permanent building erected for the 1951 Festival of Britain. The designers, LCC architects Sir Leslie Martin and Sir Robert Matthew, were concerned first and foremost with acoustics and visibility. The result is one of the most successful examples of modern architecture in London, providing comfortable seating for 3,000 people, spacious foyers, fine river views (the frontage was enlarged in 1962–5), and a platform which can accommodate a choir of 250. The hall has been completely insulated against noise from nearby Waterloo Station. The complex was completed when, in 1967, the Queen Elizabeth Hall and the Purcell Room were built. They seat 1,100 and 400 people respectively.

Royal Opera House

Covent Garden, WC2

The present building had two predecessors, the second one being the scene of the famous Old Price Riots – the public's protestations against the sharp increase in the cost of seats. The theatre officially opened as an opera house in 1847 and opera has flourished here ever since, achieving its greatest peaks between 1859 and 1939 when it was the leading entertainment of 'society'. Productions today are most lavish and still attract a great following who come to see and hear the very best names in the world of opera. Thomas Beecham brought ballet to the theatre in 1911 and it became the headquarters of the Royal Ballet Company.

Above: Lynn Seymour and Anthony Dowell in a *pas de deux* from the 1976 production of *A Month in the Country*.

Left: The Royal Opera House, Covent Garden, is world-famous for the high standards it sets both in opera and ballet. The world's most distinguished singers and dancers have worked here.

Below: A scene from Verdi's opera, *Aida*, set in ancient Egypt. The lavish set and glittering costumes are worthy of this tragic royal love story.

It is hard to think of London without such famous landmarks as Piccadilly Circus, Big Ben, Buckingham Palace or St Paul's springing instantly to mind. Yet there are more recent landmarks that have, inexplicably, become as much a part of London life as the Changing of the Guard. For more than one generation of theatregoers, *The Mousetrap*, Agatha Christie's famous thriller, has become an established tradition. Right: The playbill from the first production with Richard Attenborough and Shelia Sim. The play continues to attract theatregoers by the coachload.

Below: The London Palladium near Oxford Circus, originally a music hall in the Edwardian era, is now the home of top variety shows and reviews.

Bottom of the page: A scene from *Peter Pan*, a favourite with children since J M Barrie created 'the little boy who never grew up' more than 70 years ago. Most London theatres stage either a pantomime or a children's entertainment every Christmas. This performance was at the Shaftesbury Theatre.

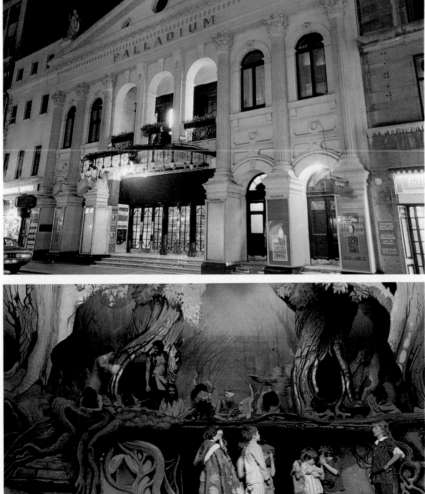

Sadler's Wells
Rosebery Avenue, EC1
The well or natural spring, discovered by Mr Sadler in 1683 and developed as a spa, is still preserved within the theatre. The theatre was noted for its Shakespearian productions during the mid-19th century and for the performances of Joe Grimaldi, the famous clown, a few years earlier. The threatened extinction of the theatre was avoided by the campaigning of theatrical manager Lilian Baylis who was instrumental in getting the building renovated and re-opened in 1931. Sadler's Wells then acquired fame as a ballet and operatic centre and it was here that the Royal Ballet first achieved world-wide status under the guidance of ballerina and artistic director Ninette de Valois.

Savoy
The Strand, WC2
This theatre, now incorporated in the famous Savoy Hotel, was commissioned by the great D'Oyly Carte and it was here that his productions of Gilbert and Sullivan's popular operettas were staged between 1881 and 1889. The Savoy Theatre was the first public building to be lit by electricity.

Shaw Theatre
Euston Road, NW1
Opened in 1971, the Shaw Theatre is the permanent home of the National Youth Theatre of Great Britain and its professional offshoot, The Dolphin Theatre Company. The Shaw Theatre aims to provide good theatre at prices young people can afford, and there are special reductions for students and people under 21. The Dolphin Theatre Company concentrates mainly on traditional and modern classics.

Theatre Royal
Haymarket, SW1
This building, designed by John Nash and opened in 1821, has regal columns which extend across the pavement, lending the theatre an imposing appearance. The interior is cool and elegant in royal blue, white and gold.

Windmill
Great Windmill Street, W1
Standing on the site of an old windmill, the theatre earned its 'We never close' slogan by operating throughout the London Blitz under the management of Vivian Van Damm. The shows were renowned for their risqué flavour and this tradition continues today. Many famous actors began their careers at the Windmill and remember the war years with affection.

A map locating central London's theatres, concert halls, and cinemas will be found on page 187.

Great Men and Monuments

London has more statues than any other city in the world, while in some parts it seems that every other house is marked by a blue plaque. Throughout London the statues, monuments, and houses of great men stand in silent commemoration of the prominent figures in the nation's history. Described on the following pages is a selection of London's more interesting monuments and statues, featuring eight men who made their homes in London and who, in their different ways, changed the face and course of Britain's history.

Prince Albert
The Albert Memorial, Kensington Gore, SW7
This enormous and imposing memorial is a monument not only to Prince Albert, but also to the benevolent aspects of Victorian Imperialism. The memorial was commissioned by Queen Victoria in memory of her husband, and was designed by Sir Gilbert Scott in 1872. The sculpture of the Prince, which was made by John Foley, sits under an ornate and intricately decorated canopy. The Prince is depicted reading a catalogue of the Great Exhibition of 1851, for which he was largely responsible.

Alfred the Great
Trinity Church Square, off Trinity Street, SE1
Thought to date from 1395, this is the oldest statue in London. It was brought here from the old Palace of Westminster in 1822.

Queen Anne
Queen Anne's Gate, SW1
Dating from the early 18th century, this little statue was probably moved here from the Church of St Mary-le-Strand. The Queen is depicted in state robes.

Queen Boadicea
Westminster Bridge, SW1
Thomas Thornycroft made this statue of Queen Boadicea, or Boudicca, in 1902. She is depicted in her war chariot, accompanied by her daughters, and appears to be defiantly waving her spear at the Houses of Parliament.

George Canning
Parliament Square, SW1
This 19th-century statue by Sir Richard Westmacott is chiefly notable for the fact that while it was still in the sculptor's studio it fell over and killed a man.

Thomas Carlyle 1795–1881

Born in Ecclefechan, Scotland, Thomas Carlyle was a member of a strictly Calvinistic family which had plans for him to enter the Church. Carlyle, however, was more attracted towards journalism and writing, and became a regular contributor to the *Edinburgh Review* while he privately compiled *Sartor Resartus*, a philosophical work based on his own confusion over religious doctrine. In 1834 he and his wife, Jane, moved to London where they occupied 24 Cheyne Row for the rest of their lives. Here Carlyle wrote his major historical works, all of which were liberally spiced with his own thoughts and earned him the title 'Sage of Chelsea'. He died on 5th February 1881 and was buried in Ecclefechan, according to his express wishes, and despite the offer of a burial place in Westminster Abbey. He is regarded as one of the most distinguished essayists in the English language.

Carlyle's House
24 Cheyne Row, Chelsea, SW3
This small 18th-century house, now owned by the National Trust, contains much Carlyle memorobilia. The attic study and the kitchen where he often entertained Tennyson are preserved exactly as Carlyle knew them.

Above: It was here that Carlyle wrote his major historical works, including *The French Revolution*. The sound-proofed study where he could take refuge from 'dogs, cocks, pianofortes and insipid men' is faithfully preserved. Below: The 'Sage of Chelsea' sits, pensive, in Cheyne Walk gardens.

William Hogarth 1697–1764

Hogarth was 60 when he painted this self-portrait, now in the National Portrait Gallery. In 1749 he moved to the house in Chiswick that he called 'a little country box by the Thames'. Now heavy traffic roars past on the Great West Road.

Hogarth's House

Hogarth Lane, Great West Road, Chiswick, W4
Paintings, prints, and personal relics are displayed in this 17th-century house, which was Hogarth's home for 15 years.

A native of London, Hogarth began his career as an apprentice silverplate engraver, and later set up as a designer and publisher of popular prints and as a book illustrator. He began to paint portraits and what he referred to as 'dramatic' paintings – a series of pictures telling a story – notably *A Harlot's Progress* and *The Rake's Progress*. He was made a governor of the Foundling Hospital (now the Thomas Coram Foundation for Children), which was founded by Captain Thomas Coram in 1739, and was commissioned to paint a number of portraits, including one of Coram. Hogarth returned to his 'dramatic' work in 1744, producing his most famous paintings, the six scenes which make up *Marriage à la Mode*, and finally, in 1754, the four pictures of *An Election*. Throughout his life Hogarth championed the cause of English art. He helped to establish an art school in London and set up a permanent exhibition of works by the rising generation of painters at the Foundling Hospital; this was a forerunner of the Royal Academy, which was founded shortly after Hogarth's death.

Charles Dickens 1812–1870

Dickens started work as a reporter, first at the Law Courts and then in Parliament, and began to contribute articles to various magazines. His first full length novel, *The Pickwick Papers*, grew from what amounted to a magazine strip cartoon. The cascade of brilliantly descriptive novels which followed reflected his acute observations of society and sympathy for his often grotesque characters. In his later years Dickens embarked on an exhausting series of public readings at which he read his own works, and toured America in 1867. He pushed himself beyond the limits of physical endurance and died at Gads Hill on 9th June 1870, leaving his final novel, *Edwin Drood*, uncompleted.

Dickens' House

48 Doughty Street, WC1
Dickens and his family lived here from 1837 to 1839, during which period he completed *The Pickwick Papers*, and wrote *Oliver Twist* and *Nicholas Nickleby*. There is a reconstruction of Dingly Dell Kitchen, as described in *The Pickwick Papers*, in the basement.

Dickens lived in many houses in London, but only the one at Doughty Street survives. The photograph shows the reconstructed kitchen described in the *Pickwick Papers*.

Charles I
Trafalgar Square, SW1
Cast in bronze in 1633, this statue was to have been melted down during the Commonwealth, but was hidden and re-erected in 1660. It was moved to Mentmore in Buckinghamshire during World War II and was replaced in 1947 with a new sword. The original sword is said to have been dislodged by a photographer in 1867 and stolen while a procession was in progress.

Sir Winston Churchill's statue by Ivor Roberts-Jones.

Sir Winston Churchill
Parliament Square, SW1
This statue of the great statesman and war leader was unveiled in 1973 and depicts Churchill in a typically pugnacious attitude.

Sir Henry Irving
St Martin's Place, WC2
Irving is regarded as being one of the greatest actors who ever lived. This statue was erected in 1910, and is the only one in London of an actor.

James II
Trafalgar Square, WC2
Usually regarded as the finest statue in London, this figure of the King was made by Grinling Gibbons.

James II in Roman dress stands in front of the National Gallery.

Lord Nelson

Trafalgar Square, WC2

This 17ft 4in statue by E H Bailey stands on the top of the famous column. Together they reach a combined height of almost 185ft. Four identical lions, cast from a single original by Sir Edwin Landseer, guard the base of the column. This memorial to the nation's greatest sailor was set up between 1842 and 1867.

Sir Walter Raleigh

Banqueting House, Whitehall, SW1

Raleigh was beheaded near this spot in 1618. The statue, which was erected in 1959, is extremely small, reflecting Raleigh's diminutive stature.

Richard I

Old Palace Yard, SW1

Baron Carlo Marochetti made this spirited equestrian statue of Richard the Lionheart in the mid-19th century.

Queen Victoria

Queen Victoria Memorial, The Mall, SW1

This elegant group of statuary stands in front of Buckingham Palace. It was designed by Sir Aston Webb, and the sculptures were made by Sir Thomas Brock.

Kensington Gardens, WC2

Princess Louise, one of Queen Victoria's daughters, made this statue in 1893.

The 1st Duke of Wellington

Hyde Park Corner, W1

The Duke is shown here riding Copenhagen, the horse he rode throughout the Battle of Waterloo. Copenhagen was buried with full military honours at the Duke's country home, Stratfield Saye, Hampshire.

The figures at the base of Wellington's statue were cast from captured French cannons.

Duke of York

Carlton House Terrace, SW1

Sir Richard Westmacott's 13ft-high statue of 'The Grand Old Duke of York' crowns a lofty column overlooking St James's Park. Both column and statue were erected in 1833.

John Keats 1795–1821

Born in London, Keats was apprenticed to a surgeon and worked for a time at Guys' and St Thomas' hospitals. By 1817 however, he had forsaken his profession and devoted his life to writing poetry. His first work, *Poems*, was published that same year, and *Endymion*, a lengthy poem based on Greek legends, appeared in 1818. From 1818 to 1820 Keats lived at Wentworth Place with his friend Charles Brown, while next door lived his lover and nurse Fanny Brawne. It was here that Keats produced his greatest poetry, including the famous *Odes*. By 1820 he was crippled by tuberculosis, and not even a journey to the more equable Italian climate could halt its progress. Keats died in Rome on 23rd February 1821, leaving behind, in addition to his poetry, what is probably the most spontaneous and revealing collection of letters written by any English poet.

Keats' House

Wentworth Place, Keats Grove, Hampstead, NW3

The two regency houses occupied by Keats and Fanny Brawne have now been made into one. They are furnished in period style and contain manuscripts, letters, and relics. *Ode to a Nightingale* was written in the garden.

Dr Samuel Johnson 1709–1784

Johnson studied literature from an early age, but was unable to complete his degree course at Oxford because he ran out of money. Johnson moved to London in 1737 and worked on political articles and a 'Turkish tragedy' which was later staged in the city. It was not a success, and closed within two weeks. In 1747 he was commissioned to work on the now famous dictionary, but was obliged to produce essays and other writings continuously to keep himself out of debt. The dictionary took $8\frac{1}{2}$ years to complete, and it contained 40,000 words, with more carefully researched definitions and shades of meaning than had ever been thought possible. Johnson next undertook the mammoth task of editing the complete works of Shakespeare. In 1763 he met James Boswell. They became firm friends, and the diary which Boswell kept contains most of the quotations which are attributed to Johnson. The man who was to become the most frequently quoted Englishman after Shakespeare died in London on 13th December 1784 and was buried in Westminster Abbey a week later.

Johnson's House

17 Gough Square, EC4

Johnson lived in this handsome 18th-century house between 1749 and 1759 and it was here that he wrote the dictionary.

Samuel Pepys 1633–1703

Pepys went to university at Cambridge, and held several clerical positions before beginning work at the Admiralty in 1660. He began to keep a diary at about this time, using a system of shorthand, and when he was forced to discontinue his daily recordings in 1669, due to the deterioration of his eyesight, the journal ran to 1,250,000 words. It has been called a descriptive work of art and is undoubtedly the best account of life in Charles II's London, with its eyewitness accounts of the Coronation, the Plague, and the Great Fire, not to mention revealing pen-portraits of his contemporaries. Pepys' continuing dedication to his work at the Admiralty was rewarded in 1673 when he was appointed administrative head of the navy. He immediately began to attack the corruption which had been spreading throughout the service, thus making enemies who were determined to bring about his downfall. In 1678 an attempt was made to implicate him in a murder and when this failed, a false charge of treason was brought against him and he was sent to the Tower, only escaping with his life because the current Parliament was dissolved. Charles II reinstated Pepys in 1683 and he held his former post at the Admiralty until his retirement in 1689. The diarist spent his final years among his books, researching a history of the navy, which remained incomplete at his death in 1703. Samuel Pepys lived at *12 Buckingham Street, WC2*, from 1679 until 1688. The house is marked with a blue plaque but is not open to the public. No. 14, where he lived from 1688 to 1700, has been demolished.

Arthur Wellesley, 1st Duke of Wellington 1769–1852

After the Battle of Waterloo, Wellington lived at Apsley House near Hyde Park Corner. People referred to his house as 'No 1 London'.

Born in Dublin, Wellesley completed his early military training in France, and for the next few years divided his time between the army and the Irish House of Commons. Active service in India at the turn of the 18th century earned him a knighthood, but it was the Peninsular War, which began in 1808, that enabled him to demonstrate his military expertise to the full. Within five years he had driven the French out of Portugal and Spain and defeated Napoleon's army in 1814 at Toulouse. Wellesley received his dukedom, plus other decorations, following this campaign. His final strategic confrontation with Napoleon took place the following year, culminating in the Battle of Waterloo on 18th June 1815. The Duke then resumed his political career and in 1828 became Prime Minister. His staunch opposition to sweeping change made him extremely unpopular and the windows of Apsley House were broken so many times that they had to be covered with iron shutters. He retired from public life in 1846, and died six years later at Walmer Castle, his official residence as Lord Warden of the Cinque Ports.

Wellington's House
Apsley House, 149 Piccadilly, W1
This mansion was designed by Robert Adam in the late 18th century and was the property of the Duke from 1817 until his death. It was opened to the public as the Wellington Museum in 1952.

Legendary Figures

The Whittington Stone is supposed to mark the spot where Dick Whittington and his cat heard Bow Bells calling him back to be Lord Mayor.

Achilles
Hyde Park, W1
This statue of the most famous of the Greek heroes was designed by Sir Richard Westmacott. It was made from a cannon captured during the Peninsular Wars and erected in 1822.

Eros
Piccadilly Circus, W1
One of London's most famous landmarks, this figure of an archer was erected as a memorial to the Victorian reformer and philanthropist, the Earl of Shaftesbury. The archer actually represents the Angel of Christian Charity, not Eros.

The Griffin
Strand, EC4
The Griffin, the unofficial badge of the City of London, stands at the point where the Strand ends and Fleet Street begins. Originally this was the site of the Old Temple Bar gateway, and the spot traditionally marks the western limit of the City.

Peter Pan
Kensington Gardens, W2
This statue of Sir James Barrie's immortal character has delighted several generations of children. It was made by Sir George Frampton in 1911.

The Whittington Stone
Highgate Hill, N19
Dick Whittington is supposed to have sat on this spot and heard Bow Bells chiming: 'Turn again Whittington, Thrice Mayor of London'. Whittington actually was mayor of London three times during the 14th century.

Commemorative Monuments

The Burghers of Calais

Victoria Tower Gardens, SW1

Rodin's superb group of figures represents the citizens of Calais who surrendered to Edward III in 1340 to save their town from destruction.

The Fat Boy

Giltspur Street, EC1

This peculiar gilded figure marks the spot, originally known as Pie Corner, where the Great Fire was halted in 1666.

Monument

Monument Street, EC3

Sir Christopher Wren designed this 202ft fluted Doric column as a memorial of the Great Fire of London, which started exactly 202ft from it in Pudding Lane. Superb views over the City can be obtained from its viewing gallery, reached by climbing 311 steps.

Sir Christopher Wren   1632–1723

Originally from Wiltshire, Wren studied science at Oxford, and later became a professor of astronomy, a subject in which he always kept an active interest. He visited France in 1665, primarily to study architectural styles, and on his return to England formulated plans for the re-modelling of St Paul's Cathedral. Before these plans could come to fruition fate took a hand and the Great Fire engulfed the cathedral and a large proportion of the City. Wren submitted a plan for the complete reconstruction of the City as soon as the Fire had been extinguished, and although it was not accepted, he was subsequently selected to join the rebuilding committee and was appointed general surveyor in 1669. Never before, or since, has one architect undertaken the simultaneous rebuilding of a major cathedral and as many as 50 churches. He died on 25th February 1723 and was buried in the cathedral. His epitaph reads simply: 'If you seek a monument, look about you.'

Wren's House

49 Bankside, SE1

A plaque on the wall of this 17th-century house marks the building in which Wren lived while supervising the rebuilding of St Paul's.

Below: Wren's model for St Paul's Cathedral. His original plans were considered too outrageous and he had to modify them but, during the building, he quietly incorporated many of his first ideas.

London's Churches

London's Churches

The Great Fire of London in 1666 destroyed over 100 churches in the square mile of the City, and many were never rebuilt. All of the churches that eventually rose from the ashes were designed by Sir Christopher Wren. Bombs wreaked further havoc in World War II. Of the churches which stand today, most date from the 17th and 18th centuries, but there are some earlier survivals, and a number of superb Victorian examples. On the following pages will be found a selection of the most outstanding churches in central London.

All Hallows-by-the-Tower
Byward Street, EC3
Preserved in the crypt here is part of the wall of a church which stood on this site in the 7th century. Also in the crypt are fragments of Roman paving, and the remains of two Saxon crosses. The shell of the church dates from the 12th to 15th centuries, but the interior, which was gutted during the Blitz, was rebuilt in the 1950s. A superb font cover designed by Grinling Gibbons escaped destruction, as did the exquisite memorial brasses in front of the altar. Samuel Pepys watched the Great Fire of London from the tower.

All Hallows
London Wall, EC2
Forming part of the boundary of the churchyard here is a stretch of the ancient wall which once surrounded the City of London. The church itself was designed by George Dance the Younger in the 18th century and has an elegant and sumptuously decorated interior. It was severely damaged during the Blitz, but was restored in the 1960s and now houses exhibitions of church art.

All Saints
Margaret Street, W1
This striking brick-built church was erected in 1849 to the designs of William Butterfield. He was the most original architect of his time and produced plans that were initially inspired by Gothic architecture. The interior of the church is decorated with coloured bricks, and the decoration becomes much richer nearer the roof, reflecting the Victorian idea that Gothic architecture becomes more elaborate the nearer it gets to heaven.

All Souls'
Langham Place, W1
John Nash designed this large church and had it built in this position to close the northward vista of Regent Street. It was built in 1822 and has a Classical portico surmounted by a needle spire. The interior is designed in such a way that the whole congregation can view all aspects of the services.

The brick spire of All Saints, Margaret Street, a striking pattern of geometrical planes.

Brompton Oratory
Brompton Road, SW7
This imposing Roman Catholic church was built in an Italian Renaissance style at the end of the 19th century. Its interior is rich in marble and mosaic decoration and the nave is a remarkable 51 ft wide.

Chelsea Old Church (All Saints')
Cheyne Walk, SW3
Almost totally destroyed during the Blitz, this church has been restored to its original appearance. The More Chapel, however, survived almost intact. It was built in 1528 for Sir Thomas More and his family, but it is doubtful if he was buried here. The church is extremely rich in monuments, and in the churchyard is an urn commemorating Sir Hans Sloane, the great 18th-century collector and benefactor.

Holy Trinity
Sloane Street, SW1
This church was designed by J D Sedding, one of the principal architects of the 19th-century Arts and Crafts Movement. The interior of the church is based on 15th-century Gothic architecture and is lit by magnificent stained-glass windows designed by Edward Burne-Jones and made by William Morris.

All Souls, Langham Place, formed an important part of Nash's overall design for Regent Street but his grand plan no longer survives.

St Alfege
Church Street, Greenwich, SE10
Built in 1718 to the designs of Nicholas Hawksmoor, this church broods gloomily over its surroundings. It was badly damaged during the Blitz, and many of the treasures which it had contained were destroyed. The church was restored in the 1950s and houses a memorial to General Wolfe and the tomb of the 'father of English church music', Thomas Tallis (d.1585).

St Andrew
Holborn Circus, EC1
Although this church escaped the Great Fire, it was nonetheless rebuilt by Sir Christopher Wren, and is his largest parish church. It did not escape the Blitz, however, and had to be largely rebuilt. It contains a delightful memorial to Thomas Coram, who founded the Foundlings Hospital in the 18th century. The church's pulpit, font, and organ came from the chapel of the hospital. St Andrew's is a non-parochial guild church and no Sunday services are held here, but it is open for prayers on weekdays.

St Andrew-by-the-Wardrobe
Queen Victoria Street, EC4
Only the shell of this church survived the Blitz. It takes its name from the Great Wardrobe, or royal storehouse, which used to stand nearby. Now the headquarters of the Redundant Church Fund, the church was restored in the late 1950s and contains furnishings from other London churches.

St Andrew Undershaft
St Mary Axe, Leadenhall Street, EC3
The strange name of this church is derived from the fact that a famous maypole once stood opposite it. It is essentially a 16th-century building, although the tower was restored during the 19th century. Its most notable monument is to John Stow, a 16th-century historian who wrote the first topographical description of London. Concerts are frequently held in the church, and the nave is converted into a restaurant for City workers between 1pm and 2pm on most weekdays.

St Anne and St Agnes
Gresham Street, EC2
Wren rebuilt this attractive little church after the Great Fire. It has a square tower and a spacious interior with a central vault supported by elegant columns. The church contains a fine collection of ecclesiastical antiquities, but is only open to the public on Sundays, when it is used for Lutheran services.

St Anne Limehouse
Stepney, E1
This was the first of Nicholas
Hawksmoor's spectacular Classical-
style churches, of which there are two
others in the East End. It was built in
1712 and is especially notable for its
imposing tower. Hawksmoor was a
pupil of Sir Christopher Wren, and
followed closely in the footsteps of his
master.

St Bartholomew the Great
West Smithfield, EC1
St Bartholomew's is one of the few
surviving examples of Norman
architecture in London. It dates from
the 12th century and is the chancel of
a great Norman monastery church
which once stood here. After the
dissolution of the monasteries it
became private property, and for 300
years was put to a variety of uses,
including a factory and stables. It
reverted to its original use during the
19th century and was restored by Sir
Aston Webb. Its interior is dominated
by huge Romanesque pillars, and
contains the tomb of Rahere, the
founder of the church and of St
Bartholomew's Hospital. The church
has a particularly interesting
gateway, consisting of a half-timbered
gatehouse above a battered 13th-
century arch which was the original
entrance to the nave.

St Bartholomew-the-less
West Smithfield, EC1
This is the chapel of St
Bartholomew's Hospital, in whose
grounds it stands. All that remains of
the original 15th-century building is
the tower and vestry, which were
incorporated into an octagonal
church designed by George Dance the
Younger in the 18th century.

St Benet's
(Welsh Metropolitan Church)
Paul's Wharf,
off Queen Victoria Street, EC4
Wren put the finishing touches to this
handsome little church in 1683. Its
exterior has elaborately decorated
window surrounds and the interior
has an abundance of carved
woodwork, including the galleries
and altar. The church has been used
by Welsh Episcopalians since 1879
and is only open for Sunday services.

St Botolph
Aldersgate, EC1
Founded in 1291, but rebuilt at the
end of the 18th century, this church
stands near the site of one of the old
City gates. It has a square tower with
a cupola capped by a wooden bell
turret. The beautifully decorated
interior is lit by an odd mixture of
stained glass windows, the best of
which is undoubtedly an 18th-
century representation of Christ in
the Wilderness.

The altar of Our Lady in Brompton
Oratory is an overwhelming example
of the Italian Baroque style.

St Botolph Aldgate
Aldgate High Street, EC3
A church has occupied this site for more than 1,000 years, but the present building dates from the 18th century, when it was rebuilt by the architect George Dance the Elder. J F Bentley, the architect responsible for Westminster Cathedral, added the figured ceiling in 1889, and further extensive alterations were made after a fire in 1965.

St Botolph
Bishopsgate, EC2
St Botolph's was rebuilt in the 18th century by James Gold with the help of George Dance the Elder. It is an impressive brick building surmounted by a clock tower and steeple. The interior was altered in the 19th century and has a coved ceiling supported by huge Corinthian columns.

St Bride
Fleet Street, EC4
This famous church is known as 'the Parish Church of the Press' because of its associations and position. It was originally built by Wren, but all that survived World War II was the façade and Wren's magnificent steeple. The traditional three-tiered wedding cake of today is a replica of the steeple, and was first copied by a local baker in the 18th century. An interesting museum of church antiquities and architectural finds is contained in the crypt.

St Clement Danes in the Strand, a very ancient church rebuilt by Wren, burnt out in World War II, and restored in the 1950s. It is now the Royal Air Force's church.

St Clement Danes
Strand, WC2
A church has stood on this site since the 9th century. Sir Christopher Wren rebuilt it in the 1680s, and it was rebuilt once more after it had been virtually destroyed during World War II. It is the memorial church of the Royal Air Force, and the crests of some 900 squadrons and Commonwealth air forces are let into the flooring. Many of the church's fixtures and furnishings have been donated by overseas air forces. The 115-ft tower houses the bells that are immortalised in the famous lines of the nursery rhyme: 'Oranges and Lemons say the bells of St Clement's'.

St Clement Eastcheap
King William Street, EC4
Of particular interest in this little church is the beautiful 17th-century woodwork, seen at its best in the canopied pulpit. The church itself was built by Wren in 1683.

St Dunstan-in-the-West
Fleet Street, EC4
Although founded in the 13th century, the present church on this site dates only from the early part of the 19th century. It is an octagonal building with a prominent lantern tower. Many monuments from the church that once stood here have been preserved, and include one to the mythical King Lud and his sons. Also of interest is the clock, which was made in 1671, and was one of the first clocks in London to have minute divisions. The famous angler Izaak Walton is depicted in the north-west window, and it was in Fleet Street that *The Compleat Angler* was published.

St Edmund The King and Martyr
Lombard Street, EC3
This church is dedicated to a king of East Anglia who was killed by the Danes in AD870. It was rebuilt by Sir Christopher Wren in 1670, and has a distinctive spire.

St Ethelburga-the-Virgin
Bishopsgate, EC2
Entered by a 14th-century doorway, this tiny medieval building is one of the best preserved of the City's pre-Fire churches. It was once famous for the picturesque shops which obscured the front, but were demolished in 1932.

St Etheldreda, or Ely Chapel
Ely Place, EC1
Originally built in the 13th century, this little chapel was allowed to deteriorate over the centuries, and was finally almost totally destroyed during the Blitz. Only the façade and some Roman foundations survived, and these have been incorporated into the present structure. The chapel is two-storeyed and has a massive vaulted undercroft dating from 1252. It is the oldest pre-Reformation Roman Catholic church in London.

St Ethelburga, Bishopsgate.

St George
Bloomsbury Way, WC1
Noted for its striking façade, this 18th-century church was built by Nicholas Hawksmoor. It has a Corinthian portico supported by six columns, and a tower and spire crowned by a statue of George I wearing a Roman toga.

St George
Borough High Street, Southwark, SE1
Rebuilt by the architect John Price in 1734–36, this church has a spired tower with octagonal upper stages. The galleried interior is watched over by Victorian carvings of cherubs affixed to the ceiling.

St George Hanover Square
St George's Street, W1
Many fashionable weddings have taken place in this church since it was built in the early part of the 18th century. It is an impressive Classical-style building with a galleried interior lit by 16th-century Flemish windows. Among those married here have been Benjamin Disraeli and Theodore Roosevelt.

St Giles Cripplegate
Fore Street, EC2
Only the nave and tower of the original church built here in the 14th century survive. It was largely rebuilt in the 16th century, with further additions made to the tower a century later, and was badly damaged during World War II. It has now been restored. Among the many famous people buried here are Sir Martin Frobisher and the poet John Milton.

St Giles-in-the-Field
St Giles High Street, WC2
This church's fine 161-ft Baroque steeple makes it a prominent landmark. A church was founded on this site by Matilda, the wife of Henry I, in the 12th century, but the present building dates from the 18th century. It was beautifully restored in 1952–53, and has superb interior decorations and fittings.

St Helen Bishopgate
Great St Helen's, EC3
One of the largest churches in the City, this magnificent structure was built in the 13th century and was originally two churches joined by an arcade of pillars. There are two naves, one of which served a monastery, and the other for the parish. The church is famous for its beautiful brasses, which are usually protected by carpets. Permission must be obtained before rubbings can be made. There is much else of interest in the building, including several excellent monuments, two fine sword-rests (one dating from 1665 and very rare), and a Jacobean pulpit which is beautifully carved.

St James's
Piccadilly, W1
This church was originally built for the Earl of St Alban by Wren in 1676. It was extensively damaged during the Blitz, and was restored to its former glory in 1954. It has a magnificent galleried interior beneath a barrel-vaulted ceiling. The font, reredos, altarpiece, and organ case are all the work of the master-woodcarver, Grinling Gibbons. The organ itself was a gift from Mary II in 1690, and came from Whitehall Palace.

St James Garlickhythe
Upper Thames Street, EC4
Founded as long ago as the 12th century, the present church on this site was built by Wren after the Great Fire, and is one of his more elaborate designs. Its most distinguishing exterior feature is the handsome spire. The interior, which was restored after bomb damage, has excellent woodwork, as well as ironwork hat racks and sword rests. The church reputedly owes its name to the fact that garlic was once sold nearby.

St James-the-Less
Thorndyke Street,
off Vauxhall Bridge Road, SW1
G E Street, one of the most accomplished of Victorian architects, designed this splendid church in 1858. Its plain exterior encases a majestic vaulted interior which is lit by windows made by the famous firm of Clayton and Bell.

St John
Smith Square, SW1
When the architect of this church, Thomas Archer, asked Queen Anne what style she would like it built in, she is reputed to have kicked over a stool, pointed at it, and said 'build me one like that'. In fact the four large towers at each corner of the building serve a strictly functional purpose, in that they were specially designed to prevent the whole structure sinking into the marsh upon which it was built. The church was gutted during World War II, and now serves as a music and cultural centre.

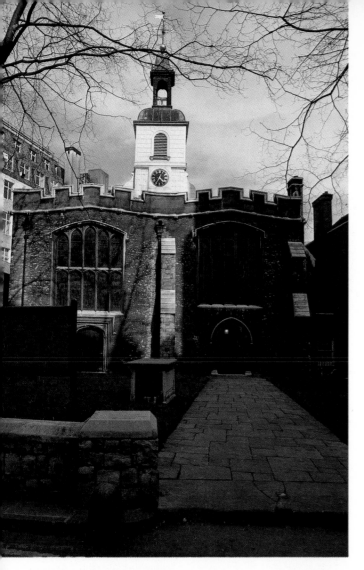

Left: Great St Helen's lies hidden behind the office buildings of Bishopsgate.

Right: The five octagonal stages of the steeple of St Bride.

Below: St Margaret, Westminster, may have been founded in the 11th century but the present building dates from the 15th century, with later additions.

St Katherine Cree
Leadenhall Street, EC3
This church was built in 1631, and is one of the few London churches that escaped damage both in the Great Fire and World War II. It is built in the Classical style, and is now the headquarters of the Industrial Christian Fellowship.

St Lawrence Jewry
Gresham Street, EC2
Rebuilt by Wren on the site of a medieval church, this church stands in the forecourt of the Guildhall. The name Jewry has survived from the period between 1066 and 1290 when the neighbourhood had a large Jewish population. The church was rebuilt after bomb damage, and the present spire incorporates a replica of the incendiary bomb which gutted the interior. It is the guild church of the Corporation of London, and pews are set aside for the lord mayor, sheriffs, and other City dignitaries.

St Leonard
Shoreditch High Street, E1
Restored by George Dance the Younger between 1736 and 1740, this church has an imposing portico and a 192-ft steeple. There have been subsequent renovations following bomb damage in World War II, but the organ console dates from 1756. Old stocks and a whipping post are preserved in the churchyard.

St Magnus the Martyr
Lower Thames Street, EC3
The church which originally stood on this site, dating from Saxon times, overlooked the northern approach to the old London Bridge. It was destroyed in the Great Fire, and was rebuilt by Sir Christopher Wren. A portion of timber from an 8th-century Roman wharf, and a stone from the first arch of old London Bridge, dating from 1176, are preserved in the churchyard near the main entrance. Today the church is hemmed in by tall buildings, but its fine tower is still prominent. Inside, much of the 17th-century woodwork and wrought ironwork has been preserved, including Wren's pulpit.

St Margaret's Lothbury
Lothbury, EC2
Rebuilt by Wren between 1686 and 1690, this church contains a good deal of ancient woodwork from other City churches, including the screen and pulpit from All Hallows the Great, Upper Thames Street, which was demolished in 1894. The Scientific Instrument Makers' Company hold their services here, and the church is also a venue for music recitals.

St Margaret's Westminster
Parliament Square, SW1
Dating from the late 15th century, St Margaret's has been the official church of the House of Commons since 1614. Although it is rather overshadowed by its mighty neighbour, Westminster Abbey, it is equally worthy of attention, and is especially notable for its wealth of monuments. The glass in the east window, 16th-century work from the Netherlands, is considered to be the finest in London. Chaucer and William Caxton were famous early parishioners, and both Samuel Pepys and Sir Winston Churchill were married here.

St Margaret Pattens
Rood Lane, Eastcheap, EC3
This church was redesigned by Wren, and contains much interesting woodwork, including the only 17th-century canopied churchwardens' pews in the City, and a beadles' pew complete with a low punishment bench where members of the congregation who misbehaved were made to sit for the remainder of the service. The name Pattens is thought to derive from the wooden soles, mounted on iron rings called pattens, designed to raise the wearer above the debris of London's streets, which were made and sold in a nearby lane.

St Martin-within-Ludgate
Ludgate Hill, EC4
It is thought that a church stood on this site some 13 centuries ago, but reliable records date only from the 12th century. It was rebuilt in 1437, destroyed in the Great Fire, and subsequently rebuilt by Wren in 1684. He incorporated the remains of the old tower into the fabric of the new church. The interior is magnificently decorated, and contains much carved woodwork by Grinling Gibbons, and a double 17th-century church warden's chair, believed to be the only one of its kind in existence.

119

St Martin-in-the-Fields
Trafalgar Square, WC2
The medieval church on this site, then surrounded as its name suggests by open fields, was extensively remodelled by James Gibbs in the early 18th century. It has an imposing temple-like portico, and a spacious galleried interior. Buckingham Palace is within the parish boundaries, and there are royal boxes at the east end of the church. The vaulted crypt contains a 16th-century chest and an 18th-century whipping post, but is better known for the fact that it is opened each night as a shelter for the homeless. This carries on the tradition of H R L Sheppard, a World War I army chaplain, who, on his return from the Front, always kept the church open for servicemen or others who were stranded.

St Mary
Rotherhithe, SE16
Rebuilt during the 18th century, this church has close connections with the sea and sailors. The altar table and sanctuary chairs are made from timber from the 18th-century warship *Fighting Temeraire*, and the nave columns are made from ships' masts enclosed in plaster.

St Mary Abchurch
Cannon Street, EC4
Wren rebuilt this church about 15 years after the Great Fire had destroyed the original, and subsequent renovations have done nothing to alter the late 17th-century appearance. It stands in a secluded courtyard, and is noted for its painted ceiling by William Stow, and rare Grinling Gibbons reredos. Most of the original fittings have survived, notably the pulpit, font, and finely carved pews.

St Mary Aldermary
Queen Victoria Street, EC4
One of the few churches that Wren rebuilt in the Gothic style after the Great Fire, this church was greatly altered during the 19th century. However, the beautiful fan-vaulted ceilings survive, as do Wren's pulpit and font.

St Mary-at-Hill
Eastcheap, EC3
Since it was damaged during the Great Fire, this church has been restored and rebuilt several times, beginning with Wren's work of about 1672. Its modest exterior encloses one of the finest church interiors in the City. There is much fine plasterwork, and the fittings are superb. The only complete set of box pews in the City can be seen here, and there are some magnificent Georgian sword rests.

The interior of St Mary-le-Bow with its hanging rood, designed by John Hayward, and so placed to allow an uninterrupted view of the altar and the episcopal throne behind it.

St Martin-in-the-Fields originally faced into St Martin's Lane but it was remodelled in the 19th century. Gibb's combination of classical portico and tower was a novelty in its day and has since been widely copied.

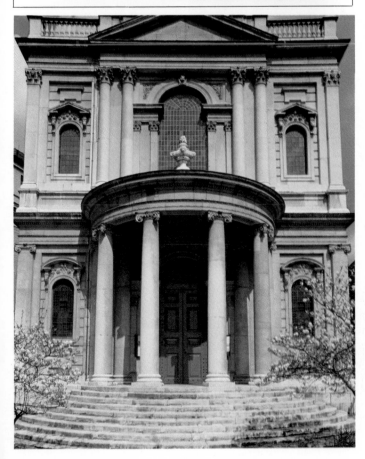

St Mary-le-Bow
Cheapside, EC2

Restored by Wren after the Great Fire, this church was extensively fire-damaged during the Blitz. Wren's steeple survived, however, and its lofty spire, crowned by a 9-ft weathervane in the form of a dragon, still towers over Cheapside. The famous Bow Bells originally rang as a curfew. Those born within their sound are said to be true Cockneys, and it was their distinctive peal which is said to have recalled Dick Whittington from Highgate Hill. The bells were recast after severe damage in 1941, and rang out anew in 1961.

St Mary-le-Strand
Strand, WC2

The present building on this site, designed by James Gibbs in the early 18th century, is one of the best examples of Italian-influenced church architecture in London.

St Mary Woolnoth
King William Street, EC4

Partly damaged in the Great Fire, and subsequently restored by Wren, this church was completely rebuilt by Nicholas Hawksmoor between 1716 and 1727 in a highly original, almost fortified, style. The interior has a tremendous feeling of sumptuous spaciousness which is heightened by the groups of Corinthian columns supporting the ceiling.

St Michael-upon-Cornhill
Cornhill, EC3

This church was built by Wren after the Great Fire, and its fine Gothic tower was added by Hawksmoor in 1721. Sir George Gilbert Scott added many Victorian embellishments. The font and the altar-table date from the late 17th century, but the most unusual, and decorative, object is the carved wooden pelican by George Patterson, which dates from 1775.

St Michael Paternoster Royal
Upper Thames Street, EC4

Dick Whittington met the cost of rebuilding this church in 1409 and he was buried here in 1423, but his tomb was destroyed during the Great Fire. Wren rebuilt the church, but it was badly damaged by a flying bomb in 1944, and the restored building was not consecrated until 1968.

St Nicholas Cole Abbey
Queen Victoria Street, EC4

One of the first churches which Wren worked on after the Great Fire, St Nicholas was gutted by incendiary bombs in 1940. The architect Arthur Bailey undertook the rebuilding in 1962, adhering to Wren's design, and preserving the unusual spire, which has an inverted trumpet shape and is crowned by a weathervane in the shape of a ship.

The lovely church of St Mary-le-Strand stands on an island site in the Strand.

St Olave
Hart Street, EC3

Samuel Pepys and Admiral Sir William Penn saved this 15th-century church from the Great Fire by having the surrounding buildings torn down. No one, however, could prevent bomb damage in 1941, and the rebuilding was subsequently carried out by Ernest Glanfield. Access to the church from Seething Lane is via an unusual gateway decorated with skulls, which Dickens describes as belonging to the church of St Ghostly Grim in his *Uncommercial Traveller*. Pepys and his wife Elizabeth are buried here.

St Paul
Deptford, SE14

Built between 1712 and 1730 to a distinctive Baroque design by Thomas Archer, this church has a fine circular portico supported by Tuscan columns and surmounted by a slim tower. The square interior is galleried and has many Dutch oak fittings.

St Peter-upon-Cornhill
Bishopsgate Corner, EC3

This church, which stands on the highest ground in the City, is believed to occupy a site on which a church has stood since the 2nd century. This makes it by far the oldest church site in London. The present church was built by Wren after the Great Fire, and contains many fine fittings, including a 17th-century font and two Wren-type churchwardens' pews. However, the most outstanding feature is the chancel screen, designed by Wren and his 16-year-old daughter. Lunchtime recitals are held in the church, and the Players of St Peter-upon-Cornhill perform colourful plays selected from medieval mystery plays.

St Sepulchre
Holborn Viaduct, EC1

Wren assisted in the rebuilding of this church after the Great Fire. It is the largest of the City parish churches, and contains some 17th-century pews and a fine Renatus Harris organ, dating from 1677. The churchyard was so popular with bodysnatchers during the 18th century that a Watch House was erected so that the corpses could be guarded. This was restored following war damage. St Sepulchre's is known as the Musicians' Church, and the Musicians' Chapel contains the ashes of Sir Henry Wood, founder of the Promenade Concerts.

St Stephen Walbrook
Walbrook, EC4

This church is one of Wren's masterpieces, and has what is believed to be the first dome built into any English church. It was badly damaged during World War II, and restored during the 1950s. At the time of printing this superb church was undergoing extensive repairs and was temporarily closed to the public.

St Vedast
Foster Lane, EC2
The most noteworthy feature of this Wren church is its elegant steeple. Inside there are a number of ancient fittings from defunct City churches.

Southwark Cathedral
Borough High Street, SE1
A church has stood on this site since the 7th century, but it was not until 1905 that the basically 16th-century parish church of St Saviour was elevated to cathedral status. Despite rebuilding, particularly during the 19th century, its medieval Gothic style has remained largely intact, and parts of the church date back to at least the 13th century. There are many monuments in the building, including an unusual one to a 17th-century quack doctor called Lyonell Lockyer. Ancient tombs include that of Edmund Shakespeare, William's younger brother.

Westminster Cathedral
Ashley Place, Victoria Street, SW1
This is the principal Roman Catholic cathedral in Britain, and was built between 1895 and 1903 in an Italian-Byzantine style by the distinguished architect J F Bentley. It is an imposing building, with a 273-ft campanile and the widest nave in England. The interior is lavishly decorated with yellow, red and white marble, and there are several chapels dedicated to British saints. Eric Gill's early 20th-century Stations of the Cross adorn the main piers and are the most outstanding works in the cathedral.

Left: The nave of Southwark Cathedral was rebuilt in the late 19th century by Sir Arthur Blomfield in a pleasing Gothic style.

Below: A 15th-century boss of a devil's head swallowing a human figure, now to be seen in the south aisle.

London's Shops
and Markets

The City of London has surprisingly few famous shops – the capital's well-known shopping areas are mostly in the West End, with such world-famous names as Oxford Street, Regent Street, Bond Street, Piccadilly and Knightsbridge. In some cases, shops along a particular road specialise in certain types of goods, as in Charing Cross Road and Edgware Road. Other roads have a more general mixture of shops, where, in a short distance, almost anything can be purchased. London also boasts a wide range of specialist shops – a selection of which is given on pages 126–129.

Oxford Street

Justifiably famous, Oxford Street is the backbone of London's shopping area. There are no particular specialities, but it is the home of many of London's big department stores and has many clothes, shoe, and fashion shops.

The busiest stretch is between Marble Arch and Oxford Circus, and not far from Marble Arch is **Marks & Spencer's** largest branch, a favourite with shoppers from all over the world for reasonably-priced good quality clothing and other goods. Nearby is **Selfridges**, London's second-largest department store and especially popular for its food hall, restaurants, kitchenware and cosmetics departments. Other department stores along Oxford Street include **D H Evans**, **Debenhams**, **Bournes**, and **John Lewis**, which has a slogan 'never knowingly undersold', and has a reputation for competitively priced household goods and fabrics.

Other inexpensive clothing stores include **British Home Stores** and **C & A**, while nearly every fashion and shoe store chain has at least one branch in Oxford Street. The **HMV** record shop with its four floors of records and tapes is the largest in Europe, and an interesting shop just outside Oxford Circus Underground station is the **Goldsmiths & Silversmiths Association**, displaying Wedgwood pottery, glass and other gifts.

Regent Street

More department stores and fashion shops are to be found in Regent Street, which crosses Oxford Street at Oxford Circus. The department stores include **Dickins & Jones**, **Swan & Edgar**, **Liberty & Co**, world-famous for its fabrics, and **Waring & Gillow**, renowned for beautiful furniture and furnishings. Classic British-style clothing will be found at shops such as **Jaeger**, **Austin Reed** and **Aquascutum**. Also on Regent Street is the well-known **Hamleys** toy store and **Garrard**, the Queen's jeweller, which is responsible for the upkeep of the Crown Jewels.

The Christmas lights in Regent Street are always a great attraction.

London's Shops and Markets

From stunningly unique fashion and bespoke suits to low-cost everyday wear, from exquisite hand-made jewellery to cheap souvenirs, from things to make the connoisseurs drool to a strange selection of bric-a-brac, London is the shopping centre for Europe, if not the world. On the following pages are introductions to the capital's main shopping areas, its specialist shops, and its street and trade markets, all of which make London a uniquely exciting place to shop.

Bond Street

New Bond Street runs down from Oxford Street to Burlington Gardens, where it becomes Old Bond Street, and continues to Piccadilly. This is one of London's most expensive streets, where leading names in fashion, jewellery, and beauty salons alternate with premises of famous art dealers. Fashion shops such as **Yves Saint Laurent**, **Ted Lapidus**, **Gucci**, **Kurt Geiger**, and **Magli** are the sort of establishment where anyone who has to ask the price can't afford it. **Asprey & Co** specialises in the fine, rare, and beautiful in leather, gold, silver, jewellery, and antiques, and there is one department store – **Fenwick** – which sells mainly women's fashions. **Elizabeth Arden**, **Max Factor**, and **Yardley** each have a beauty salon and there are a number of photographic shops in New Bond Street, notably **Dixons** and **Wallace Heaton**.

Piccadilly

There seem to be more airlines and tourist boards represented in Piccadilly than shops, but those that are here are some of the most important names in London. On the opposite side of Piccadilly Circus from Swan & Edgar is the old-established clothes and sportswear store of **Lillywhites**.

Piccadilly itself was a fashionable area in the 19th century, and the shops here reflect it. Almost opposite the Royal Academy is **Fortnum & Mason** which stocks the finest food and drink as well as a variety of other goods. **Swaine, Ardeney, Brigg & Sons** nearby is the place to go for high-quality leather goods, umbrellas and riding equipment. Burlington Arcade, off Piccadilly, has some of the most elegant small shops in London, where ties, woollen goods, and antique and modern jewellery can be bought.

Simpson is a first-class tailor and outfitter in Piccadilly, but the well-heeled gentleman will buy his clothing in streets off either side of Piccadilly. He will have his shirts hand-made in Jermyn Street, and his suits supplied from a Savile Row or Sackville Street tailor. Those who can't afford such things will go to **Moss Brothers**, on King Street off the Strand, where men's and women's dress clothing for any occasion can be hired or bought.

Tottenham Court Road

Running up from New Oxford Street to Euston Road, Tottenham Court Road was once thought of as the furniture centre for London. Today it is predominantly known for its hi-fi and electrical equipment shops such as the many branches of **Lasky** and **Lion House**, which has a hi-fi department store on the corner of Store Street. There are still, however, a number of good furnishing stores, the largest being **Heal & Son Ltd**.

Top left: Mr Fortnum and Mr Mason greet each other on the Fortnum and Mason's clock, Piccadilly.

Top right: Marks & Spencer's largest branch, near Marble Arch.

Above: Savile Row, home of some of the world's most exclusive tailors.

Right: Uniformed beadles ring handbells before locking up the elegant Burlington Arcade at 5.30 pm.

Newer and smaller, but no less striking, is **Habitat**, whose popular furniture and furnishings are of a modern design. Other interesting shops on Tottenham Court Road are **Paperchase**, which has a unique range of cards, posters, wrapping paper and other stationery, and **The Reject Shop** which stocks a wide range of seconds in pottery and household goods.

Edgware Road

Shops here, such as **Henry's Radio**, stock a wide range of electrical and electronic goods, from tiny components and kits to complete equipment.

Charing Cross Road

Charing Cross Road is at the southern end of Tottenham Court Road and is the home of a great variety of new and second-hand bookshops as well as shops selling music and musical instruments. Of the bookshops, **Foyles** must be the most famous, and **Macari's** and **Scarth** are two of the many shops stocking musical instruments, though these days most of their trade is in guitars, electric keyboards, and amplifiers. Shaftesbury Avenue, which crosses Charing Cross Road at Cambridge Circus, also has many music shops.

Knightsbridge

Though the Knightsbridge, Brompton Road and Sloane Street area has some of the most luxurious fashion boutiques, antique shops and department stores in London, they all tend to be overshadowed by the magnificence of **Harrods**, the largest department store in Europe. The legend of Harrods is that it sells everything – from fresh octopus to travelling rowing machines, from alabaster bathtubs to gold-plated xylophones. Equally notable, but not as comprehensive, is the **Harvey Nichols** department store in Sloane Street. It is a luxurious store particularly noted for women's and children's wear as well as all kinds of furniture and furnishings. Also popular is **The Scotch House**, which specialises in Scottish woollens, knitwear, and woven tartans.

Kensington High Street

At the western end of Hyde Park, the two roads of Kensington High Street and Kensington Church Street make up this lively and fashionable off-centre shopping area. The department store **John Barker** specializes in household goods. Going down Kensington High Street, chain clothing stores like **C & A**, **Marks and Spencer**, **British Home Stores**, and individual fashion shops such as **Crocodile** and **Feathers** mingle with supermarkets and exotic restaurants to give a unique atmosphere. Kensington Church Street is a haven for antique collectors at its eastern end, and at its western end for those looking out for the most up-to-date in clothing.

Carnaby Street and the King's Road

Perhaps one of the most well-known names in London, Carnaby Street is a pedestrian precinct behind Regent Street which in the 1960s had the most adventurous boutiques selling the trendiest gear in town. It still has a lively atmosphere and a number of modern men's and children's fashion boutiques, but the spirit of Carnaby Street has moved over the last few years to the King's Road in Chelsea. Along here, among some very sophisticated antique, furnishing and fashion shops, are astounding eye-openers in clothes shops.

Ancient and Old Established Shops

There are a number of small, old-fashioned shops dotted around London's streets which typify the Victorian 'gaslight' image of the capital. Those mentioned below have retained their essential character, together with their original façades and fittings.

R Allen and Co
117 Mount Street, W1
This butchers' shop has a dark sculptured exterior and has served the residents of Mayfair for almost 200 years. It retains the mosaic wall tiles and threshold for which butchers' shops were once famous.

Arthur Beale
194 Shaftsbury Avenue, WC2
Rope has been made by this company for something approaching 400 years. The premises were originally located on the old Fleet River. Arthur Beale is now a general chandlers' selling wire rope, rigging and charts.

J Floris
89 Jermyn Street, SW1
Established in 1739, J Floris continues to sell perfume from its small but impressive premises, which are presided over by descendants of the original founder. It is considered to be London's leading perfumer.

Fribourg and Treyer
31 Haymarket, SW1
The oldest building in the Haymarket, these low-windowed premises date from the 18th century. Fribourg and Treyer have sold snuff and tobacco since 1720, and they also specialise in cigars, and the full range of smokers' requisites, including lighters and pipes.

Below: Cheeses of every variety can be bought from Paxton and Whitfield

London's Specialist Shops

The section which follows contains details of some of the ancient and specialist shops which may be found in central and outer London – some well known, some more obscure. Their prices range from the sublime to the fairly ridiculous – £6,000 for a pair of hand-made shotguns to a matter of pence for a false moustache. They all have one indisputable factor in common – they are an essential part of London's infinite variety.

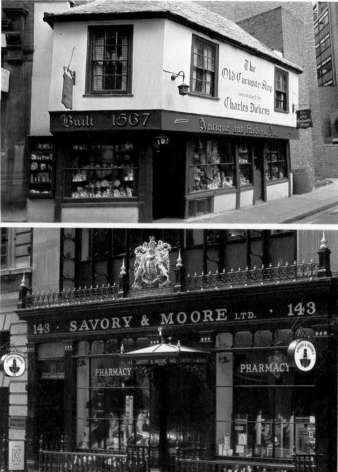

Fulham Pottery
210 New King's Road, SW6
Founded in 1671, this is said to be the oldest pottery in the country. Nowadays clay, tools and other equipment are on sale and complete beginners kits are also available.

Inderwick's
45 Carnaby Street, W1
Established in 1797, Inderwick's are the country's oldest pipe-makers. Their extensive stock includes briars, hookahs and meerschaums.

James Lock
6 St James's Street, SW1
Established as hatters for over 200 years, Locks made the first bowler hat, known as the *Coke* after its inventor. Bowlers are still made to measure on the premises.

The Old Curiosity Shop
Portsmouth Street, WC2
This antique shop, dating from around the 17th century, claims to have been the model for Charles Dickens' *Old Curiosity Shop*, although some scholars insist that it was actually located opposite the National Portrait Gallery.

Paxton and Whitfield
93 Jermyn Street, SW1
An old-established cheese shop, crammed with cheeses of the highest standard from all over the world. An unmistakeable aroma guides patrons to its portals.

Purdey
57 South Audley Street, W1
For more than 100 years, Purdey's have been the foremost makers of sporting guns. Each weapon is hand-made and today an order takes around four years to be completed.

Savory and Moore
143 New Bond Street, W1
These 19th-century premises are said to contain the oldest chemist's shop in London.

G Smith
Charing Cross Road, WC2
An old-established tobacconists, specialising in snuff.

Below: R Allen's is a traditional English butcher's shop.

James Smith
53 New Oxford Street, WC1
Umbrellas and sticks of all kinds have been made and sold here since 1830. Smith's is notable for its old-fashioned signs and for the variety of its stock, which includes custom-made sword sticks and ceremonial maces for African chiefs. They also undertake repairs.

Antique Shops

Spink
5 King Street, SW1
Famous as coin and medal dealers since the mid-17th century, this shop has a wide selection of ancient and modern coins and decorations from all parts of the world.

Lock's still retains the reputation for superb headwear that it established over 200 years ago.

Strike One
1a Camden Walk, N1
These specialists in English 18th- and 19th-century clocks also undertake repairs.

Winifred Myers
91 St Martin's Lane, WC2
A dealer in autographs. The stock includes the correspondence of famous men and women in the field of the arts, politics, etc, and covers a period of 500 years. Apart from Napoleon, all the subjects are English.

Through the Looking Glass
563 King's Road, SW6
Specialists in 19th-century mirrors which come in all imaginable sizes.

Troll
27 Beauchamp Place, SW3
The only genuine Scandinavian antique shop in the country. It sells 18th-century furniture, pine tables, and chairs.

Art and Handicraft Shops

Candle Makers Supplies
28 Blythe Road, W14
Candle-making kits are sold here together with moulds and all materials associated with the craft. Books on the subject are also available.

Handweavers Studio and Gallery
29 Haroldstone Road, Walthamstow, E17
This shop sells and hires looms, spinning wheels, and weaving materials. Instruction for weavers is also available.

Phillips and Page
50 Kensington Church Street, W8
This shop sells everything connected with brass rubbing. Information on the locations of suitable brasses is available together with instructions for obtaining permission to rub.

Alec Tiranti
21 Goodge Place, W1
All materials required for sculpting and wood-carving may be obtained here including goggles, tools and casting equipment.

Edgar Udny
83–85 Bondway, SW8
Specialise in all kinds of ceramic and mosaic tiles together with laying and cutting tools.

Button, Bead, and Stone Shops

Baku Trading Company
80 Portobello Road, W8
African trading beads are sold here.

The Button Queen
23 St Christopher's Place, W1
Antique and ornamental buttons are the speciality in this shop.

Eaton Bag Co
16 Manette Street, W1
All kinds of sea shells are on sale here together with fossils, dried starfish, and other exotic specimens.

Ells and Farrier
5 Princes Street, W1
These small premises carry an unbelievable stock of all kinds of beads and sequins suitable for stringing or decorating.

A brass rubbing of Sir Humphrey Stafford in Philips and Page.

Gemrocks
7 Brunswick Shopping Centre, WC1
Stones of all kinds, precious and semi-precious, are on sale here. Gemrocks also sells tumblers, polishers, cutters and books on jewellery making.

A Taylor
1 Silver Place, W1
The most all-embracing stock of buttons in London, if not in the country, is to be found here – leather, horn, plastic, etc.

Books and Records

Bloomsbury Bookshop
31 Great Ormond Street, WC1
One of the best-known secondhand bookshops devoted to literature on jazz, this shop is owned by jazz trumpeter John Chilton.

Children's Book Centre
229 Kensington High Street, W8
The entire floor space of this shop is devoted to books for children up to the age of thirteen. Talks by authors and artists are often given and a quarterly newsletter dealing with new children's books is also available.

Floris is London's leading perfumer.

Cinema Bookshop
13 Great Russell Street, WC1
As the name implies this shop is filled with books and magazines covering all aspects of the world of cinema, including biographies of stars and directors.

Dobell's Folk Record Shop
75 Charing Cross Road, WC2
Dobell's is said to have the largest collection of 'blues' records in England.

Dobell's Jazz Record Shop
77 Charing Cross Road, WC2
A companion to the Folk Record Shop, covering all types of jazz. New and secondhand records and tapes are available.

John Faustus
Jermyn Street, SW1
Rare books and prints are the speciality here.

Foyles
119 Charing Cross Road, WC2
The best known, and probably the largest, bookshop in London with a stock of over 4 million volumes. There is a large secondhand department where books of all kinds are bought and sold.

Samuel French, *26 Southampton Street, Strand, WC2*
Famous primarily as publishers of plays, French's also has a theatrical bookshop. Plays of all kinds are available for sale. Part of French's premises were once occupied by David Garrick, the famous actor.

HMV
363 Oxford Street, W1
HMV is said to carry the largest stock of records and tapes in the country, if not in Europe. Most general LPs are available and international artists are also featured.

Moondogs
400 High Street North, E12
Specialists in old recordings of popular music, notably rock and roll and rhythm and blues.

A Moroni and Son
68 Old Compton Street, W1
Newspapers and magazines from all over the world are sold here.

Motor Books
33 St Martin's Court, WC2
Literature on all aspects of the motor car is available here, together with volumes dealing with motorcycles and aircraft.

Zwemmer
76–80 Charing Cross Road, WC2
Zwemmer's carry the most extensive stock of English and foreign books on art and architecture in the country.

Clothing Shops

Berman and Nathan
18 Irving Street, WC2
An old-established theatrical costumiers where wigs and all kinds of costumes may be hired. Children are also catered for.

John Lobb
9 St James's Street, SW1
Craftsmen can be seen at work in this old established bespoke shoemakers.

Moss Bros
Bedford Street, WC2
This is the most famous clothing hire firm in Britain. Clothes for all occasions are available and can be altered to suit individual requirements. They can also be purchased. Despite Moss Bros' predominantly male image, ladies' evening wear including fur coats and stoles, wedding and bridesmaids dresses are also in stock.

E H Rann
21 Sicilian Avenue, WC1
Specialists in school and regimental ties and badges.

Scotch House
2 Brompton Road, SW1
The principal suppliers of Scottish knitwear and tartans in London.

A very nonchalant lion from Theatre Zoo.

Theatre Zoo
8 New Row, WC2
Animal costumes of all descriptions are available for hire here.

Food Shops

Bendicks Chocolates
53 Wigmore Street, W1
Some 32 varieties of handmade chocolates are on sale here including bittermints and mint crisps.

Below: Prestat is a high-quality confectioners in South Moulton Street.

Dein's Food Stores
191 Shepherds Bush Market, W12
Specialises in West African and West Indian foods – live snails and salted pigs ears to name but a few. Dein's supply delicacies by post to customers as distant as Moscow and Australia.

Markovitch
371–373 Edgware Road, W2
Specialists in kosher food – meat, groceries, hot beef sandwiches, etc. A takeaway service is available on Sunday nights.

Moore Bros Ltd
248 Fulham Road, SW10
Freshly ground coffee is sold here, together with coffee making equipment. Old scales and grinders are also available.

Parmigiani Figlio
43 Frith Street, W1
London's largest selection of Italian cheeses and foods is sold here. Pasta, salami, herbs and seasonings are also on sale.

Furnishings and Flower Shops

Aquarius
571 King's Road, SW6
All kinds of waterbeds, including king-sized, are on sale here.

Bedlam
114 Kensington Church Street, W8
811 Fulham Road, SW6
All kinds of hanging and space-saving beds are on sale here, including bunks and folding models. They can be made to individual specifications. Old-fashioned nightshirts and caps are also available.

F H Brundle
75 Culford Road, N1
Specialists in nails. All kinds available – wire nails, square nails, lath nails, etc.

This fine brass bell is one of many manufactured by the Whitechapel Bell Foundry.

Fribourg and Treyer is the discerning smoker's paradise.

Chivers Flowers of London
43 Charlotte Street W1
63 Marchmont Street, WC1
129 Tottenham Court Road, W1
Florists who provide a unique service in that bunches of flowers may be obtained from vending machines outside all three branches after the shops have closed.

The Glasshouse
65 Long Acre, WC2
Glassblowers may be seen at work on the premises. All kinds of handblown articles are on sale.

Thomas Goode
19 South Audley Street, W1
This company has produced top quality china for around 150 years, with numerous crowned heads, including Queen Victoria, among its customers. Personal crests or monograms can be provided.

C E Henderson
48 Leadenhall Market, EC3
Specialists in Japanese miniature bonsai trees. Evergreens, apple trees, etc, are available.

Knobs and Knockers
61–65 Judd Street, WC1
Specialise in fittings (knobs, fingerplates, etc) with which to embellish doors. A large range is available in brass, aluminium and china.

Model, Sport and Toy Shops

Barnums Carnival Novelties Ltd
67 Hammersmith Road, W14
Masks, false noses, and many varieties of false beards and moustaches are on sale here.

Beatties
112 High Holborn, W1
Perhaps the largest model shop in existence. Model railways are a speciality here, with a secondhand department, but car, aeroplane and boat kits are also on sale.

Below: Tradition specialises in model soldiers.

Chess Centre
3 Harcourt Street, W1
Specialists in chess sets, carrying a virtually unrivalled stock constructed from a variety of materials.

Davenports
51 Great Russell Street, WC1
The sign showing a rabbit emerging from the traditional top hat proclaims an abundance of conjurers' equipment (professionals get their supplies here).

Kaye Desmonde
17 Kensington Church Walk, W8
A huge collection of English, French and German dolls, mostly dating from the early 20th century and before is on sale here.

The Doll's House
4 Broadley Street, NW8
Antique and reproduction doll's houses are displayed here, but it is very much a collectors' shop. Miniature dolls and furnishings are also available.

German porcelain pipe bowls at Astleys of Jermyn Street.

Hamleys
200 Regent Street, W1
One of the world's largest toy shops. Games, puppets, dolls, etc, can be found here in great quantities at a wide range of prices.

Hardy
61 Pall Mall, SW1
This shop is world-famous for fishing tackle and has sea, game and coarse fishing equipment. Advice on fishing is readily available.

Just Games
1 Lower James Street, W1
Specialists in adult board games, war games, card games and puzzles.

Kites
69 Neal Street, WC2
Sells ready-made kites, kits for building them and books on the subject.

Pollock's Toy Museum
1 Scala Street, W1
Well-known as a museum (see page 99) but a shop is included in the premises where the toy theatres for which Mr Pollock became famous are still on sale, together with many traditional toys.

Steam Age, Mechanical Antiquities
59 Cadogan Street, SW3
Engines, railways and steamboats, mostly collectors items, are available in this shop.

Tradition
5 Shepherd Street, W1
All kinds of lead soldiers are sold here. The stock ranges from Greek and Roman to modern soldiers and includes painted and unpainted items. Antique uniforms and swords are also available.

Miscellaneous Shops

Anything Left-Handed
65 Beak Street, W1
Just what the name implies. Scissors, tin-openers, pen nibs, gardening, kitchen and needlework aids are all available, along with left-handed playing cards (with the symbols on all four corners).

L Cornelissen and Son
22 Great Queen Street, WC2
Artists materials are sold here but an interesting speciality are the quill pens and quills from which pens can be made.

The Folk Shop
Cecil Sharp House,
2 Regents Park Road, NW1
Folk music books and records are available together with a variety of traditional folk instruments such as dulcimers, tabors and melodeons.

Keith Harding
93 Hornsey Road, N7
Specialists in musical boxes of which they hold an extensive stock. Repairs and restoration are also undertaken and books on the subject are sold.

G B Kent and Sons
174a Piccadilly, W1
Kent's have been making hair brushes and toothbrushes, etc, since the 18th century.

London Transport Posters
280 Old Marylebone Road, NW1
Inexpensive and historical posters are available here, mostly depicting the capital's tourist attractions.

Above: A craftsman at work at The Glasshouse

Left: Davenports box of magic tricks

129

Street Markets

There is very little that cannot be purchased in London's street markets. Items on display range from garish junk of dubious usefulness to antiques worth thousands of pounds; from sets of dinner services to some of the best meat and vegetable produce to be found in the country. Many of the markets consist of no more than a few stalls at street corners, but some of them stretch for miles and are stamping grounds for many of London's most colourful characters.

Berwick Street Market
Berwick Street, W1

This cheerful, cluttered market, with its stalls on either side of the road, runs through the heart of Soho. The stallholders are noted for their generally good-humoured banter as they clamour to attract customers. Fruit and vegetable stalls predominate here, but shellfish, clothing, and household goods are also available, and some of the stalls are attached to neighbouring shops. The market is especially crowded at lunchtimes, as shoppers queue up at stalls which are reputed to sell some of the best quality fruit and vegetables in London.

Monday–Saturday

Brixton Market
Electric Avenue, SW9

As this market is set in an area with a large West Indian population, it is not surprising that many of its stalls are stocked with Caribbean fruit and vegetables. There are also second-hand clothes and household goods stalls, and the entire market is enlivened by the compulsive rhythms of West Indian music.

Monday–Saturday (Wednesday am only)

Right: Flowers in Berwick Street Market.
Below: Further along Berwick Street, shoppers are intent on purchasing appetising products.
Below right: A stall at Covent Garden's street market.
Bottom: Local Brixton housewives busy with their weekly shopping.

Camden Passage
Camden Passage, N1
A vigorous campaign conducted during the early 1960s raised funds which saved this area from demolition. It is a rich and varied mixture of antique shops and stalls, most of the latter appearing on Wednesdays and Saturdays. A holiday atmosphere pervades the market, largely because the majority of the traders give the impression of thoroughly enjoying their work. A few of the shopkeepers have been known to carry relaxation to the extreme by conducting their business from the Camden Head, the market's adopted pub, leaving a note on the shop door to direct prospective customers to their temporary premises. The arcades of the market become very crowded on Saturdays, and only those arriving early can hope to find a bargain. The goods on display are liberally sprinkled with bric-à-brac and Victorian curios, but Camden Passage is as good a place as any for a wide variety of antiques, with dealers specialising in furniture, jewellery, prints, pottery, books, pub mirrors, period clothing, and silverware.
Monday–Saturday (Sunday am only)

Chapel Market
White Conduit Street, N1
This rather congested market is very popular with the locals at weekends. Fruit and vegetables are always available, and there are usually stalls selling fish, groceries, and household goods.
Monday–Sunday am (Thursday am only)

Club Row
Sclater Street, E1
Part of the East End's famous Petticoat Lane complex of street markets, Club Row has stalls selling general household items, but is most famous for its pet market. Creatures on sale range from commonplace domestic pets to exotic animals such as crocodiles, and birds like toucans.
Sunday am

The serious business of selling cloth in Club Row Market.

Above: Shops in Camden Passage display high-quality *objets d'art*.

Left: A stallholder examines his wares at Chapel Market.

Columbia Road Market
Shoreditch, E2
An enormous variety of flowers, plants, and shrubs make this market a Mecca for all gardening enthusiasts.
Sunday am

Dingwalls Market
Camden Lock, NW6
Many of the stalls here are presided over by young and enthusiastic traders. Antiques, bric-à-brac, period and Asian clothes are generally available, and there are also craft and food stalls.
Saturday

East Lane Market
Walworth, SE17
This is an old established general market with some bric-à-brac stalls. Plants, shrubs, and fruit are usually available on Sundays.
Tuesday–Sunday am (Thursday am only)

Farringdon Road
Clerkenwell, EC1
Second-hand books and prints cover the kerbside stalls here. This was once a hunting ground for rare bargains, but most of the elderly gentlemen who rummaged eagerly through the piles of books are no longer in evidence.
Monday–Saturday

Jubilee Market
Covent Garden, WC2
Partly under cover, this small general market opened in Covent Garden at about the time that Covent Garden Market moved to Nine Elms. There are fruit, vegetable, and bric-à-brac stalls, but the greater part of this market contains souvenirs, clothes, craft, jewellery, and record stalls.
Monday–Friday

Leadenhall Market
Gracechurch Street, EC3

There has been a market in the general area of this site since the 14th century, probably established by Edward III in an effort to stamp out a flourishing black market in poultry by compelling all sellers to congregate in the same place. Whatever its origins, Leadenhall, which takes its name from the lead-roofed 14th-century mansion of Sir Hugh Neville that once stood nearby, was a thriving meat and poultry market by the mid-17th century. Samuel Pepys recorded in his diary that he purchased 'a leg of beef, a good one, for sixpence' here. In 1881 Sir Horace Jones built the ornate glass-roofed arcade which covers the 70 or so shops between Leadenhall Street and Lime Street. During the excavations it was discovered that the site occupies what was the centre of Roman London, as the remains of the basilica and other administrative buildings were uncovered. Formerly purely a wholesale market, today Leadenhall is open to the general public and, while still specialising in meat and poultry, also offers fish, vegetables, and plants. The Victorian arcade, containing cafes and pubs in contrast to the rows of carcasses which are suspended on tiers of hooks outside the shops, is noted for its old-time market atmosphere, and is a favourite haunt for City office workers, whether intent on buying, or simply watching the world go by.
Monday–Friday

Leather Lane
Holborn, EC1

Fruit, groceries, vegetables, clothing, household goods of all descriptions – particularly crockery – are always on display here, and some of the most vociferous and quick-witted stallholders in the capital provide a feast of noisy entertainment for the vast crowds who throng the market during the lunch-hour. Bargains abound and the sight of an entire dinner service being expertly tossed in the air is a regular occurrence.
Monday–Friday

Lower Marsh and The Cut
Lambeth, SE1

This busy general market nestles in the shadow of Waterloo Station and becomes very popular during the lunch period.
Monday–Saturday (Thursday am only)

New Caledonian Market
Bermondsey Square, SE1

The old Caledonian Market moved to this site from Islington after the end of World War II, and its modern offspring is now primarily a dealers' antique market. An enormous selection of articles is on view, set out on closely-packed stalls, but those in search of a bargain need to be early risers as a great deal of the trading takes place between 5am and 7am (when the market officially opens). Although something of a closed

Above: An imposing piece of Victorian stonework spanning the arcade of attractive Leadenhall Market.

Right: Held over the heads of the indifferent crowds in Petticoat Lane, the banner of doom.

Above: New Caledonian Market. Evidence of the diverse range of articles on sale is this mixture of china doll's heads, keys and trinkets.

Right: This piece of jewellery demands closer scrutiny from one who has the air of a professional dealer.

community, run principally by dealers for dealers, private collectors and casual visitors are made very welcome. Bric-à-brac, silver, jewellery, clocks, pottery, and porcelain are always available, and furniture, coins, and medals are also featured, but stallholders tend to avoid specialisation, displaying oddments and curios of all descriptions. A pleasant, friendly atmosphere pervades the market, which abounds in colourful and unusual characters.
Friday

Newport Place
Soho, W1

A busy general market where clothes are the predominant articles on sale.
Monday–Saturday

Northcote Road
Battersea, SW11

A bustling fruit and vegetable market situated near Clapham Junction.
Monday–Saturday (Wednesday am only)

North End Road
Fulham, SW6

This general market specialises in fruit and vegetables, and flowers and plants are on sale during the summer months. Other stalls in this cheerful market offer clothes, and household goods.
Monday–Saturday (Thursday am only)

Petticoat Lane
Middlesex Street, E1

Middlesex Street lies to the north of Houndsditch, which was once the habitat of carpenters and glaziers, but is now filled with cut-price warehouses. The street acquired the name Petticoat Lane during the 17th century because of the number of old clothes dealers who congregated here. Despite the fact that it officially became known as Middlesex Street as long ago as 1846 the old name has lived on, at least as far as the Sunday market is concerned. It is one of the most famous of all London markets, and opens around 9am, but all the stallholders begin to set up their premises about 7.30am before an interested audience of sightseers. Despite its present-day cosmopolitan atmosphere, engendered by the Indian, West Indian, and Jewish communities which are prevalent in the area, Petticoat Lane still retains its essential Cockney character. The maze of stalls occupies every available corner, and there is very little in the way of household goods and clothes of every description that cannot be purchased.
Sunday am

Portobello Road
Notting Hill, W11

Named after Puerto Bello on the Gulf of Mexico, where Admiral Vernon won a victory over the Spanish in 1735, Portobello Road has been noted for its antique shops and stalls since the 1950s. It reached the height of its fame during the late '60s and early '70s when it became the centre of London's hippy community. The atmosphere has changed now, although it is just as bizarre, with a heady mixture of shoppers, punks, surviving hippies, antique collectors, tourists, and eccentrics belonging to no identifiable group. A general market with fruit, vegetable and meat stalls operates all the week, but it is on Saturdays that all the stalls and arcades are opened. The stalls and shops, of which there are more than 2,000, contain all kinds of furniture, clothes, jewellery, ancient gramophones and records, books, bottles, coins, medals, toys, a great deal of Victoriana, and an endless selection of junk. Buskers, street singers, photographers (some with monkeys), and street performers jostle with and cajole the crowds. Reggae and punk music fills the air in some parts of the road, and everywhere there are sounds of usually good-natured haggling. It is rare to find a genuine bargain in the antique stalls at the lower end of the road these days, since all the traders are experts, but real finds can sometimes be made amongst the piles of junk on the stalls beyond the Westway Flyover.
Monday–Saturday (Thursday am only)

Right and above: Portobello Road is a street of considerable contrasts. Along it can be found everything from expensive antique stalls presided over by knowing proprietors to street music provided by a host of buskers.

Ridley Road
Hackney, E8

One of the better known of London's East End markets, the stalls here are patronised by the local Jewish and West Indian communities. It is a general market, with many fruit and vegetable stalls, and becomes very crowded on Saturdays.
Tuesday–Saturday (Thursday am only)

Roman Road *Tower Hamlets, E3*
A busy market with stalls on either side of the road. There is a good variety of wares, and a 'pie and mash' shop provides traditional Cockney refreshment.
Monday (am only)–Saturday

Shepherd's Bush *W12*
Stalls specialising in West Indian food, pets, and household goods will be found in the market here. It extends as far as Goldhawk Road beside a railway viaduct.
Wednesday, Friday, and Saturday

Walthamstow *The High Street, E17*
This extensive general market straggles along either side of Walthamstow's main street. It is particularly busy on Thursdays.
Monday–Saturday (Wednesday am only)

Wembley Stadium *Wembley, NW10*
A large open-air market is held here every Sunday on part of the stadium car park. A large variety of goods is sold, and usually there is free parking.
Sunday am

Wentworth Street
Tower Hamlets, E1

This general market is engulfed by Petticoat Lane on Sundays. For the rest of the week it caters for locals, and has some excellent stalls selling Jewish and West Indian foods.
Daily

Whitechapel Road
Tower Hamlets, E1

Stalls line the pavements of this famous East End thoroughfare, multiplying on Saturdays when the market really comes to life.
Monday–Saturday

Whitecross Street
Islington, EC1

A busy market which caters, to a large extent, for lunch-time shoppers. It is particularly crowded on Wednesdays and Fridays.
Monday–Saturday

Woolwich Market
Beresford Square, SE18

This small market is very popular and has a wide variety of stalls.
Monday–Saturday (Thursday am only)

Left and far left: An archetypal cockney street trader getting down to work with relish one Sunday morning in Petticoat Lane, and a rather specialised display of footwear – the Lane is renowned for material and clothing.

133

Trade Markets

Noise, a rich variety of smells, and seeming confusion typify London's trade markets. In fact all the business is carried out with literally breath-taking efficiency and speed, and only those who arrive at dawn will see the markets operating at full spate.

A Billingsgate porter wearing his traditional 'bobbing hat'.

Billingsgate Market
Lower Thames Street, EC3
The first official mention of this historic wholesale fish market was made as long ago as the end of the 13th century, when a royal charter was granted to the Corporation of London for the sale of fish, but a market is known to have been held on this site at least 400 years earlier. For hundreds of years it was held in the jumble of narrow streets which once made up this area; the fish, and other products which used to be sold here, having been landed at the nearby medieval wharf which was located nearby.

The arcaded building which stands on the site today was built to the designs of Sir Horace Jones in 1875 and brought under one roof the sale of all types of fish – 'wet, dried and shell'. Constructed of yellow stock brick, it is adorned with a figure of Britannia supported by dolphins and has weathervanes in the form of fish.

From about 5am the market becomes a hive of activity and the air is pervaded by a pungent aroma of fish and the uninhibited language of the porters. By 8am most of the business is over and about 300 tons of fish will have changed hands. Some of the porters still wear the traditional headgear called 'bobbing hats' which are believed to be similar in style to those worn by the archers at Agincourt. They are made of tough leather and wood, with flat tops and turned-up brims, and enable each porter to carry about one hundredweight of fish on his head.

After all the transactions have been completed the whole area is washed down and becomes quiet and deserted until the following morning when the hub-bub begins all over again.

The fish trade is a well organised commercial concern despite the old traditions which characterise it. The professional packing, and sorting of this top-quality fish indicates the sophistication of this lucrative business.

Borough Market
Stoney Street, SE3
This fruit and vegetable market claims a direct descent from the market which was held on the old London Bridge for local people to sell their own produce. This ancient market was replaced by a second, founded by Edward VI in the 16th century, and was located in Borough High Street, which was, in its turn, removed to the present location in 1757. Today the market occupies buildings beneath the railway arches of the viaduct serving London Bridge Station, to the south of Southwark Cathedral.

It operates from Monday to Saturday, with traders commencing business as early as 3am. Activity builds up to a crescendo of noise and bustle between 6 and 7am, and most of the business has been completed by the middle of the morning.

Covent Garden
Nine Elms, SW8
The original Covent Garden (the area to the east of Charing Cross Road) owes its name to the fact that the monks of Westminster Abbey had a 40 acre walled garden here.

Following the dissolution of the monasteries in 1537 the land at Covent Garden was eventually granted to the 1st Earl of Bedford in 1552. In 1631 the 4th Earl obtained a licence from Charles I to erect a group of buildings on the site. The architect Inigo Jones was commissioned to design houses which would be suitable for the gentry, and he built these round a piazza modelled on those he had seen in Italy. The square, and the covered walks in front of the buildings, attracted market traders from near and far, and by 1670 the market had received official recognition.

It grew to become the most important fruit, vegetable, and flower market in the country, and in 1830 the first specially-built market premises were erected on the site. These buildings were rapidly outgrown, and by the middle of the 20th century wholesalers had taken over all the streets in the area. Traffic congestion had become a serious problem by this time, and it was decided that the only solution was to move the market to specially-built premises at Nine Elms. The move was made in 1974, to the sorrow of many people, as Covent Garden had a unique and irreplaceable character.

Strenuous efforts have, however, been made to preserve something of the feel of the old market area. The 19th-century Flower Market building has been renovated and will eventually house the London Transport Museum and the Theatre Museum.

The market has now settled into its new home at Nine Elms, and there is no doubt that the vast building makes up in increased efficiency what it lacks in character.

Above: Painted by John Collet in about 1750, this picture shows stalls in Covent Garden's piazza. In the background can be seen the 'actors church' of St Paul's, designed by Inigo Jones, and used as a background by George Bernard Shaw in *Pygmalion*.

Right: Heaving trays of fruit and vegetables about at the market's new home at Nine Elms is as much a part of daily life as it has been for centuries.

Below: Flowers are the most perishable items sold at Covent Garden, so florists must examine the blooms carefully before placing orders that may involve hundreds of pounds.

Smithfield Market

Charterhouse Street, EC1

Smithfield is London's principal wholesale meat market, and its annual turnover of some 200,000 tons of produce makes it one of the largest meat, poultry, and provision markets in the world. The total area covered by all the market buildings is over eight acres.

Smithfield, which is derived from 'Smoothfield', was originally an open space located just outside the old city walls. The site has great historical significance as the scene of tournaments, fairs, and the location of a horse and cattle market from the 12th to the 19th century. One of the most famous of all English annual fairs, St Bartholomew's, was held here every August, and attracted traders and customers from all over Europe. Medieval fairs like St Bartholomew's tended to concentrate on single commodities, and the more important fairs contributed substantially to international trade.

Nearly 300 people were burnt at the stake at Smithfield in religious persecutions during the reign of Queen Mary. It is not surprising, therefore, that numerous reports of groans, shrieks, and the sound of crackling flames have been made by startled pedestrians passing through the area late at night.

Up until the middle of the 19th century all cattle sold at Smithfield were driven through the narrow and congested streets of central London. At one time the number of beasts flowing in and out of the market amounted to 70,000 a week. It was not until 1867 that a government statute placed restrictions on the droving of cattle through the capital's thoroughfares. It was at this time that the present Central London Meat Market was constructed. It was designed by Sir Horace Jones and is a Renaissance-style building consisting of iron and glass arcades fronted with red brick and flanked by domed towers. To the west of the cattle market is the Poultry Market building, which was built in 1963 to replace a Victorian structure that was destroyed by fire in 1958.

The meat porters at Smithfield are traditionally called 'bummarees', and are highly skilled at manoeuvring heavily-laden barrows through the bustle and hurly-burly of the early morning market.

Smithfield's market buildings cover over eight acres.

Spitalfields Market
Commercial Street, E1

Named after the priory of St Mary Spital which was founded here in 1197, Spitalfields refers both to the area and to the wholesale market, which trades in fruit, vegetables, and flowers.

The market covers five acres to the east of Liverpool Street Station, on a site which was once a Roman burial ground. When Tudor brickmakers were digging the clay for which this area was once famous, they found a number of stone coffins, pots, and coins. In 1682 Charles II granted letters-patent to John Balch and his heirs authorising them to hold a market here on two days each week.

In those days Spitalfields was a fertile agricultural area, and the market sold all kinds of local produce together with goods made in the vicinity. During the 18th and 19th centuries Spitalfields was swallowed up by the dense ranks of urban housing which became some of the worst slums in London. It was here that Jack the Ripper committed his last and most horrific murder.

The market site was bought in 1902 by the City Corporation, who built upon it the New Market buildings which were opened in 1928 by Queen Mary. The buildings have been extensively modernised, and now provide stands for 150 wholesale merchants. There are extensive underground chambers, used principally for ripening bananas, beneath the market. Trading begins at 5.30am every weekday and is generally completed by 9am.

Above: Fruit and vegetables from far-flung places such as Israel, the Caribbean and the Mediterranean countries adorn the stalls of Spitalfields Market.

Right: Well-worn wooden handbarrows in unfamiliar repose. They last for years – a sound argument for clinging to traditional materials.

Below left: Taking a brief respite to watch the world go by.
Below right: The administration behind the scenes – a sight that has changed little since Dickens' day.

Green London

Green London

Escape from the crowded streets of London lies within the capital itself. It is in the cultivated 'wildness' of the great parks; the secluded shrubberies of the squares; in the riverside walks and gardens, and through the ancient gates of the Inns of Court. Even more so, it is in the marvellous breathing spaces of London's heaths, commons, and the wonderfully unspoiled crescent of Epping Forest. London may well be one of the greenest cities on earth, and the greenness keeps it sane.

Autumn light gives St James's Park a magical look that makes it seem far from city turmoil.

Crocuses in St James's Park are one of the first and most welcome signs of spring.

The Royal Parks

St James's Park

Here, on the fringe of one of London's busiest shopping and entertainment centres, is a green oasis of peace.

St James's is a reminder of the countryside, a great contrast to the city greyness that surrounds it. In autumn it is one of the few places in the West End where the commuter can see the first frosts; in summer it is full of relaxing office workers, many of whom have made a habit of feeding the park's flourishing population of birds.

Medieval St James's was a vastly different place, a brooding, marshy waste where the morning breeze stirred mist round a hospital for female lepers. Things changed in the 16th century when Henry VIII swept away the hospital, built St James's Palace and converted the surrounding area into a deer park. The Stuart kings drained the marsh and formed the lake, and Charles II transformed the land into a Versaille-type formal garden. At this time the lake was a featureless strip known as the Canal, but it was waterscaped in 1828 when the great architect John Nash was employed to remodel the park. Today pleasant walks and paths thread through a mixture of flower borders, shrubs, and trees. The nucleus of the park is formed by the lake, which is almost oriental in flavour with its fringe of weeping willows and resident ornamental ducks floating serenely upon it. Duck Island in the centre provides a lush haven for water birds, the most famous being the pelicans which parade its banks with a proprietary air.

The ornamental gates of Green Park.

Green Park

This is indeed a green park. Its close turf, graduating towards a more carefree rankness round the roots of lovely old trees, might have been borrowed from the sheep-cropped slopes of the Sussex Downs. There are no flowerbeds, though in springtime the grass is sprinkled with the flowers of daffodils and crocuses. There is no visible water in the park, but the Tyburn Stream flows just beneath the surface and is the reason for the park's verdancy.

Just across the thin tarmac boundary of The Mall is St James's Park, but even without the road the two areas would be distinct from one another. It is easy to forget their shared history in picturesque St James's, where the magical combination of water and flowers masks the memory of violent crimes that have been enacted on its lawns. In the slightly severe greenness of Green Park, however, stories of past events spring easily to mind.

The ghosts of duellists battle in the damp shadows of the trees at twilight, the slightest breeze entices an almost human sigh from the gnarled plane tree near Piccadilly, and occasionally the setting sun turns patches of grass an unsettling red.

The times of violence have gone from the park now, along with Charles II's constitutional stroll that gave its name to Constitution Hill, and the walls of the ice house that he built to keep his wines cool in summer.

Hyde Park

Hyde Park merges imperceptibly with Kensington Gardens, which makes it seem a lot larger than it is, but there is a marked character difference between the two parks.

Before Henry VIII enclosed the area as a hunting chase, the park was a wild tract of countryside that once formed part of a vast primeval forest. It was watered by the little River Westbourne, a tributary of the Thames. After it was dammed to form the enchanting Serpentine lake the Westbourne vanished underground.

The Serpentine is undoubtedly the main feature of the park. It is the habitat of wild creatures that find scant sanctuary elsewhere in the city centre. It is also a source of pleasure to humankind, a large silvery flatness that rests easy on the eye and murmurs to the dip of oars or swish of sailing dinghies. Its shrub-covered islands are the homes of breeding waterfowl, sanctuaries guarded from the tread of man. At the eastern end of the Serpentine is the Dell, often considered the park's most picturesque feature. At its centre is a large block of granite called the Standing Stone; it is in fact all that remains of a 19th-century drinking fountain.

Here the horse is still welcome, whether it be of the King's Troop of the Royal Horse Artillery come to fire a salute, or a civilian out for a casual canter along the *Route du Roi* – now known as Rotten Row. There was once an enclosure in the park called The Tour where courtiers drove a circular route in an ostentatious parade of fashion. Ever since the

The Serpentine framed in the balustrades of the bridge.

Stuart Kings threw open the gates, Hyde has been a people's park. Its history is one of gaiety, of racing and sports, folk dancing, and minor self indulgence. This spirit of relaxed tolerance, of democratic freedom, is nowhere more typified than at Speaker's Corner. Here, at the Marble Arch corner of the park, anyone can stand up and say just what they please, so long as they can tolerate the remarks of their audience.

A carpet of leaves in Hyde Park.

Kensington Gardens

The boundary between Kensington Gardens and Hyde Park, which were one and the same place before William III enclosed his palace garden, runs north to south across the Serpentine Bridge. Both parks have the Serpentine waters in common, though in Kensington Gardens it is called The Long Water.

It is not until the walker has penetrated some distance into the gardens that the individual characteristics of the areas become apparent.

Prim school children sitting in the shadow of the Albert Memorial.

The gardens become more orderly. The manicured greenery of Hyde Park gives way to colourful regimentation. Avenues of trees shade the pathways, and sculpture adds excitement to the views. Kensington Palace is the focal point providing a dignity characterised by the unmistakable workmanship of Sir Christopher Wren, which can be glimpsed through a cloak of trees. The beautiful sunken gardens round the rectangular pond in front of the palace is the culmination.

There is fantasy here too. In the children's playground the pixies and other small creatures of Ivor Innes' imagination rampage over the Elphin Oak in the frozen motion of carved wood near playground swings donated by the writer J M Barrie. A statue of Barrie's eternal youth Peter Pan stands beside The Long Water, and serves as a reminder of his enchanting story, much of which is set in the gardens. The tranquillity of Kensington Gardens is as deliberate as its formality; note the 'sail only' rule for model boats on the Round Pond.

Regent's Park

After the execution of Charles I, the great royal hunting ground of Marylebone Park fell into the hands of Oliver Cromwell, who sold its timber and deer to pay his war debts. Further erosion occurred when Charles II sold leases on the ground to various noblemen, and it was not until the early 19th century that any attempt was made to regain what had been lost. Then, however, it became part of the Prince Regent's grand design for a vast neo-classical redevelopment under the talented hand of John Nash – hence 'Regent's' Park. Nash's original plans were never completed. That would have meant building on the park itself, and the Prince Regent decided that the open space was preferable to more development. The focus of the overall design was the Inner Circle. This now encloses the lovely Queen Mary's Garden, which has an attractive little lake, cascades of delicate and many-hued rockery plants, and one of the most beautiful rose gardens in the capital.

The subterranean Tyburn River fills the lake and pours into the boating pond from the only visible stretch on its route to the Thames.

The park's other waterway, the Regent's Canal, makes a much more definite impact on the landscape. A pleasure-boat service carries passengers to Regent's Park Zoo from the terminal in Little Venice. The elegant charm of the park is enhanced by several Victorian garden ornaments, notably two large flower vases on the Broad Walk. Near the lake is a group of fossil tree trunks which are the only surviving reminders that the Royal Botanical Gardens were once situated here. The park has many public amenities, including games fields, facilities for archery and tennis, and sailing on the lake.

Regent's Park's shaded avenues offer many pleasant walks. Above: Sir William Reid Dick's statue of the Boy with the Frog in Queen Mary's Garden, within the Inner Circle.

One of a group of fossilised tree trunks that stand beside the lake.

Primrose Hill

Once part of the same hunting forest as its neighbour, Regent's Park, Primrose Hill retains in its name the rural character that it undoubtedly had in the past. It lost a great deal of its charm during World War II, when it was cleared and used for allotments, but it is gradually recovering its attractiveness. The view from the summit is panoramic and encompasses virtually the whole of central London.

The hill's height made it prominent in the otherwise flat farmland that surrounded it, and it became an obvious place for the quenching of revenge by dark deed or duel.

In 1842 it gained gaslights, a gymnasium, and respectability as a Royal Park. It also gained a fence to keep the public out, but nowadays its 62 acres are open to anybody wishing to enjoy them.

Below: Pink and white masses of cherry blossom delicately scent the springtime breezes.

Greenwich Park

It is difficult to consider Greenwich Park without involving the magnificent Wren buildings that rise from the foot of the valley. It is a matter of taste; those interested in architecture will find the park an apt foil to those masterly designs, while others might thank providence that they complement rather than spoil the Thames-side greenness lapping at their walls.

The park was enclosed in medieval times, used as a hunting chase by the Tudor monarchs, and formalised by the Stuarts. Several tumuli, traces of a Roman villa, and records of a castle demolished by Charles II show that the area now occupied by the park was inhabited fairly constantly from prehistoric times.

The view up into Greenwich Park, laid out by the French King Louis XIV's gardener, Le Nôtre, for Charles II. Flamsteed House is the former home of the Royal Observatory, now based at Herstmonceux in Sussex. The timeball on the turret mast falls daily at exactly 1 p.m.

Looking down towards the river from the Royal Observatory.

The most extensive changes were made by the great French landscaper Le Notre, who was commissioned by Charles II. His love of symmetry, and of the straight line opposed by the curve, is very much in keeping with another of the park's aspects – as a place of science. Here stood the old Royal Observatory, now pensioned off as a museum, and here also is the Meridian – a stone-set strip of brass that marks zero degrees Longitude, the point on which such measurements all around the world are based.

Away from all this, in the park's eastern corner, is the Wilderness, 13 acres of bracken and wild flowers inhabited by a herd of fallow deer. Close by is a delightful flower garden. Everywhere there are trees, and the sense of not being far from running water. On the park's northern perimeter is the largest children's playground in any of the Royal Parks, facilities for cricket and football near the Ranger's House, and, in the centre of the park, the historic 20ft stump of Queen Elizabeth's Oak.

Richmond Park

This vast tract of virtually wild countryside on the very doorstep of London's urban sprawl remains from an ancient forest that once covered much of southern England.

Charles I enclosed the park area as part of a royal estate, and successive monarchs have shaped the land to suit their hunting needs. The deer that they so avidly sought no longer display the furtive timidness of the hunted. Instead they wander unharmed among copses and spinneys high above the Thames Valley, and are not averse to bullying the picnicking tourist into parting with a sandwich or two. The ultimate irony must be the deer's freedom of the slopes of King Henry VIII's Mound, which the monarch had built so that he could watch their slaughter.

In the 18th century severe restrictions on public access to Richmond Park were imposed by the Crown, but – thanks to a brewer called John Lewis – today's public can wander there at will. Lewis fought to preserve a public right of way through the park, and won.

A formal garden can be seen at Pembroke Lodge, and the various plantations show a wealth of exotic shrubs and wild flowers. Model sail boats are allowed on Adam's Pond, where the deer drink, and 18-acre Pen Ponds have been specially made for angling (a fishing permit is required).

Deer graze beneath sun-dappled foliage in Richmond Park, a reminder of the days when the royal parks were truly the preserve of the monarch.

Through the Lion Gate, situated north of Hampton Court's famous maze, Wren had planned to have his main entrance to the palace from Bushy Park.

Hampton Court

Before Macadam made the biggest single revolution in road building since the Romans, the River Thames was the main access to London. That, and the sylvan beauty of its wild valley, must have been the deciding factors in Cardinal Wolsey's choice of site for Hampton Court, the most magnificent house of the Tudor age.

Nestling inside an elbow of Britain's premier river is an outstanding collection of formal gardens and little architectural conceits – stunning herbaceous borders and long, shaded walks lined by ancient trees. The combination of flowers, statues, and fountains in the Privy Garden is considered to show formal gardening at its very best, and the heady breath of the elaborate Herb Garden intoxicates the senses.

There is water here too. The magnificent Long Water was created by Charles II in French-canal style, and the very old Pond Garden demonstrates that strange, botanical no-man's land between dry and submerged habitats.

The Rose Garden grows in what was once the hoof-hammered lists of Henry VIII's Tiltyard, and the modern Knot Garden recreates the almost tortured complexity that was sought after by gardeners during the 16th century.

Above all Hampton Court is a place of opposites, contrasts that are summed up in just two of its features – the charming Wilderness dell which is surrounded by a carpet of daffodils in springtime and the geometric perfection of the famous Maze.

For more details of Hampton Court also see pages 17 and 77.

Bushy Park

Hampton Court Road separates its namesake park from less formal acres of Bushy Park, an engagingly pastoral area that recreates the seeming randomness of the real countryside. With one notable exception, that is – Sir Christopher Wren's magnificent Chestnut Avenue. This superb double row of enormous trees is best seen in spring, when the candle-like blooms form a frothy pink and white line that bisects the park from north to south.

Close to the Hampton Court end of the avenue is the Diana Fountain, which once stood in the grounds of the great house, but now marks the junction of the chestnut way with an avenue of limes. The latter is a smooth, formal highway through an otherwise wild part of the park.

North of the limes is the Longford River. Although it looks entirely natural, it was in fact built on the order of Charles I to supply Hampton Court with water, and still feeds many of the park's water features. At one point it flows through the mature woodland and picturesque glades of Waterhouse Plantation, where it hurls itself over an artificial ledge in the heart of one of the most beautiful rural retreats in the country.

Most visitors to the park congregate near the cricket ground and children's playground – both well worth visiting, but not to the exclusion of all else. Bushy House, a handsome 18th-century building, contains the National Physical Laboratory.

The gardens at Hampton Court are after the French 17th-century manner and were laid out for William III by pupils of the great French gardener Le Nôtre.

The famous Chestnut Avenue runs for a mile through the centre of Bushy Park and is ideal for horse riding.

The Public Parks

of London legend, and its earthen 'laboratory' beds have been laid out to be pleasing to the eye.

The first nine acres of gardens were laid out by George III's mother, Princess Augusta, some 200 years ago, and they really began to flourish during the reign of her son. Their present-day success is largely due to the eminent 19th-century botanist Sir Joseph Banks, a close friend of the king, who worked with Head Gardener William Aiton to lay the basis for the superb collection that now exists. Royal patronage continued, even after

the gardens came into public ownership in 1841. Today's visitors can be thankful for this as they enjoy the conserved wildness of the Queen's Cottage and grounds – a gift from Queen Victoria.

The largest living collection in the gardens is the Arboretum, where many species of trees and shrubs grow harmoniously. The Tropical and Palm Houses are interesting too, while magnificent flower borders of the Herbaceous Section are a constant delight. Great cushions of alpines grow amongst sandstone outcrops and beside the stream of the Rock Garden, and the woodland garden around The Mound exudes a green coolness that is at once relaxing and tonic.

The Chinese Pagoda in Kew Gardens was designed by Sir William Chambers purely for decorative effect. It is 10 storeys high, each successive storey decreasing by 1 ft in diameter and height.

Decimus Burton's magnificent Palm House built 1844–8 to house palm trees from all over the world.

Kew Gardens, Borough of Richmond

London Zoo may be the showcase of the animal kingdom, but when it comes to plants there is nowhere to beat the Royal Botanic Gardens at Kew. Here, firmly established on 300 acres of Thames-side London, are exotics from all over the world – the mice and the mammoths of botany.

The garden's facilities for research are unrivalled, but it is not as a purely scientific establishment that Kew is known. The great beauty and strangeness of its charges are part

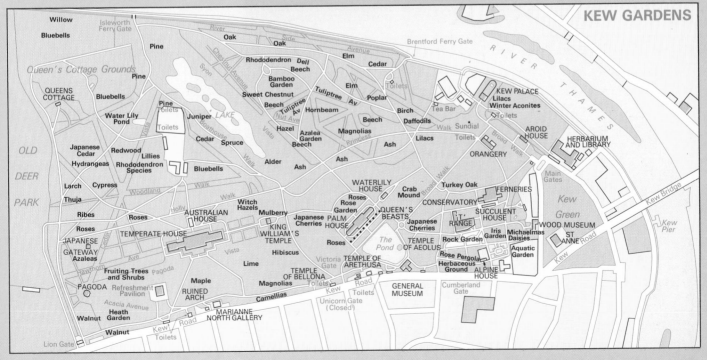

The conservatory at Syon Park.

Syon Park, Isleworth

Close to Kew Gardens in spirit, but divided from it by the waters of the Thames, is Syon Park – the country's first national gardening centre.

Its horticultural reputation goes back to the 16th century, when the use of trees as purely decorative contributions to its layout was looked upon with amazement. The park that exists today, however, is the work of that master of landscape design – 'Capability' Brown. As such it is a valuable cultural record, as well as a beautiful retreat from the bustle of modern town life.

There is water in plenty. The capital's major artery flows sedately past the 16th-century exterior of Syon House, and the picturesque lake supports large colonies of water-loving plants. Here beauty is combined with practicality.

The focal point of Syon, if not the house, must certainly be the Great Conservatory. This vast crescent of metal and glass, with small pavilions at either end and a lofty central dome, was the first construction of its type in the world. It was also the inspiration for the ill-fated Crystal Palace, but apart from all this it houses one of the finest private collections of tropical plants in the country. It is the only place in Britain where the coconut palm has reached full maturity. Here the visitor will find the rare and the exotic, but will also recognise the familiar house plants that nestle behind curtains on millions of window ledges throughout Britain.

A particularly beautiful – if somewhat overwhelming – feature of the park is the six-acre Rose Garden. At the appropriate time of year some 1,200 of these queens among flowers assault the eye with their unselfconscious colour.

All this, just nine miles from the centre of London, is open to the public – though admittance to the house and park is by separate entrances.

The landscaped gardens of Osterley Park on the western outskirts of London, were laid out during the 18th century.

Osterley Park, Osterley

Osterley is indeed a 'green lung' for London, or at least for the city's heavily built-up western suburbs. Nearby the M4 motorway carries its never-ending metallic stream into the warrens of the capital, growling to itself in a constant monotone of labouring car and lorry engines. Yet nothing detracts from the park.

Its delightfully informal landscape preserves the character and tranquillity of the English countryside. The 120 acres of level ground that it covers have been cleverly and sympathetically landscaped so that the flatness is not apparent. Trees have been planted singly and in copses to break the lie of the land still further, and the whole is complemented by enchanting lakes.

Osterley House – the reason for all this carefully contrived rurality – stands amid smooth lawns and fragrant stands of old cedars. The building that can be seen today owes much of its appearance to the architect Robert Adam, who refaced the original 16th-century structure in the mid 18th century. It was originally built by the Tudor financial wizard Sir Thomas Gresham, the richest merchant of his times and a firm favourite of Queen Elizabeth I.

The house and park complement each other well. Adam's elegant lines rise grandly from the formal gardens laid out around the house, throwing the 'wild' parkland into a rugged relief that it might not have achieved on its own. Both house and grounds are open to the public.

Wild deer can be seen at Battersea Park.

Tulip time at Holland Park.

Battersea Park, SW11

Amongst the attractions in this riverside park are a deer park, sub-tropical garden, and wildflower garden. Facilities specifically for children include playing fields, a small zoo, and a miniature railway.

Crystal Palace Park, SE19

This 70-acre park is named after the huge glass-and-iron structure that was built in 1851 for the Great Exhibition. It was moved here from Hyde Park in 1854, and destroyed by fire in 1936. Situated in the park, whose hill-side site commands extensive views, is an Olympic-standard swimming pool and a superb sports stadium.

The only survivors of the old Crystal Palace are these monsters occupying an island on the lake.

Holland Park, W8

Less than 30 years ago Holland Park was the garden of a private house, and even now it retains that air of intimacy that is so peculiar to the inviolate. Its flock of peacocks and gaggle of geese mount solemn guard for long-gone inhabitants of the house, and visitors stroll on smooth lawns where open-air Kensington teas may have been held not too many summers ago.

In the 18th and 19th centuries the house here was a popular meeting place for the literary and political personalities of the day. Only part of it now faces across the elegant quadrangle that it once dominated, but it is easy to imagine the intellectuals of the time threading through lighted rooms at the end of a summer evening. Macauley called Holland Park the 'Favourite resort of wits and beauties, painters and poets, scholars, philosophers, and statesmen'. Such people, jaded by the effort of creation or wearied by their excursions into the labyrinthine politics of high social life, must have found the park easy on the eye and relaxing to the mind.

That feeling remains, though the sparkling company and locked gates have gone. In springtime the Dutch and Iris Gardens are a constant delight to the visitor – especially the person who has unexpectedly stumbled upon this strange little haven while lost in the masonry heart of Kensington. Other flowerbeds show a wide range of plants, including the original Caroline Testout roses, and a charming show of native British plants. Also here is a *yucca* garden, where the Mexican *yucca* plant guards its delicate clusters of white flowers with bunches of spear-like leaves.

In contrast with the formal path-and-lawn layout, given a military air by the uniformed nannies who take their small charges for walks here, is the free-play area. This is woodland that has been left to its own devices for the benefit of older children.

The zoo's founder was Sir Stamford Raffles, an extensively travelled stalwart of the British Empire, who had a thorough and largely self-taught knowledge of natural history. He and other eminent naturalists of the day formed the Zoological Society, a body which began a small collection of animals on a five-acre site in Regent's Park. Thus, in 1828, the foundations were laid for one of the world's greatest zoological collections – a collection that still receives no aid from the government, and subsists entirely on the proceeds of its ticket sales.

The first major increase in the collection occurred when the entire Tower of London menagerie was transferred to Regent's Park. Subsequent additions arrived thick and fast, causing great excitement amongst the local population as exotics of all shapes and sizes were herded through the streets to their new homes. One of the most famous of these was Jumbo the elephant, who was so well known that his name became absorbed into the English language as a descriptive word.

London Zoo was opened to the public (as the Zoological Gardens) in 1847, and has never been short of visitors since. Neither has it stood still. It opened the first insect and reptile houses in the world, kept the first aquarium, and today is able to show a staggering 6,000 living species of animal, many in environments that are hardly a whisker away from their natural habitats.

Bighorn goats roam the brilliantly sculpted tiers of the Mappin Terraces.

London Zoo

There can be few modern institutions that hold the interest and nostalgic charm of the zoo. Of all zoos, the great and intricate complex in Regent's Park must be the king. It is one of the world's foremost zoos, and has a reputation for the care of its charges that is second to none. It is also unfailingly popular with the millions of people from all over the world who visit it each year.

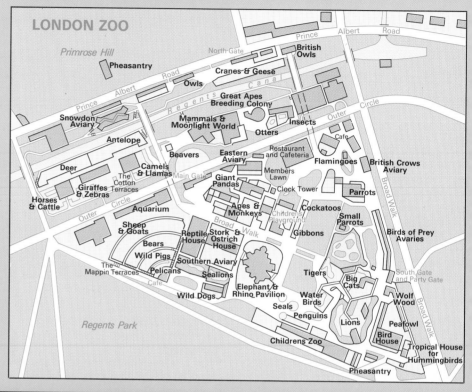

Some of the creatures are such as might be encountered on a country walk in Hampshire; others are endangered species that would be difficult to find anywhere in the world.

The Children's Zoo is a charming area where youngsters can walk among domestic animals, stroking, patting, and even riding the inmates. Feeding times, always a great attraction, are posted on the notice board.

Somewhat different are the large, superbly designed Lion Terraces, which were opened exactly one century after the building of the previous 'big cat' accommodation.

The rest of the zoo architecture is just as stunning: the walled-and-ditched Mappin Terraces, where visitors can enjoy unrestricted views of animals that think they are in the wild; the Freshwater, Seawater, and Tropical Halls of the Aquarium; the Reptile House; the Michael Sobell Pavilion for Apes and Monkeys; the Elephant and Rhino Pavilion; and the amazing night-time world of the Charles Clore Pavilion for Small Mammals, where day and night have been reversed so that visitors can see the denizens of the dark.

Deer and Antelope roam the Cotton Terraces above the Regent's Canal. The best views of them are obtained from the British Waterways Board's Waterbus, which cruises along the canal between Little Venice and the zoo. Elsewhere are camels and llamas, giraffes, and a worldwide selection of cattle.

One of the most famous, if controversial, structures in the whole complex is Lord Snowdon's aviary. Some people may throw doubt onto the aesthetics of its futuristic shape, but nobody can deny that it is an ideal place to see birds. Inside the enclosure is a cantilevered bridge from which visitors can watch free-flying birds in a number of re-created habitats – nesting, fighting, and feeding as they would in the wild. There are other, more conventional aviaries dotted around the zoo, but for many this is the high spot of their visit.

London Zoo is not just a place to idle away a few enjoyable hours in satisfying a vague sense of curiosity, although it is very good for that. It is also a serious scientific institution dedicated to the study and preservation of all forms of wildlife – an institution that has already saved numerous rare animals from extinction by encouraging them to breed in captivity.

It is also part of London legend, a repository of apocryphal tales about such unlikely creatures as the intractable Jumbo, the lovable Guy (the gorilla), and the old-time Chimps' Tea Parties.

Right: An elephant in the Elephant and Rhino Pavilion.

Below right: Feeding time at the Penguin Pool, which was built in 1934 and is now a protected building because of its revolutionary use of pre-stressed concrete.

Below: Only glass separates this leopard from his young admirer.

Below left: Giraffes share their quarters with another distinctively-patterned African animal, the zebra.

The Heaths and Commons

Hampstead Heath
NW3 and NW11

If the parks of London were once a hotbed of criminality and violence, where no 'decent' person would dare risk his neck or purse after dark, then the heaths and commons of the capital were even more so.

Their scrubby slopes and dark thickets provided ample cover for highwaymen, who preyed on travellers using the lonely roads into London. This was a different class of criminal from the murdering footpads and sly slitpurses of the city, however – the highwaymen were figures of romance that history tolerates and the 20th century views with a kind of misplaced nostalgia. Long gone are the days when Sixteen String Jack, the dashing Claude Duval, and Dick Turpin haunted Hampstead Heath, striking fear into the hearts of men and women.

Modern Hampstead is a 'fossil' village that has been preserved against the urban sprawl of the metropolis by the money and resistance to change of its traditionally 'arty' inhabitants. Similarly, the heath is a tract of open countryside that should not really exist – it owes its existence to providence rather than design. Its 790 acres include some of the highest ground in the capital, and the views of London that can be enjoyed from the heath are famous.

There are extensive tracts of open grassland dotted with majestic old trees, and carefully planned formalised areas that were originally set out during the Regency period. Part of society's interest in Hampstead was due to the springs which rise from its depths. These were claimed to have health-giving properties, and the 18th century fad for 'taking the waters' ensured its popularity.

Two of London's all-but-lost rivers rise on Hampstead Heath – the Fleet and the Westbourne – later to sink again and flow through sunless conduits to the Thames.

The heath has a strong tradition of fairs, and their garish, unpretentious clamour still fills the air on most Bank Holidays. The Buckland family, who have been associated with the fairs for many years, once stayed here in the beautifully painted caravan that stands near the rustic mushroom of Dr Johnson's Summer-house.

Among the interesting buildings on the heath are 17th-century Kenwood House (open, see page 102), whose 200-acre grounds include a lakeside platform for open-air concerts. It was once the home of Lord Mansfield, who was (fortunately) prevented from developing the heath as building land by Parliament. It is to that august body that the modern visitor must give thanks for the heath's survival.

Parliament Hill Fields
NW3, NW5 and NW6

According to tradition the 319 ft eminence of Parliament Hill was to be the grandstand from which Guy Fawkes' fellow conspirators expected to watch the final 'dissolution' of Parliament.

The Fields are really part of Hampstead Heath, but they have an entirely different character and offer a very comprehensive range of sporting facilities. These include an athletics track, a lido, and the bowling green where the Greater London championship bowls finals are held each September. Views from Parliament Hill Fields take in Highgate Ponds and London's skyline.

Blackheath
SE3

This was an important meeting place in the days when the Roman Watling Street was the best way to get from the Channel coast to London. That ancient highway ran right through Blackheath, and for many centuries important visitors were met here by the mayor, aldermen, and many of the citizens of London.

The heath has seen celebratory meetings of victorious monarchs and their grateful subjects, but it has also been the scene of sadder, more poignant occasions. One such was when Anne of Cleves and her entourage made camp here – a glittering event which sadly impressed the crowds far more than the bride-to-be impressed King Henry VIII. A less royal but more influential happening here was Wat Tyler's rallying for the Peasants' Revolt in the 14th century.

Happily the Blackheath of today is a quieter place. Its green openness, where James I first played golf, provides a vast garden for the 'village' of Blackheath.

Wimbledon's windmill was built in 1817.

Wimbledon Common
SW19

Wimbledon Common is part of a large green area in the south-western suburbs of London. It was once a lonely, isolated place where travellers rarely ventured after dark for fear of highwaymen. Even today people with a mystical bent do not venture here after dark, for those same highwaymen are still said to roam as earthbound spirits.

The common, however, and the adjacent Richmond Park and Putney Heath, are no longer isolated. On all sides tarmac and masonry are encroaching, and far from being places of dread these open spaces are now places of pleasure to the local people. Mature woodlands punctuate large expanses of grassland here, and there are several attractive ponds. A special area has been set aside for organised games.

The lawns of Kenwood House, on the northern edge of Hampstead Heath, are covered with daffodils in early spring.

Caesar's Camp is an ancient earthwork situated in the south-west corner of Wimbledon Common.

Clapham Common
SW4

Flat and park-like, with a few small areas of wild ground and large areas of open grassland, this triangle of open ground lies at the end of Clapham High Street and is a valuable amenity in a very crowded part of South London. Many fairs and circuses are held here, and there are several ponds and games areas. The Greater London Horse Show is held on the Common over the weekend of the late summer Bank Holiday.

Streatham Common
SW16

A common in name, but in fact a delightful combination of heath and garden, Streatham Common covers some 68 acres and boasts a grass theatre for open-air performances.

Its large areas of open grassland offer plenty of scope for the casual walker and children at play. A lovely flower garden nestling in a hollow in the south part of the common is sheltered by tall trees that support a rookery, and the oddly soothing cawing of those birds is never far away.

Other features include a garden where all the blooms are white, and charming little retreats where rock and water have been used to complement a variety of plants.

Wandsworth Common
SW11

Reclaimed from marshland during the 19th century, Wandsworth Common is an astonishing contrast to the industrial riverbank usually considered typical of this area. Its attractive lake pleases the eye and provides sport for anglers, while the monotony of a town landscape can be momentarily forgotten in its woods.

Tooting and Tooting Bec Commons
SW16 and SW17

Tooting Common runs into Tooting Bec Common, forming a large area of wild and semi-wild countryside. It is a fascinating and varied landscape, with overgrown marshes, small copses, thickets of gorse, and open grassland. There are also several artificial ponds. The commons' many amenities include an open-air swimming pool and an athletics track. Near the south side of Tooting Bec Common is Streatham Park, home of the Thrales, where Dr Johnson was a frequent visitor.

Tulips make a bold contrast to the sombre foliage of the cedars in the Rookery, Streatham Common.

Putney Heath
SW15

Thickets of furze, golden yellow with bloom in summer, characterise the sandy expanses of this heath and distinguish it from adjoining Wimbledon Common.

Duellists once came here to satisfy their honour, and its dark corners were haunted by highwaymen. Later it became a very fashionable place, where society held bowling meetings and the royal family raced its horses.

Hounslow Heath
Borough of Hounslow

This lovely place once had the worst criminal record of any public open space in London. Highwaymen there were in plenty, plus a lesser class of criminal called footpads – who hunted in packs and would often murder to steal.

Major General William Roy of the Royal Engineers chose Hounslow Heath as the place to start his triangulations, which were to become the basis of the entire series of Ordnance Survey maps. The actual starting place is marked by a tablet fixed to the muzzle of a gun.

London Fields
E8

At one time London Fields were used for grazing sheep, but as the capital expanded they became much more valuable as the nearest open space to the City of London. In fact, they were so popular that their grassy surface became worn away right down to the earth. What was once a pleasant urban 'meadow' became a dustbowl or a quagmire, depending on the weather. Nowadays the area is carefully tended, and its turf is protected for the enjoyment of the City's workers.

Barnes Common
SW13

Grassland, gorse patches, and heather combine to form a pleasantly varied landscape here in what has been called London's best-kept common. Adjoining it is Barnes Green, a large public garden laid out around a pond.

Peckham Rye
SE15

The first-time visitor to Peckham Rye is in for a very pleasant surprise. It is a delightful little retreat with its cultivated garden looking like an ideal combination of all that is most beautiful in the wild. Its triangle of open grassland is fringed by trees, and its stream-fed lake laps round a tiny island. Flower-decked banks slope down to pleasant walks that wend from open grass to shaded woodland, and here and there the anarchy of the wild gives way to the straight lines of formal gardening. It also has tennis courts and a bowling green.

Epping Forest

London's parks and heaths are places where lungs and legs can be stretched, where the eye can remember that landscapes are not always of angular brick, and the ear can be soothed by birdsong rather than assaulted by motor-metallic din.

They are valuable reminders of the countryside, but though they come very close to it, they are *not* the countryside.

The same cannot be said for Epping, London's only real forest – an astonishing survivor of the tide of urban development that has been creeping out from the capital since Victorian times.

For many Londoners, particularly those from the East End, Epping Forest is a large haven of greenery, peace, and tranquillity to which they can escape from seemingly endless terraces and high-rise flats – but it has not survived unscathed. Its southern parts have been severed from the main body by tentacles of linear development, and have in turn been chopped into small green oases surrounded by streets of houses. Sometimes the oases are not just green, because this is the low part of the forest's 12-mile spread and is therefore prone to flooding. Such places as Leyton Flats, for instance, become positively waterlogged in the winter. It can be said that the 'real Epping Forest' is the northern part. Here are grassy plains and wild thickets, dense coverts of fine old hornbeams and beeches punctuated by open grassy glades.

There are animals here too, perhaps not so many as when this was just a small part of a vast forest that covered most of southern England, but certainly more than are found elsewhere in the capital. The smaller inhabitants include foxes, stoats, hares, rabbits, the ever-present grey squirrel, and the furious little weasel.

The largest and by far the most unusual animals here are the black fallow deer that have probably roamed this area for many centuries. Actually a very dark brown rather than black, these lovely and timid creatures are peculiar to Epping Forest. They were almost wiped out by poachers in the 19th century, and after a brief rise to a population of some 300 they began to succumb to the noise and traffic of the 20th century. Sensible creatures that they are, the deer wandered off into the comparative peace of private estates. The trend has been stopped by the establishment of a 109-acre sanctuary on the edge of the forest, and once more the population of this unique strain is building up to healthy proportions.

The preservation aspect of man's activities in the forest is a reflection of the area's status as an Area of Special Scientific Interest – thus designated by the Nature Conservancy Council. The Council's job is difficult and unenviable, and the great natural treasure in its charge is constantly at risk.

Conservationists of the 19th century had to fight off the determined advances of land grabbers, each sure of his right to enclose common land. In fact the enclosures were illegal, and had it not been for the efforts of a poor local villager, the forest might have disappeared entirely. This hero was Thomas

Queen Elizabeth's Hunting Lodge in fact dates from the late 15th century.

Willingale, who was so outraged by the erosion of his free-grazing and wood-gathering territory that he started legal proceedings to bring the forest back into public ownership. His efforts, made at a time when Epping had been whittled away to a mere 3,000 acres, prompted the authorities into concrete and sustained action. The forest was not only saved, but it also regained much of the land that had been stolen from it.

Many of the rights that Thomas Willingale enjoyed are still exercised by the 'forest people'. Anyone who owns half an acre or more of undeveloped land in one of the forest parishes is allowed to graze horses, sheep, cattle, and pigs in the woods and glades. This is why the unwary walker might be surprised by the contemplative gaze of a cow as he rounds a bush, or find himself nudged by an over-friendly horse.

There is plenty of water in the forest – in fact some 150 ponds and lakes ranging from the sweeping expanse of artificial Connaught Water to the smaller reaches of Bulrush Pond and Hollow Pond, as well as the Heronry and Perch Ponds of Wanstead Park. The River Roding flows along the forest's eastern perimeter as it makes its way to the Thames, and the Gothic ruin of a magnificent boathouse stands by another of the park's waterways.

Pollarded beeches in Little Monk Wood, Epping Forest.

EPPING FOREST

The grotto in Wanstead Park at the southern edge of Epping Forest was once the boathouse of the Ornamental Water.

Ambresbury Banks is an iron-age earthworks. Recent archaeological digs show that it was thrown up between 300 BC and AD 10.

lake and densely wooded banks of Higham Park; the rhododendron-filled expanse of the once-private Knighton Wood; and the estate-like acres of Wanstead Park, which was once attached to the long-gone mansion of Wanstead House.

Epping Forest is important as a recreational area. As well as peace and beauty, it offers facilities for many outdoor sports and pastimes. Anglers and inland sailors can enjoy the lakes and ponds, horse riders can follow the special trails that have been laid out for them, and the surrounding villages have the use of numerous cricket and football pitches. It is also an area of great educative value, where wildlife observation and field studies are pursued by student and teacher alike.

A great source of information is the Epping Forest Museum, which is housed in Queen Elizabeth's Hunting Lodge (see also page 98), a timbered building of the 15th century. Inside are exhibits relating to the history and natural history of the area, and it contributes to the work of the Conservation Centre set up for the benefit of schools and study centres. The centre, managed by the Field Studies Council, is a complex of teaching laboratories, lecture facilities, and staff accommodation at High Beech.

The 73 Conservators of Epping Forest, staff of the Corporation of London, take their responsibilities very seriously. They have to walk the narrow bridge between preservation – to which they are committed – and the maintenance of the public's right of access, given by Queen Victoria in 1882. It is the responsibility of every one of the thousands who come to Epping to help them in their task.

The water is not what it was, however. Pollution has taken a terrible toll of the varied plant and animal life that once thrived here, and the Roding has to be carefully filtered before it can be used to top up Connaught and the lesser ponds. Careful monitoring and clean-up programmes have saved the lakes, which still support a wealth of wild life and fish, but pollution is still a serious problem.

It is the same story throughout the forest, which is why there are so many seemingly petty restrictions regarding access and traffic. One piece of 'pollution' that may become a valuable historical relic in time is the line of tank traps that stretches across the area. One wonders if Boadicea, who is traditionally supposed to have embarked upon her last battle with the Romans from here, would have approved of such restrictions to the vehicles of war.

The character of the forest changes to suit the type of ground which it covers, and the overall effect is one of pleasant variety. The wild thickets and low marshes have already been mentioned, but there is also the lovely

The Squares

London's squares form an essential part of the capital's overall character. Many of them were originally surrounded by the elegant town houses of the gentry, and some of these mansions still stand. It is their look of refined gentility, combined with the formal elegance of the central gardens, which gives these areas their unmistakable aura.

Belgrave Square, SW1

Sheer size robs Belgrave of its square-like characteristics, because it is not possible to see from one side to the other. To all intents it is a small park, but the carefully tended lawns and gardens have an un-park-like air of exclusiveness undoubtedly lent by the elegant cream-coloured terraces that surround it. The square is one of the largest in London, and centres on attractive private gardens enclosed by ironwork entirely in keeping with the local architecture.

Berkeley Square, W1

Modern development has detracted somewhat from the original charm of this very famous square. It is doubtful whether the nightingales assigned to it in the song actually existed, though the huge plane trees in which they would have perched are there for all to see. The trees were planted in 1790, a decade before the building of the quaint Pump House that is still so much a part of the square's character. Also very much in keeping with the atmosphere of slightly time-worn elegance is the garden fountain – a nymph with a pitcher.

Dorset Square, NW1

Long before Dorset Square was laid out its site was occupied by the original Lord's Cricket Ground. Here the MCC – the country's most famous cricket club – was begun in the 18th century. However, the grass in the square is no descendant of that upon which early matches were played, for when the square was being developed groundkeeper Thomas Lord left, taking his turf with him.

Above: The plaque which marks Dorset Square as the first home of the Marylebone Cricket Club.

Right: Dorset Square today, bereft of all its cricketing memories, even down to the original turf.

Below: Golden Square dates from the 18th century. It is now the home of the cinema and television industry.

Sylvan peace in Portman Square.

Fitzroy Square, W1

Designed by the famous Adam brothers in the 18th century, Fitzroy Square preserves well-built terraces typical of their designers' work, particularly on the eastern side.

Golden Square, W1

According to popular legend, this Soho square had its name changed from 'Gelding' to 'Golden' by some of its more society-conscious residents. It is now a centre for the woollen trade.

Sculpture by Naomi Blake in Fitzroy Square.

Grosvenor Square, W1

Built and rebuilt on the site of a 17th-century citizen's blockade against Charles I, Grosvenor Square is now largely in the hands of a foreign power. This is immediately apparent in the vast brooding eagle that stretches its 35ft wingspan protectively over the American Embassy, at the same time managing to encompass most of the square in that expansive gesture. The area is popularly known as 'Little America'.

The open garden around which the square is formed was designed by William Kent, a distinguished 18th-century architect and designer, and occupies some six acres. It is a pleasant patch of green amongst the buildings that loom from all sides, and echoes the transatlantic feel of the place in a memorial to one-time US President, Franklin D Roosevelt.

Manchester Square, W1

The leafy centre of Manchester Square contrasts prettily with the dark brick of the Georgian architecture that surrounds it. It is a quiet place, situated just far enough away from Oxford Street to be unaffected by the noise, yet close enough to be a haven for those weary of shopping in the famous thoroughfare.

Portman Square, W1

Once second only to Grosvenor Square in the eyes of high society, Portman took 20 years to build during the 18th century. The centre of the square is occupied by a garden in which grass, shrubs, and trees combine effectively.

Tavistock Square is the home of the British Medical Association and also of Woburn House, the small but interesting museum of the Jewish Communal Centre. Dickens once lived in the Square and so, later, did Virginia Woolf.

Ranelagh Gardens, SW3

These delightful gardens are adjacent to the Royal Hospital, and are in fact owned by that famous 'Chelsea Pensioner' institution. The hospital bought the original gardens after they had been closed down in the 19th century. Before this they had been used in spring only for concerts in the Rotunda.

Perhaps the most famous event held in the gardens nowadays is the Chelsea Flower Show, when thousands of visitors come to enjoy the colour and perfumes of thousands of blooms.

Russell Square, WC1

James Burton laid out Russell Square in the early 19th century, but few of his original buildings have survived. An exception is No 21, on the north side, which is considered a good example of his work.

The pleasant central garden was originally designed by the architect Humphrey Repton, but his layout was later altered. The sculptor Richard Westmacott made the impressive statue of the 5th Duke of Bedford.

St James's Square, SW1

At the centre of this orderly and elegant square, originally created by architect Henry Jermyn, is a garden which is particularly noted for its lovely trees. An equestrian statue of William III forms the central focal point for ranks of tall plane trees, the pastel softness of flowering almond and cherry blossom, the fragrant pyramids of lilac bloom, and golden crowns of laburnum.

The Inns of Court

Barristers in the Middle Temple.

and buildings, or as premises whose function has changed. A notable example of the latter is the old Inn of Chancery (Staple Inn) which stands at the junction of High Holborn, Holborn, and Gray's Inn Road. It is one of the finest examples of half-timbered building in London.

Gray's Inn

A late 17th-century gatehouse opens from Holborn into the quiet, sequestered confines of Gray's Inn Square. Groups of buildings of such varied heights and styles that they seem to have grown where they stand are separated by sheltered pavements and smooth lawns.

Mature plane trees add their pale green to the picture, standing sentinel over the lovely gardens and casting dappled shadows across the grass. Charles Lamb said that these were the best gardens of the Inns of Court. They may have been designed by Francis Bacon, whose bronze statue stands in South Square, but the nature of their origins seems unimportant. It is enough to know that they are there.

Lincoln's Inn

Rightly known for its fine architecture and long history, Lincoln's Inn is inseparable from that much-loved lunchtime haven of city workers, Lincoln's Inn Fields.

This large, leaf-embowered area is the largest modern square in London, and as such should perhaps be included in the 'Squares' section of this chapter. It is an essential part of the Inn, however, and echoes the tranquillity of that ancient establishment.

The central gardens cover a surprising 12 acres and are well laid out with paths and lawns. Office escapees can play tennis on several courts here, and the two full-sized netball courts are very well used. The

A lunchtime break in Lincoln's Inn Fields for both players and spectators. The netball teams come from the office buildings nearby.

popularity of this little 'green lung' became apparent some years ago when a proposal was made to build new courts there. The public outcry was so great that the plans had to be dropped (see also Walks 7 and 8).

The Temple

The best way to enjoy this Inn of Court, named after the Knights Templar who occupied the riverside site from about 1160, is to walk through its lanes and alleys. The buildings are very fine and generally very old, and the sense of space is well married to that indefinable air of peace peculiar to all the Inns.

The main entrances are from Fleet Street, near the Law Courts. Between Fleet Street and the Thames are the Middle and Inner Temples, whose finely manicured lawns slope gracefully down to the Thames. The lovely garden of the Middle Temple is not accessible to the public, but can be seen from the road.

Fine old trees grace Fountain Court, close to Middle Temple Hall. Architecture by Sir Christopher Wren can be seen in King's Bench Walk, part of the residential complex, and a 14th-century precursor to 20th-century Inner Temple Hall can be seen from Elm Court. One of the most notable buildings in the Inn is the ancient round church of the Knights Templar, which was consecrated in 1185. Temple Inn sustained a great deal of bomb damage during World War II, but this has since been skilfully repaired (see also Walk No 8).

To pass through the doorway of an Inn of Court is to step back in time. The peace and tranquillity of their courtyards is anachronistic, more in keeping with their monastic origins than the blatantly secular hubbub outside their walls.

They were founded for the education and lodging of lawyers, and even today nobody can enter that profession without being accepted by an Inn of Court – even if they already have a law degree. Their student charges literally eat their way to success, because an old Inn tradition decrees that prospective barristers must eat three formal dinners there each term for 12 terms. They also have to pass their exams, of course.

There used to be 12 Inns of Court, but only three still exist in their traditional capacity – Gray's Inn, Lincoln's Inn, and Temple. The others survive only in the names of streets

Quiet corners are a well-loved feature of the Inns of Court.

156

Relaxing in London

London's Pubs

There are over 7,000 pubs in London. They cater for every conceivable taste, and range in appearance from labyrinthine coaching inns to basic bars on humble street corners. On the following pages is a selection of the most interesting of them. Descriptions of several riverside pubs are also given in the part of this book called London's River (see pages 74–89). It should be remembered that many City pubs are not open at weekends.

The Anchor
Bankside, Southwark, SE1
Shakespeare's Globe Theatre was sited near this historic pub and its Clink Bar is a reminder that it stands close to the site of the old Clink Prison from which the slang term 'in clink' is derived. Instruments of torture are on display in the bar – a gruesome reminder of the days when prisons were places of extreme cruelty. The pub has known river pirates and smugglers as well as the Press Gang who hauled men off to serve in the Navy. Beams, open fireplaces and natural brick and stone walls form a really old world interior, but the restaurant, where English and French dishes are served, is a modern addition. The remainder of the building dates from the 17th century and commands fine views across the river to the City.

The Black Friar
174 Queen Victoria Street, EC4
Occupying a sharply-angled corner site, this wedge-shaped building is a splendid example of a Victorian pub, with wrought-iron balustrades on the upper storeys and a large Black Friar perched on the corner above the entrance. A nearby Dominican Priory founded in the 13th century was the inspiration for this tavern's name and visual theme. Hand-beaten copper murals in the bar depict jolly friars carousing, fishing and otherwise enjoying themselves. Gold leaf on the ceiling, gas lighting, open fireplaces with brass firedogs, and some good *art nouveau* decorations combine to make The Black Friar a most unusual and interesting pub.

Bunch of Grapes
207 Brompton Road, Chelsea, SW3
The ornate exterior of this pub contrasts sharply with its interior, which provides a quiet haven from the bustling street, with some fine woodcarving and Victorian mirrors to add visual interest.

Designed by the architect H Fuller Clark in 1897, the Black Friar is ornately decorated, outside as well as in.

Dirty Dick's
202–4 Bishopsgate, EC2
The original Dirty Dick was one Nathaniel Bentley, an educated and well-travelled 18th-century gentleman, who went totally insane when his bride-to-be died on the day they were to have been married. The room where the wedding feast was set out was closed at his order and he became ragged and unkempt, in direct contrast to his former elegance. This story which has obvious affinities with that of Miss Haversham in Dickens' novel *Great Expectations*, which leads one to believe that Dickens knew the place and its legend. Bentley actually lived in Leadenhall Street and at his death the landlord of the pub – known at that time as The Gates of Jerusalem or The Old Port Wine House – bought the contents of the room and had them removed to his hostelry. The collection has since been altered and added to and its main point is indescribable filth. It's worth having a drink in this room just for the experience. Elsewhere in the establishment good pub food is available in a pleasant (clean!) atmosphere.

The Flask
77 West Hill, Highgate, N6
Highgate is one of London's prettiest 'villages' and the Flask has the atmosphere of a country pub, in winter log fires adding cheery comfort to the pub's always-friendly welcome. The site has been occupied by a tavern since the 15th century, but the present building dates from 1663.

George Inn
77 Borough High Street, SE1
Eleven years after the Fire of London a similarly disastrous fire destroyed many buildings south of the Thames, among them the George Inn, which Shakespeare once frequented. After the fire, the inn was rebuilt as an exact replica of the medieval hostelry, with galleries overlooking a central courtyard. Unfortunately, extensions to the nearby railway marshalling yards resulted in the loss of part of the building, but one side with a gallery remains, making this the only

An intriguing pub sign.

I am the only Running Footman
5 Charles Street, W1
A modern picture hanging in the bar here shows a footman running ahead of a gentleman's carriage blowing a horn to warn people to clear the way. Another authority says that the running footman went ahead to pay tolls, make arrangements for accommodation or a change of horses, and generally ease the difficulties of a long journey. The best of them might have done well in an Olympic marathon since they were reputed to manage about eight miles an hour. The pub is an unpretentious but well-proportioned 18th-century building. Originally called The Running Horse, its name was changed by the 4th Duke of Queensbury, who may have admired the stamina of a particular footman.

The Jamaica Wine House
St Michael's Alley, Cornhill, EC3
Coffee was not sold commercially in England until 1652 and one of the partners in the company which started the trade opened the Jamaica as a coffee house – the first one in London. Pepys mentions visiting a coffee house in Cornhill in 1660. The original building was one of the many lost in the Fire of London and the present stone-built Jamaica Wine House dates back to 1668. The main bar, with its oak panelling, retains the appearance of a coffee house. Indeed coffee is still available, as well as an excellent selection of wines, spirits and bottled beers.

Lamb and Flag
33 Rose Street, Covent Garden, WC2
The Georgian frontage of this famous pub disguises the fact that it is the only surviving example of a 17th-century timber-framed building in the West End. Its unusual sign is the same as that of the Middle Temple Inn of Court but there seems to be no direct connection, though they may have a common religious derivation. The hostelry was once connected with prize-fighting and became known as 'The Bucket of Blood'. Nowadays it is a favourite haunt of theatre folk and plays are sometimes performed in an upstairs room. Paintings, prints, and satirical illustrations adorn the walls.

The interior of the Bunch of Grapes – the perfect atmosphere for a quiet lunchtime drink.

example of a galleried inn still to be seen in London. Dickens' father was detained for debt in the nearby Marshalsea prison. The author became intimate with the area and knew the inn well, afterwards using it as a location in a number of books, including *Little Dorrit*. Companies of actors play scenes from Shakespeare and Dickens in the inn's courtyard during the summer months.

The Golden Lion
25 King Street, St James's, SW1
Clamped between office blocks, this imposing Victorian building has high ornate ceilings and some interesting furniture and ornaments. During the summer months, tables and chairs are set out on the pavement in front of the pub.

The Grenadier
18 Wilton Row, Belgravia, SW1
There's a ghost in The Grenadier. Irate officers rather overdid the flogging they gave to one of their number who was caught cheating at cards, and he died as a result. This took place in the Officers' Mess at Wellington's barracks. A pub called The Guardsman was built on the site and the ghost of the officer took up residence in it. Later its name was changed to The Grenadier but old traditions linger: the barmen wear white mess jackets – so that the ghost will feel at home perhaps – and part of the original pewter bar can be seen.

The Guinea
30 Bruton Place, W1
Although The Guinea dates back to 1423, its appearance is not particularly distinctive and there are no frills inside either. This pub is also known as The Olde One Pound Note.

The Gun
27 Cold Harbour, E14
With the West India Dock on one side and a River Police jetty on the other, The Gun is very much part of the life of the Thames. It has its own boat moorings and a veranda overlooking the water. The building is predominantly 18th-century, built of brick with timber cladding to the upper storey – a style familiar in Essex villages farther downstream. Guns used at the battles of the Nile and Trafalgar were produced at a nearby foundry, which accounts for the pub's name. Upstairs there is a room where Nelson kept assignments with Lady Hamilton.

The Grenadier's bright colour scheme echoes its military connections.

The London Apprentice
Church Street, Isleworth

On the Thames, some miles west of London as it existed until the beginning of this century, The London Apprentice was the mecca of many workers from the 'Great Wen' who rowed up the river on high days and holidays. A painting in one of the bars shows apprentices resting after arriving by boat at the hostelry, but there is a second explanation of the pub's name. When Robert Adam designed nearby Syon House for the Duke of Northumberland, Italian craftsmen were employed on the building, and their apprentices worked on a beautiful carved ceiling in the room in the pub which is now used as a restaurant. Still a favourite place to get away to, this 500-year-old hostelry has many connections with history: Henry VIII, Lady Jane Grey and Charles II are all reputed to have stayed here.

The Magpie and Stump
18 Old Bailey, EC4

Lord Tomnoddy, a character in Barham's *Ingoldsby Legends*, hired an upstairs room in The Magpie and Stump where he entertained 20 friends at an all-night party, the object being to watch the public executions at Newgate Prison next morning. By morning they were all out cold and missed the 'entertainment' – which served them right. That story is fiction but the truth is not much different, for people paid £10 or more for a grandstand window on the upper floor of the hostelry. Newgate Prison has now been replaced by the Central Criminal Court (the Old Bailey) and the last public hanging took place in 1868, but lawyers and others connected with the Court still frequent the house – in fact one room is known as Court No 10, there being nine courts in the Old Bailey. The building dates back to the 17th century though the façade, which has mock-Tudor timbering on the upper storey, is a recent addition.

Mayflower
117 Rotherhithe Street, SE16

The Mayflower has such close connections with the United States that it is licensed to sell both British and American postage stamps. The story goes back to the 17th century – when the pub was as new as the colony. The famous ship *Mayflower* was moored nearby before setting sail for Southampton, Plymouth and the New World, and the pub's name was subsequently changed from The Shippe as a tribute to that brave little vessel. In 1621 the *Mayflower* returned to Rotherhithe and her master, who died shortly afterwards, is buried here. Inside, the pub is genuine 17th-century, with old beams and porthole windows, except for part of the upper floor which was damaged during World War II.

Top: The London Apprentice has a long and varied history and is now a scheduled building because of its great architectural interest.

Above: The Old Caledonia has been converted into a floating pub – a happier end than the breaking grounds where most redundant ships are sent.

Below: The Olde Bull and Bush, famed in Music Hall, is still a popular pub.

Olde Bull and Bush
North End Way, Hampstead, NW3

'Come and have a drink or two down at the Olde Bull and Bush' sang Florrie Ford in her still-popular Music Hall song, and down the years people have happily done just that. This one-time farmhouse is set in attractively wooded scenery near to Hampstead Heath, and was converted into an inn at the beginning of the 19th century. It became popular after the statesman William Pitt (who lived nearby at North End House) breakfasted there with the actor David Garrick, the painters Reynolds and Gainsborough, and the essayist Sterne. They were delighted with the place, and it has retained its popularity, through Victorian times when it was famous for concerts, until now, when it is still a favourite haunt of people from the worlds of entertainment and the arts as well as Hampstead residents and tourists.

Old Caledonia
*Waterloo Pier,
Victoria Embankment, WC2*

Moored by Waterloo Bridge, with views of Thames traffic and the impressive public buildings on the south of the river, the *Caledonia* was turned into a pub in 1969 after many years' service as a ferry boat off the Scottish coast. She is a paddle steamer, built in 1934, and her funnels and engine room have been retained.

Ye Olde Cheshire Cheese
145 Fleet Street, EC4

The original Olde Cheshire Cheese was a victim of the Great Fire and the present building rose from the ashes in 1667. The cellars, however, are much older and are partly made up of the undercroft of a 14th-century Carmelite monastery, later the London house of the Abbots of Peterborough. The first record of a tavern on the site dates from 1538, and in 1543 a certain Thomas Cheshire kept a tavern in Fleet Street. It is probably from him that the pub derives its name. Now in the middle of Fleet Street's newspaper offices and a favourite haunt of writers and journalists, the pub's literary connections reach back into the past. Dr Johnson was a regular, and Dickens mentions it in *A Tale of Two Cities*, while one of its most famous characters was verbose rather than literate. This was a parrot whose knowledge of bad language was prodigious. It died in 1926 at the age of 40 and even the BBC announced its demise. The pub's restaurant is famous for traditional English food.

The Poppinjoy
Fleet Street, EC4

This modern pub stands on the site of a house which belonged to the abbots of Cirencester in medieval times. The Poppinjoy was a model bird used for target practice by archers.

The Printers Devil
Fetter Lane, EC4

A number of models and illustrations in this pub explain the history of printing, and the pub's name is derived from an early term for printers' errand boys.

Prospect of Whitby
57 Wapping Wall, E1

The *Prospect* was a ship out of the Yorkshire port of Whitby which was laid up off Wapping, and the pub was referred to as 'the tavern near the *Prospect* of Whitby'. It has also been known as the Devil's Tavern because it was the haunt of river pirates, smugglers, and men who stole from bodies dragged from the Thames. During the 17th century hundreds of ships were moored along this stretch of the Thames, so it is no surprise that Samuel Pepys, as Secretary to the Admiralty, knew the Prospect. The Pepys Society now holds its meetings in this historic old pub.

Red Lion

2 Duke of York Street, W1

Typical of a Victorian 'gin palace', the Red Lion has a number of small bars with engraved mirrors, and a cast-iron staircase leading to the toilets.

The Salisbury

90 St Martin's Lane, WC2

Situated in the middle of London's theatreland, this opulent Victorian pub attracts many people from the world of entertainment. Its superb etched windows and mirrors, red plush seating, and abundance of polished wood, all combine to make it a fine example of a 19th-century hostelry.

The Samuel Pepys

Brooks Wharf,

48 Upper Thames Street, EC4

About the only drink you can't get at The Samuel Pepys is tea, which is strange as the building was a tea warehouse in Victorian times. The décor is mostly 17th-century, with the downstairs bar done up as a ship's chandlers, and there is a letter by Pepys and a translation of part of his diary on display upstairs.

The Samuel Pepys is a favourite place for a jolly evening out.

The Spaniards

Hampstead Lane, NW3

Before it became a pub, this 15th-century building was the home of the Spanish ambassador to the Court of James I. It is possible that after he had returned to Spain some of the Ambassador's servants stayed on to run the house as a tavern, which would explain the pub's name. It is a comfortable building with exposed beams, huge fireplaces, and displays of maps, etchings and firearms. Names connected with the place – which lies between Hampstead and Highgate on the Old North Road – include Dick Turpin, Oliver Goldsmith, Byron, Keats and Shelley, Joshua Reynolds, and Charles Dickens.

The Spotted Dog still preserves the atmosphere of the old Essex country inn it once was.

Spotted Dog

212 Upton Lane, Forest Gate, E7

This is a very old timber-frame building with weather-boarded gable-end and part-thatch, part-tiled roof, and a history which matches its appearance. Among the tales told about it is one concerning Charles II and his hunting party who inconsiderately turned up requiring refreshment after the place was closed for the night. The landlord 'blew his top' (in modern parlance), to the King's amusement, luckily. When he found out who his guests were he quickly changed his tune and Charles rewarded him with a 24-hour licence. Dick Turpin is supposed to have associations with the pub too, which is more likely to be true than some of the other stories about him, as he came from Essex and was a member of a gang which worked from Epping Forest. The pub was also used by City merchants during the plague periods of 1603 and 1665–66, and the City Arms can be seen painted on a wall here.

The Two Chairmen

39 Dartmouth Street, SW1

Situated in a street which adjoins elegant Queen Anne's Gate, this old pub retains an atmosphere that fits perfectly with its surroundings. Its one bar is everything that a typical English pub should be. The cock-fighting equipment displayed on the walls is a remainder that a cockpit was situated nearby during the 18th century.

Widow's Son

75 Devons Road, Bow, E3

Two hundred years ago this site was occupied by a cottage in which lived a widow and her sailor son. He was expected home for Easter and she baked a batch of hot cross buns for the occasion. Good Friday passed, and Easter Day, and the sailor did not come, but his mother kept a bun for him. The following year she set aside another bun for him and continued to do so until her death. When she died the buns were strung together and hung up. Each Good Friday a sailor added another bun, and the cottage became known as the Bun House. When the Widow's Son pub was built on the site in 1848 the string of mouldy and blackened buns was hung in the bar and still each year another bun is added. The pub is an interesting example of an early Victorian building, with a wooden ceiling, many ornamental mirrors, and pictures and plaques of seascapes, ships and other things connected with the sea.

Everything that tourists imagine when they think of a 'typical English pub'. The interior of the Widow's Son is a delight

161

Eating Out in London

London is a gourmet's paradise. Concentrated in the West End alone are several hundred restaurants catering for most tastes and pockets, with full meals ranging from £1.50 to £30. Most nationalities with a reputation for cuisine are represented somewhere in Soho, but it sometimes pays to look farther afield to find the best place of its kind.

There are many establishments in London which are worth visiting because they provide a special kind of treat – like afternoon tea for children of all ages at Neal's Yard Bakery in Covent Garden, or Muffin Man at 12 Wrights Lane, Kensington. Then there is the eat-as-much-as-you can set tea at Harrods Restaurant – expensive, but the children's tea costs less than Mum's and Dad's. You can eat jellied eels at the Eel Pie and Mash Shop in Wandsworth Bridge Road, or a tasty pasty at Cousin Jack's Cornish Shop in Drury Lane. There are plenty of American-style hamburger joints, and other American restaurants offering more than just fried chicken. If you want something out-of-the-ordinary try Roscoe's in Old Compton Street, or Tootsie's in Holland Park Road. Fashionable but fairly expensive is Joe Allens in Exeter Street, off the Strand, while Widow Applebaum's in South Molton Street offers a good selection of American-Jewish food. The choice is endless, but the establishments selected here reflect the best London can offer.

Classical French

Connaught Hotel
Carlos Place, W1
The restaurant and grill room of this world-famous hotel offers food of the highest classical standards. It is cooked under the direction of French-born Michel Bourdin, ex *sous-chef* of Maxim's in Paris. The dignified restaurant with its beautiful panelling offers attentive service matching the best in Europe.

Le Gavroche
61 Lower Sloane Street, SW1
According to experts this is the best restaurant in Britain. The Roux brothers, who own it, have established standards of excellence that encompass not only their cooking but every member of their staff. Every dish is an experience.

Classical International

Mirabelle
56 Curzon Street, W1
One of the last 'grand' restaurants in London, the Mirabelle is expensive, but luxurious in setting and service. Its unusual decor includes barley-sugar twist pillars and a stunning garden at one end with a retractable roof for warm weather. The cuisine represents the very best in Continental cooking, and is unrivalled in England.

Real French

Chez Solange
35 Cranbourne Street, WC2
Opened 20 years ago and owned by René Rochon and his wife, Thérèse, this restaurant is unpretentious, but elegantly furnished. The service is efficient, and the cooking authentic.

Lacey's
26 Whitfield Street, W1
This restaurant is situated in a sparkling-clean basement room, and provides first class French cooking accompanied by reasonably priced regional wines. The owner, Bill Lacey, was once a *sous-chef* at a famous French restaurant.

A mouth-watering display at Ma Cuisine.

Ma Cuisine
113 Walton Street, SW3
Fairly new on the scene, this small restaurant with cook/owner Guy Mouilleron and his wife in charge, has become very popular. The menu is simple, but the food is excellent.

Tante Claire
68 Royal Hospital Road, SW3
The owner, Pierre Kaufman, does the cooking – and includes some unusual dishes such as a pig's foot stuffed with a *mousseline* of sweetbreads. Another is *andouillette de la mer* – a slice of turbot rolled round a stuffing of fish with an exquisite sauce made from blackcurrant vinegar.

Original

Carrier's
2 Camden Passage, N1
Charm and good taste can be seen in all three small dining rooms of Robert Carrier's restaurant. The menu is a four-course, fixed price affair. The starters are especially enjoyable and main courses contain Greek, Turkish, French, and English influence.

Alonso's
32 Queenstown Road, SW8
One of the most consistently good restaurants in London. The theme and decor is Spanish, but the menu is remarkably original.

Swiss

The Swiss Centre
Leicester Square, W1
This modern complex of restaurants offers a variety from snacks to full meals. The Taverne specialises in cheese dishes, the Locarda in Italian-Swiss, and the Chesa in more expensive meals.

British

Simpson's
The Strand, WC2
Established in 1828, this is a traditional English restaurant with several rooms on two floors. The dishes to sample are the huge roasts from heated carving trolleys, but there are others – boiled chicken, tripe and onions, Lancashire hotpot, etc.

Tate Gallery
Millbank, SW1
The location and decor should not deter potential customers, since this is a very fine restaurant. The food is modelled on early traditional English dishes, some from the recipes of Elizabeth, wife of Oliver Cromwell.

Walton's
121 Walton Street, SW3
One of the most elegant and opulent restaurants in London. The English cooking is of a standard barely matched anywhere. Naturally, it is also very expensive.

Locket's
Marsham Court, Marsham Street, SW1
Within easy reach of the House of Commons, Locket's is popular with MPs. Sound basic ingredients are evident, and Lamb Shrewsbury is a good choice for the main course.

Kosher

Blooms
90 Whitechapel High Street, E1
Situated in the East End, here will be found the finest gefillte fish, salt beef, latkes (fried potato cakes), and much more. Reasonable prices, too.

Italian

Terrazza
19 Romilly Street, W1
The first of the famed Mario and Franco group, the food here shows some compromise for English tastes, but is mostly authentic, and always enjoyable. This restaurant is handy for theatreland and the West End.

San Frediano
62 Fulham Road, SW3
One of the new trattorias, the San Frediano is popular for its reliable food and animated atmosphere.

Cantonese

Poon's
King Street, WC2
The menu here is large and varied and includes many items rarely found in Britain. It is best to go in a party to sample dishes which may be suggested by Mrs Poon.

Hungarian

Gay Hussar
2 Greek Street, W1
This restaurant is full of atmosphere, and has excellent food and wine. It is situated at the Oxford Street end of Soho, and it is necessary to reserve tables.

Greek

White Tower
Percy Street, W1
Not cheap, but a value-for-money restaurant. The menu includes dishes from other Balkan countries.

Japanese

Masako
6 St Christopher's Place, W1
An authentic atmosphere with charming Japanese waitresses. Included on the menu is *Sashimi*, a dish of raw fish which is in fact delicious when served with a special sauce and mustard.

Above: Almost as much attention is paid to pleasant surroundings as to the preparation and presentation of the food at Carriers.

Left: Japanese food still comes as a rare and surprising delight to most Westerners.

Sporting London

London is the centre of much British sport. Every Saturday afternoon during the season hundreds of thousands of voices roar in support of London's 12 Football League Clubs. The football match of the year – the FA Cup Final – is held at Wembley in May, at Twickenham the world's Rugby giants lock in fierce combat, and for a hectic midsummer fortnight heads twist left and right watching the Wimbledon Lawn Tennis Championships. For those wanting something a little quieter, the two major Test Cricket grounds, Lord's and the Oval, are both popular places to spend an hour, a day, or even a few days when the Tests are on.

Scotland invades England. Scottish football fans in Trafalgar Square on the way to see Scotland v England at Wembley.

Association Football

Football is so old a sport that no-one is quite sure of its origins. It has always been popular in England, where legend has it that the severed head of a marauding Dane was once used as a ball. In 1385 Edward III had to ban the game because his troops were spending more time playing than training for war.

Football in London was well established by the 17th century when street games were regularly played between rival groups of apprentices in Covent Garden, Cheapside and the Strand.

The Football Association (FA) was not founded until 1863, and the first FA Challenge Cup Final was played at the Oval, Kennington, in 1872. Today London has 12 teams in the four divisions of the Football League, and it has had at least one team in the top category, Division One, every year since 1904. In addition, London boasts Britain's foremost football stadium – Wembley.

Wembley Stadium
Empire Way, Wembley
Built in 1923 as part of the British Empire Exhibition, the 100,000-capacity Wembley Stadium held its first FA Cup Final in the same year, and has been the Cup Final venue ever since. Also used for the Football League Cup Final and the majority of England's International fixtures, it is every footballer's dream to 'go to Wembley'.

A host of other events take place each year, including the Rugby League Cup Final, Women's Hockey Internationals, Schoolboy Soccer Internationals, the Gaelic Games, pop festivals, Speedway Championships, and regular twice-weekly greyhound racing. In 1934 an indoor sports building, the Empire Pool and Sports Arena, was built, and though no longer used for swimming, the arena is adaptable for staging ice shows and ice hockey, boxing, badminton, tennis, gymnastics, basketball, cycling and horse shows.

Almost every major event at Wembley goes down in the history books, but perhaps the two most notable events in Wembley's history were in 1948, when the Olympic Games were held here, and in 1966, when it was the ground on which England won the World Cup Soccer Final against West Germany in a game that will never be forgotten.

Above: The Royal International Horse Show, held at Wembley in July.

Below: The FA Cup Final, the big day at Wembley Stadium.

London's Football Clubs

Arsenal
Arsenal Stadium, Highbury, N5
Arsenal have won the FA Cup five times, the most recent being in 1979. They have achieved a total of eight League Championships, including four between 1931 and 1935. In 1971 they were the second team this century to win the League and Cup double, ironically beating Spurs who had done the same ten years earlier.

Brentford
Griffin Park, Braemar Road, Brentford
Brentford have spent most of their time in the lower echelons, apart from a spell in the First Division just before and after World War II.

Charlton Athletic
The Valley, Floyd Road, Charlton, SE7
Charlton Athletic played in the first post-war Cup Final in 1946. Their player Bert Turner scored for each side in Derby County's 4–1 victory and the ball burst. Charlton redeemed themselves the following year, beating Burnley 1–0. The ball burst again.

Chelsea
Stamford Bridge, Fulham Road, SW6
Chelsea, currently undergoing a lean spell, won the League Championship in 1955 and the FA Cup in 1970. This was the first Wembley final to require a replay, which was played at Old Trafford, Manchester, where Chelsea beat Leeds after extra time. The following year they beat Real Madrid in the European Cup-Winners Cup Final, again in a replay.

Crystal Palace

Selhurst Park, Whitehouse Lane, SE25
Crystal Palace, then in the Third Division, reached the semi-final in 1976, but were beaten by Second Division Southampton. Palace, as they are known, won the Second Division Championship in 1979 to gain long-sought promotion to the First Division.

Fulham

Craven Cottage, Stevenage Road, Fulham, SW6
Fulham, a Second Division club, went to Wembley in 1975 for an all-London final against West Ham, but found their First Division opponents too much for them, losing 2–0.

Millwall

The Den, Cold Blow Lane, New Cross, SE14
Millwall have yet to gain promotion to the First Division, having spent most of the last two decades in the Second Division.

Orient

Leyton Stadium, Brisbane Road, Leyton, E10
Orient's fine Cup form in 1954, when they reached the 6th round as a Third Division side, was surpassed in 1978 when they reached the semi-final – only to lose to Arsenal in an exciting match.

Queen's Park Rangers

South Africa Road, W12
Queen's Park Rangers' supreme moment came in 1967 when they appeared in the first Wembley League Cup Final – a Third Division club facing First Division opponents West Bromwich Albion. Rangers were losing 0–2 but staged a dramatic fight-back to win 3–2.

Tottenham Hotspur

748 High Road, Tottenham, N17
Tottenham Hotspur have probably been the most successful London club over the last two decades, their total of five FA Cup triumphs including wins in 1961, 1962 and 1967. In 1961 they were the first team this century to achieve the League and Cup double by winning both trophies in the same year. Tottenham, or Spurs as they are popularly known, became the first English club to win a European trophy when they defeated Athletico Madrid 5–1 in the 1962–63 European Cup-Winners Cup Final. Since then they have added two League Cup Final victories (1971 and 1973) as well as winning the EUFA Cup in 1972.

West Ham United

Boleyn Ground, Green Street, Upton Park, E13
West Ham United have never been League Champions but they won the FA Cup in 1964 and 1975, and defeated Munich 1860 in the European Cup-Winners Cup Final at Wembley in 1965.

Wimbledon

Plough Lane Ground, Durnsford, Wimbledon, SW19
Wimbledon were elected to the Football League in 1977 after three consecutive Southern League Championships. Earlier that year they had a splendid FA Cup run, disposing of First Division Burnley away from home and holding Leeds United, one of the country's leading sides, to a draw on their own ground before losing the replay.

Athletics

Crystal Palace National Sports Centre
Crystal Palace Park, Sydenham, SE19

New River Sports Centre
White Hart Lane, N22

Parliament Hill Fields
Gospel Oak, NW3

Victoria Park
Victoria Park, E9

West London Stadium
Wormwood Scrubs, W12

London has witnessed many great moments in athletics history, including the staging of the 14th Olympic Games at Wembley in 1948. The White City stadium has also been the scene of many memorable events. Built at the beginning of this century, the stadium was the venue for the 4th Modern Olympic Games and was London's principal athletic stadium for more than half a century.

In 1964 the Crystal Palace National Sports Centre opened and the White City finally ended its long and honourable association with athletics.

The purpose-built Sports Centre has an all-weather track and covered accommodation for spectators, and stages all manner of athletics ranging from major international matches to county championships.

The Boat Race

The Boat Race, a contest between two crews of eight rowers and one coxswain representing the universities of Oxford and Cambridge, is one of the most famous sporting events in the world. The first Boat Race took place at Henley-on-Thames in 1829, but in 1845 the event was moved to its present location in London. The course runs on the Thames from Putney to Mortlake, a distance of over 4 miles, and it takes place annually on a Saturday shortly before Easter.

Thousands of people flock to the riverside to take up vantage points, many paying for the privileged positions near the finish at Duke's Meadows, Chiswick, or on floating barges. The current score in victories stands at 68 to Cambridge and 56 to Oxford. There has been one dead heat (in 1877) and each crew has twice suffered the indignity of sinking before completing the course.

Above: Rosettes for the Boat Race. The world-famous contest between Oxford and Cambridge universities is a gruelling upstream pull on a four-mile stretch of the Thames.

Below: Middle-distance record breaker Steve Ovett wins another race for Britain at the Crystal Palace National Sports Centre.

Above: The last wicket falls. Old Father Time draws stumps on the Lord's Cricket Ground weathervane.

Right: A record of a historic match at Lord's in 1837 between the North and South of England. The Lord's Cricket Museum houses a fine display of cricket memorabilia.

Cricket

Lord's Ground
St John's Wood, NW8

The Oval
The Oval, Kennington, SE11

Cricket was first played in Tudor times but it was not until 1744 that the rules were formally drawn up. Nevertheless, it had become, and still is, one of the most widely played games in England. Even the smallest village will probably have its team and its own ground where the quiet of a Sunday afternoon is broken only by the slap of leather on willow and a gentle ripple of applause.

Cricket is equally widely played in London, on commons and playing fields, but the two major venues are Lord's Cricket Ground in St John's Wood and the Oval in Kennington.

Lord's is probably the best-known ground in the country and is the home ground for two clubs – Middlesex County Cricket Club and the famous Marylebone Cricket Club, perhaps even better known by its initials, MCC. Until recently the MCC was effectively the governing body for the game, and its collection of cricket memorabilia forms the Lord's Cricket Museum (see page 98).

The MCC started out as the White Conduit Club, named after its ground in Islington, and moved several times before finding its permanent ground. Lord's is named after Thomas Lord, a groundsman, who was instrumental in finding the site and even moved the hallowed turf from ground to ground.

The game of cricket accompanied the British to the colonies and it became equally popular in Australia, New Zealand, the West Indies, India and Pakistan. It is these countries who play England in the Test Matches, which are played here and in their own countries. A Test Match is usually five days long and there can be as many as six in a series, played on various pitches throughout the country. Both Lord's and the Oval are traditional venues for Test Matches, the latter being the site of the first-ever Test in 1880.

The Oval is the home ground of Surrey County Cricket Club, and today it is usually the venue for the final Test in a series.

Lord's, too, has Test Matches, and many other countries as well as the six Test countries are being drawn into international cricket by the new Prudential Cup competition. Begun in 1975, it takes place every four years, with the final being played at Lord's in June. The many other matches played at Lord's include county cricket, the finals of the Gillette Cup and the Benson and Hedges Cup, and the annual match between Eton and Harrow.

Greyhound Racing

Catford
Greyhound Stadium, SE6

Hackney Wick
Waterden Road, E15

Haringey
Green Lanes, N4

Walthamstow
Chingford Road, E17

Wembley
Stadium Way

White City
Wood Lane, W12

Wimbledon
Plough Lane, SW19

'Going to the dogs' has always been a popular pastime, especially with East End Londoners. Pure-bred greyhounds chase after an artificial hare on an electrified rail at speeds of up to 40mph. Races, either on the flat or over hurdles, are over varying distances and attract a good deal of betting and prize money. The more famous tracks are at Haringey, Walthamstow and White City, and many have restaurants overlooking the races.

Greyhounds in their element, straining after the hare at Hackney Wick Stadium, show all the grace, power and speed of which they are capable. For many Londoners, a night at the dogs is a favourite pastime.

Rugby Union Football

Blackheath RFC
Rectory Field, Blackheath, SE3

Harlequins RFC
Stoop Memorial Ground, Craneford Way, Twickenham

London Irish RFC
The Avenue, Sunbury-on-Thames

London Scottish RFC
Kew Foot Road, Richmond, Surrey

London Welsh RFC
Old Deer Park, Richmond, Surrey

Richmond RFC
Richmond Athletic Ground, Richmond, Surrey

Rosslyn Park RFC
Priory Lane, Upper Richmond Road, Roehampton, SW15

Saracens RFC
The Pavilion, Green Road, Southgate, N14

Wasps RFC
Repton Avenue, Sudbury

Another line-out won, another advantage gained. Twickenham is the home ground for both Harlequins RFC and England, and is the venue for many rugby union championships as well as international matches. Playing at Twickenham is to rugby union what Wembley is to soccer – the highest accolade.

Rugby Football may have been born when, in 1823, W W Ellis picked up a soccer ball and ran with it – but there is no doubt it was nursed to maturity in London. Guy's Hospital claims to have the world's oldest Rugby Club, formed in 1843. Blackheath Club, the first group to come together specifically for the purpose of playing Rugby (in 1858), Richmond (founded 1861) and Harlequins (founded 1866) played important roles in shaping the game as it is now played.

Twickenham was not always Rugby Union's 'home' as it is now. Before the Rugby Union purchased the land at Twickenham in 1907, internationals involving England were mostly played at the Oval, with Blackheath, Richmond and Crystal Palace playing host on a few occasions.

Wherever one is in London, there is likely to be a rugby game worth watching. Fixtures to look out for at Twickenham are internationals (which are well publicised), the Oxford *v* Cambridge match in early December, the RFU Club Competition final in April, and the Inter-Services Championships played during March and April. Apart from the major clubs listed above there are a number of Old Boys' Clubs and teams which compete for the Hospitals Cup, as well as the many college and school teams acting as nurseries for future great players.

Speedway

Hackney Wick
Waterden Road, E15

Wimbledon
Plough Lane, SW19

Introduced to Britain in the 1920s, speedway has grown to be the largest spectator sport after football. This highly-specialised motorcycling sport, which developed from dirt-track racing in open fields, is now usually held within large football or greyhound stadiums. With thrills, spills, and the roar of machines under brilliant floodlighting, speedway racing is very exciting entertainment. The highly-powered 500cc bikes run on pure methanol, and have no brakes. The fearless riders need a great deal of skill and daring to execute the long, broadside drifts on the sweeping curves at each end of the track, sending showers of the loose shale surface into the air.

The superb control of a speedway rider at Hackney Wick Stadium.

Above: 'Wimbledon' is a fortnight of strawberries and cream, swivelling necks and hard-fought tennis on the finest grass courts in the world.

Tennis

All England Lawn Tennis and Croquet Club
Church Road, Wimbledon, SW19

'Wimbledon' – for tennis fans the world over, the name resounds with the excitement and magic of that summer fortnight when top players from across the globe converge in London to compete for the most coveted prizes in lawn tennis. In the last week of June and the first week in July, the All England Lawn Tennis and Croquet Club hosts, in effect, the world tennis championships on grass, though with typical British reserve the event is called simply the Lawn Tennis Championships Meeting.

The Wimbledon complex, to which improvements have been made since its opening in 1922 by King George V, consists of 15 grass courts with their cherished and world-famous Cumberland turf, 10 hard courts, a post office, bank, and restaurants whose speciality is strawberries and cream.

Over 2,000 members of staff cater for the 300,000-plus spectators who attend throughout the fortnight, and almost as coveted as the prizes and trophies is a ticket to the Centre Court for one of the final matches. Near-continuous TV coverage of the Wimbledon fortnight sweeps the whole country with tennis-madness, and 'Wimbledon' has become one of those great British institutions which everybody loves – or simply learns to live with.

Inner and Outer London Maps

Key to Inner London Atlas

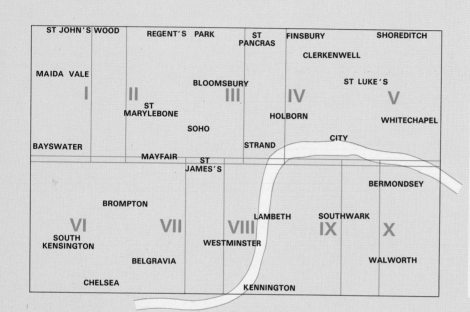

One - way street	←
Pedestrians only	
Access only	
Traffic roundabout	
Banned turn	
British Rail Station	CANNON ST STA
London Transport Station	St Pauls
Garage parking	G
Parking	P
Police	POL
Hospital	H
Post Office	P.O
Church or religious centre	†
Park or open space	
Place of interest	Museum
A A Service centre	AA
Overlap extent and number of continuing page	IX

Key to Greater London Atlas

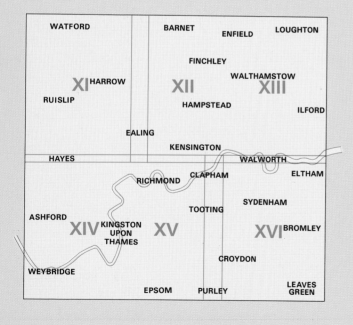

Primary route	A3
A road	A24
B road	B243
Other road	
Level Crossing	
Toll road	
Roundabout	
British Rail Station	●
London Transport Station	
London Transport and British Rail Station	
Parking (at suburban stations)	P
Garage (at suburban stations)	G
Hospital	H
A A Telephone	☎
A A Pilot meeting point	★
Service Centre (normal hours)	AA
Service Centre (24 hours)	AA 24 hour
Motorway Information Service Centre (normal hours)	AA info
Road Service Centre (normal hours)	AA 94
Place of interest	Kew Palace
Park area / golfcourse	
County boundary	

OXFORD STREET

Oxford Street, where specially marked, is closed to through traffic (except buses & taxis) 7am-7pm. Monday - Saturday

OXFORD STREET

Oxford Street, where specially marked, is closed to through traffic (except buses & taxis) 7am-7pm. Monday - Saturday

Central London's Theatreland

THEATRES
1 **Adelphi:** tel (01) 836 7611
2 **Albery:** tel (01) 836 3878
3 **Aldwych: tel (01) 836 6404**
4 **Ambassadors:** tel (01) 836 1171
5 **Apollo:** tel (01) 437 2663
6 **Arts Theatre:** tel (01) 836 2132
7 **Astoria:** tel (01) 437 6239/437 5757/734 4291
8 **Cambridge:** tel (01) 836 6056
9 **Comedy:** tel (01) 930 2578
10 **Criterion:** tel (01) 930 3216
11 **Drury Lane, Theatre Royal:** tel (01) 836 8108
12 **Duke of York's:** tel (01) 836 5122
13 **Fortune:** tel (01) 836 2238
14 **Garrick:** tel (01) 836 4601
15 **Globe:** tel (01) 437 1592
16 **Haymarket:** tel (01) 930 9832
17 **Her Majesty's:** tel (01) 930 6606
18 **Lyric Theatre:** tel (01) 437 3686
19 **National Theatre** (Olivier, Lyttleton, Cottesloe): tel (01) 928 2252
20 **New London:** tel (01) 405 0072
21 **Palace:** tel (01) 437 6834
22 **Palladium:** tel (01) 437 7373
23 **Phoenix:** tel (01) 836 8611
24 **Piccadilly:** tel (01) 437 4506
25 **Prince Edward:** tel (01) 437 6877
26 **Prince of Wales:** tel (01) 930 8681
27 **Queen's Theatre:** tel (01) 734 1166
28 **Regent:** tel (01) 637 9862/3

29 **Royalty:** tel (01) 405 8004
30 **St Martin's:** tel (01) 836 1443
31 **Savoy:** tel (01) 836 8888
32 **Shaftesbury:** tel (01) 836 6596/7
33 **Strand:** tel (01) 836 2660
34 **Talk of the Town:** tel (01) 734 5051
35 **Vaudeville:** tel (01) 836 9988
36 **Whitehall:** tel (01) 930 6692
37 **Windmill Theatre:** tel (01) 437 6312
38 **Wyndham's:** tel (01) 836 3028

CONCERT HALLS AND OPERA HOUSES
39 **Coliseum:** tel (01) 836 3161
40 **Queen Elizabeth Hall and Purcell Room:** tel (01) 928 3002
41 **Royal Festival Hall:** tel (01) 928 3191
42 **Royal Opera House,** Covent Garden: tel (01) 240 1066

CINEMAS
43 **ABC 1 & 2,** Shaftsbury Avenue: tel (01) 836 8861
44 **Academy 1:** tel (01) 437 2981
45 **Academy 2:** tel (01) 437 5129
46 **Academy 3:** tel (01) 437 8819
47 **Centa Cinema:** tel (01) 437 3561
48 **Cinecenta:** tel (01) 930 0631
49 **Classic Royal:** tel (01) 930 6915

50 **Classic Eros:** tel (01) 437 3839
51 **Classic Moulin Cinema Complex:** tel (01) 437 1653
52 **Classic** Oxford Street: tel (01) 636 0310
53 **Columbia:** tel (01) 734 5414
54 **Dominion:** tel (01) 580 9562
55 **Empire:** tel (01) 437 1234
56 **Essential:** tel (01) 439 3657
57 **Filmcenta:** tel (01) 437 4815
58 **Jacey,** Leicester Square: tel (01) 437 2001
59 **Leicester Square Theatre:** tel (01) 930 5252
60 **London Pavillion:** tel (01) 437 2982
61 **National Film Theatre:** tel (01) 928 3232/3
62 **Odeon,** Haymarket: tel (01) 930 2738/2771
63 **Odeon,** Leicester Square: tel (01) 930 6111
64 **Odeon,** St Martin's Lane: tel (01) 836 0691
65 **Plaza 1, 2, 3 & 4:** tel (01) 437 1234
66 **Prince Charles:** tel (01) 437 8181
67 **Rialto:** tel (01) 437 3488
68 **Ritz:** tel (01) 437 1234
69 **Scene 1, 2, 3 & 4:** tel (01) 439 4470
70 **Soho Cinema:** tel (01) 734 4205
71 **Warner West End:** tel (01) 439 0791

INFORMATION
Details of performances are given in most daily papers and in some weekly magazines.

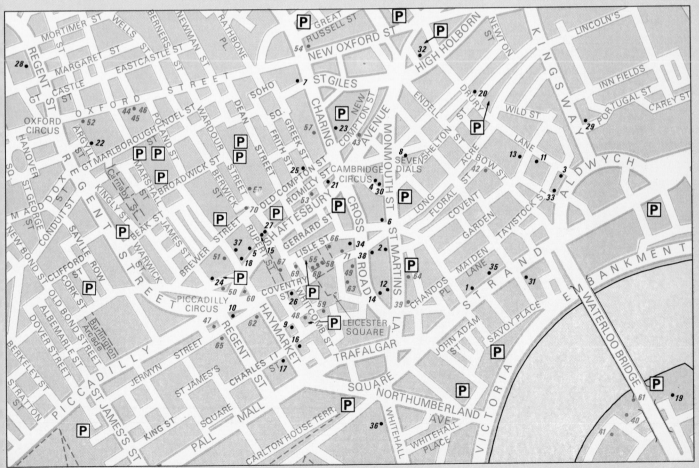

Figures on the Albert Memorial, Kensington Gardens.

Bethnal Green Museum, Cambridge Heath Road.

The Chelsea Flower Show.

Goddard's Eel & Pie House, Greenwich Church Street.

One of the King's Beasts, Hampton Court Palace, which guard the entrance gate.

Karl Marx's memorial in Highgate Cemetery.

M

N

O

Oxford Street.

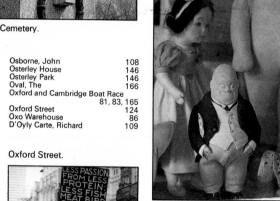

P

Pollock's Toy Museum.

Q

R

Regent's Canal.

Trafalgar Square.

The Palace of Westminster, as seen across the river from the Jubilee Walkway.

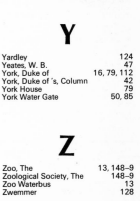

Acknowledgements

The publishers gratefully acknowledge the following for the use of photographs and illustrations:

Ambassadors Theatre, p109 *poster*. British Tourist Authority, p20 *Ceremony of the Keys*; 21 *Swan Upping*; 23 *Beating the Bounds*; 32 *Westminster detail*; 34 *Abbey*; 108 *2×Opera House*; 109 *Shaftesbury Theatre*; 158 *George pub sign*. Camera Press, p70 *woman porter*. J Allen Cash Ltd, p158 *Ye Olde Cheshire Cheese sign*. Colorsport, p164 *horse jumping & Wembley Stadium*; 165 *athletics & rosettes*; 166 *greyhounds*; 167 *rugby & speedway*. A C Cooper Ltd, p166 *cricket print*. Cooper-Bridgeman Library, p68 *Regent Street painting*. Gerry Cranham, p167 *Wimbledon*. Fox Photos, pp14/15 & 18 *State Opening*; 107 *Proms*; 112 *Dr Johnson's house*. Michael Holford Library, pp2/3 & 66/67 *Visscher panorama*; 30 *1850s print*; 67 *2×Cries of London*; 69 *Great Exhibition*; 72 *Jeremy Bentham*; 73 *operating theatre*; 96 *Greek sculpture*; 120 *int. St Mary-le-Bow*; 135 *Covent Garden painting*. Imperial War Museum, p70 *Air Raid Warden*. Arthur Lockwood, p65 *Tower in C15*; 69 *Boat Race painting*. London Transport, p9 *poster & Underground train*; 10 *tilting bus*; 9 & 10 *symbols*. London Zoological Gardens, p149 *leopard*. Mansell Collection, p66 *Plague poster*. Museum of London, pp62/63 *Sorrell reconstruction*; 64 *coin & mother goddesses*; 65 *C16 map*; 66 *Fire painting*; 67 *coffee-house*; 68 *frost fair*; 93 *2×shop fronts*. National Gallery, p100 *Leonardo da Vinci*. National Portrait Gallery, p111 *Hogarth*; 112 *Dr Johnson*. National Theatre, p106 *Gielgud & No Man's Land*. Picturepoint Ltd, p13 *waterbus*; 19 *Trooping the Colour*; 25 *Yeomen & crowns*; 69 *Frith painting*. Paul Popper, p124 *decorations, Regent Street*. Radio Times Hulton Picture Library, p70 *Tottenham Court Road*. Ronald Sheridan, p26 *chapel in Tower*; 102 *int. Kenwood House*; 114 *St Paul's model*. Spectrum Colour Library, p8 *Regent Street view*; 19 *Trooping the Colour*; 21 *Pearly Kings*; 22 *Christmas tree*; 29 *Stock Exchange*; 34 *flags in Abbey*; 71 *Coronation procession*; 94 *V&A Museum*; 95 *National History Museum*; 96 *Elgin Marbles & Egyptian Room*; 157 *kites, Parliament Hill*; 166 *Lord's weathervane*. Tate Gallery, p101 *Constable painting*. Thames Conservancy, p76 *Old Father Thames*. Madame Tussauds, p99 *wax figures*. Woodmansterne Ltd, p20 *Changing of the Guard*; 22 *Lord Mayor's Procession*; 23 *firing salute*; 27 *armour*; 33 *int. Big Ben*; 35 *vaulting, Westminster Abbey*.